FODOR'S

ALASKA

1986

Editors: Debra Bernardi, Andrew E. Beresky

Area Editor: Norma Spring

Photos: Bob Spring for Exploration Holidays & Cruises.

Drawings: Michael Kaplan, Sandra Lang

Maps and Plans: Dyno Lowenstein

Norma Spring is a Seattle-based freelance writer, whose books include Alaska, Pioneer State *and* Alaska, the Complete Travel Book. *She is also the author of numerous newspaper and magazine articles on Alaska, as well as round-the-world travel, including a book on travel in the U.S.S.R.,* Roaming Russia, Siberia, and Middle Asia, *illustrated with color and black-and-white photographs by husband Bob.*

FODOR'S TRAVEL GUIDES
New York & London

The following Fodor's Guides are current; most are also available in a British
edition published by Hodder & Stoughton.

Country and Area Guides

Australia, New Zealand
  & The South Pacific
Austria
Bahamas
Belgium & Luxembourg
Bermuda
Brazil
Canada
Canada's Maritime
  Provinces
Caribbean
Central America
Eastern Europe
Egypt
Europe
France
Germany
Great Britain
Greece
Holland
India, Nepal &
  Sri Lanka
Ireland
Israel
Italy
Japan
Jordan & The Holy Land
Kenya
Korea
Mexico
North Africa
People's Republic of
  China
Portugal
Scandanavia
Scotland
South America
Southeast Asia

Soviet Union
Spain
Switzerland
Turkey
Yugoslavia

City Guides

Amsterdam
Beijing, Guangzhou,
  Shanghai
Boston
Chicago
Dallas–Fort Worth
Greater Miami & The
  Gold Coast
Hong Kong
Houston
Lisbon
London
Los Angeles
Madrid
Mexico City &
  Acapulco
Munich
New Orleans
New York City
Paris
Philadelphia
Rome
San Diego
San Francisco
Stockholm, Copenhagen,
  Oslo, Helsinki &
  Reykjavik
Sydney
Tokyo
Toronto
Vienna
Washington, D.C.

U.S.A. Guides

Alaska
Arizona
California
Cape Cod
Colorado
Far West
Florida
Hawaii
New England
New Mexico
Pacific North Coast
South
Texas
U.S.A.

Budget Travel

American Cities (30)
Britain
Canada
Caribbean
Europe
France
Germany
Hawaii
Italy
Japan
London
Mexico
Spain

Fun Guides

Acapulco
Bahamas
London
Montreal
Puerto Rico
San Francisco
St. Martin/Sint Maarten
Waikiki

MANUFACTURED IN THE UNITED STATES OF AMERICA
10 9 8 7 6 5 4 3 2 1

CONTENTS

ARCTIC VACATIONS, 2 DAYS NO NIGHTS.

If you take an Arctic vacation this summer, we can promise you almost anything. Except a sunset.

The sun shines for eighty-some days in a row up here which gives you plenty of time to enjoy the exotic delights of Nome and Kotzebue. You can visit a working gold mining camp and try panning for gold yourself. Enjoy the famed Eskimo Blanket Toss. See native craftsmen carve ivory and jade. And watch a dog team charge across the tundra.

It's all here. And Alaska Airlines can show it to you.

Our Arctic tours of Alaska are one to three days in length, and feature comfortable sleeping accommodations and convenient flight times. For information and a free brochure call your travel agent. Because with the kinds of days we can plan for you, who needs nights?

ANCHORAGE TO THE ARCTIC.
$444.*

Alaska Airlines
Fly with a happy face.

*Price is per person, double occupancy for two-day package.

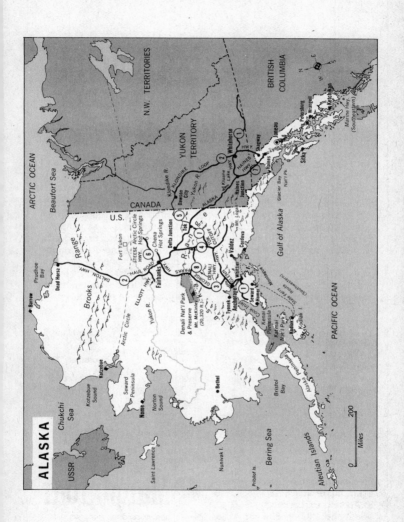

Have fun experiencing the best of Alaska on a Maupintour escorted tour!

You want to see and do and have fun, and be with people who are enjoyable companions. And, you want someone to take care of the details, give advice and take the bother out of travel. That is what Maupintour is all about. Come join our tour of Alaska and the Yukon including an Inside Passage cruise.

Discover the Maupintour difference: ☐ uncommonly good quality ☐ well-planned itineraries ☐ accompanying tour manager ☐ limited size group ☐ interesting companions ☐ a pleasant balance of activities and free time ☐ for one price everything is included ☐ outstanding value in a superior style of travel.

Maupintour escorted tour programs include :

☐ Africa
☐ Alaska / Yukon
☐ Alps
☐ Arizona
☐ Art / Culture
☐ Asia
☐ Australia
☐ Austria / Bavaria
☐ Belgium
☐ British Isles
☐ California
☐ Canada
☐ China
☐ Christmas Tours
☐ Colorado

☐ Cruise Tours
☐ Death Valley
☐ Ecuador
☐ Egypt / The Nile
☐ Europe
☐ Fall Foliage
☐ France
☐ Galapagos
☐ Germany
☐ Greece / Aegean
☐ Hawaii
☐ Historic East
☐ Holland
☐ Hungary
☐ Iceland

☐ India / Nepal Kashmir
☐ Ireland
☐ Israel
☐ Italy
☐ Japan
☐ Mexico
☐ Middle East
☐ Morocco
☐ National Parks
☐ New Year's Tours
☐ New Zealand
☐ Nile Cruise
☐ Opera Tours
☐ Orient

☐ Pacific N.W.
☐ Peru
☐ Poland
☐ Portugal
☐ Scandinavia
☐ South Pacific
☐ Soviet Union
☐ Spain / Portugal
☐ Switzerland
☐ Turkey
☐ USA East
☐ USA South
☐ USA West
☐ Winter Tours
☐ Yugoslavia

Free tour brochures! Ask your travel agent, call or write Maupintour, 1515 St. Andrews Dr., Lawrence, KS 66046. Telephone toll-free 800-255-4266.

Maupintour

quality escorted tours since 1951

FACTS AT YOUR FINGERTIPS

 FACTS AND FIGURES. The name of the 49th state came from a similar-sounding Aleut word meaning "great land of white to the east." The forget-me-not is the state flower; the Sitka spruce, the state tree; king salmon, the state fish; and the willow ptarmigan, the state bird. The state has adopted an official song, "Alaska's Flag." The state motto is "North to the Future." Juneau, in southeast Alaska, is the state capital. In 1974, Alaskans voted to move it, and in 1976 they chose a site in the interior, near the town of Willow, between Anchorage and Fairbanks. However, there was much debate over allocating funds for the building and moving. The funding measure was defeated in the November 1982 election.

Alaska ranks as the nation's biggest state—it is one-fifth the total size of the continental United States—with an area of 591,004 square miles, and a population estimated at over 516,324, living in two time zones. It is a big country in every sense: glaciers, fjords, forests, rivers, mountains, among them 20,320-foot Mount McKinley, highest on the North American continent. The Yukon is the longest river, with 1,400 of its almost 2,000 miles flowing through Alaska. The Malaspina, near Yakutat in Southeast Alaska, is the largest of 5,000 glaciers. There are more than three million lakes. Lake Iliamna, covering a thousand square miles in southwest Alaska, is America's second largest freshwater lake. The state has abundant natural resources, including oil and natural gas, timber, valuable minerals, fish and game. Industries based on these, plus growing tourism, are the foundation of the burgeoning economy.

 PLANNING YOUR TRIP. If you don't want to bother with reservations on your own, a travel agent won't cost you a cent, except for specific charges like telegrams. He gets his fee from the hotel or carrier he books for you. A travel agent can also be of help for those who prefer to take their vacations on a "package tour"—thus keeping your own planning to a minimum. If you prefer the convenience of standardized accommodations, remember that the various hotel and motel chains publish free directories of their members that enable you to plan and reserve everything ahead of time.

If you plan your own itinerary, keep in mind the size of this largest state, and the changeable nature of the land which can lead to unexpected shifts and/or delays in travel plans. Here are some helpful hints. Weigh the amount of time you have, add a day or more for delays due to unforeseeable (not necessarily disagreeable) circumstances, and give thought to some sidetrips. Then compute the mileage from your map, assess your finances, and match it all up with the available transportation.

The state of Alaska and members of the travel industry issue stacks of informational material, including maps, which pinpoint attractions, list historical sites, parks, etc. Local convention and visitor bureaus and chambers of commerce are also good sources of information. Specific addresses are given under *Practical Information* sections.

Plan to board the pets, discontinue paper and milk deliveries, and tell your local police and fire departments when you'll be leaving and when you expect to return. Ask a kindly neighbor to keep an eye on your house; fully protect your swimming pool against intruders. Have a neighbor keep your mail, or have it held at the post office. Consider having your telephone temporarily disconnected if you plan to be away more than a few weeks.

Look into the purchase of trip insurance (including baggage), and make certain your auto, fire, and other insurance policies are up-to-date. Flight insurance is often included in the price of the ticket when the fare is paid by major credit card. Before buying any separate travel insurance, check your regular policies carefully; many travelers unwittingly end up with redundant coverage. Several organizations offer coverage designed to supplement existing health insurance and to help defray costs not covered by many standard policies—emergency transportation, for example. Some of the more prominent of these organizations are: *NEAR* (Natonwide Emergency Ambulance Return), 1900 N. McArthur Blvd., Suite 210, Oklahoma City, OK 73217; (800) 654–6700. *Carefree Travel Insurance,* c/o ARM Coverage, Inc., 9 E. 37 St., New York, NY 10016; (212) 683–2622. *International SOS Assistance, Inc.,* P.O. Box 11568, Philadelphia, PA 19116; (800) 523–8930. *IAMAT* (International Association for Medical Assistance to Travelers), 736 Center St., Lewiston, NY 14092, in the US; 123 Edward St., Suite 275, Toronto, Ontario MSG IE2, in Canada. You may also want to investigate trip cancellation insurance, especially if you're flying a charter or APEX, where you might get stuck paying for a flight you are unable to be on. This insurance is usually available from travel agents. A valuable source of information on travel insurance is the *Travel Information Bureau,* 44 County Line Rd., Farmingdale, NY 11735.

Major credit cards are generally accepted, even in remote places like the Pribilof Islands. Consider converting the greater portion of your trip money into traveler's checks. Arrange to have your lawn mowed at the usual times, and leave that kindly neighbor your itinerary (insofar as is possible), car license number, and a key to your home (and tell police and firemen he has it). Since some hotel and motel chains give discounts (10%–25%) to senior citizens, be sure to have some sort of identification along if you qualify. Usually American Association of Retired Persons (AARP) membership is best. (See *Hotels and Motels* sections.)

TOURIST INFORMATION SERVICES. *AVA* and *DOT* are the backbone of the Alaskan tourist industry. The *Alaska Visitors Association* (AVA) is made up of 13 local AVA chapters throughout the state and in Seattle. Members cover most areas of the state and a wide range of activities. DOT, the *Division of Tourism,* Pouch E, Juneau AK 99811, (907)–465–2010 (Information Officer), publishes a comprehensive Travel Planner annually. The Planner includes information on Canada's Yukon. Almost every community in Alaska has a tourist contact center, convention and visitors bureau, and chamber of commerce—all eager to supply information for their areas. For instance, Alaska Highway travelers may stop for information and free coffee at the Tok Chamber of Commerce hospitality center, Mile 1314, open 7:00 A.M. until 10:00 P.M. in summer, every day.

For information and schedules for the Alaska ferries that serve southwest Alaska and connect Seattle and/or Prince Rupert with southeast Alaska ports, contact the *Alaska Marine Highway System,* Pouch R, Juneau, AK 99811, or Pier 48, Seattle, WA 98104. For reservations, necessary during the busy summer, call (907) 465–3941 in Juneau; (907) 272–7116 in Anchorage; (206) 623–1970 in Seattle; and (604) 627–1744 in Prince Rupert. Call toll-free (800) 544–2251 in the lower 48 states; (800) 551–7185 in Alaska. Payment for those with cabins has to be made at least 45 days before departure (for those with and without cabins on Seattle sailings). An Alaska-minded travel agent can help.

Some other aspects a visitor might want to know something about: Alaska Oil & Gas Assn., 505 W. Northern Lights Blvd., Ste. 219, Anchorage, AK 99503–2553; Mining Information Office, Dept. of Natural Resources, Pouch 7–005, Anchorage, AK 99510. Agricultural information is dispensed by the *Cooperative Extension Service,* University of Alaska, Fairbanks, AK 99701, and the *Alaska State Division of Agriculture,* Box 949, Palmer, AK 99645. To learn about the business climate and job possibilities consult the *Alaska Department of Commerce & Economic Development,* Division of Economic Enterprise, Pouch E.E., Juneau, AK 99801, the *Alaska State Chamber of Commerce,* 310 2nd St., Juneau, AK 99801; and if you are really serious about job opportunities, check with the *Alaska State Employment Service,* Box 3–7000, Juneau, AK 99802.

To discover Canada's Yukon, write: *Tourism Yukon,* P.O. 2703, Whitehorse, Yukon Territory, Canada Y1A 2C6; phone (403) 667–5430. Or contact the Yukon Visitors Association (YVA), Barry Redfern, Executive Director, 302 Steele St., Whitehorse, Yukon Territory, Canada Y1A 2C5; (403) 668–3331.

 WHEN TO GO. Henry Gannett, wandering mapmaker, *circa* 1900, advised, "if you are young, stay away until you grow older. . . . " He opined that Alaska's natural beauty overshadowed any world counterpart to the point that "all other scenery becomes flat and insipid. It is not well to dull one's capacity for such enjoyment by seeing the finest first."

Actually, today's answer to the question "when?" should be "now" or "as soon as possible," while there are still nostalgic touches from the past, and contrasts brought on by the old cultures adapting to the jet-age present, as they plan for a bright future.

Summer, the lightest season in the far north, is the most popular time to visit. Alaskans call it summer in early June, when even residents in the far north have usually contended with "break-up," the time when frozen ground thaws on the surface. They consider this season to last until the leaves, nipped by frost at night and starting to turn color, herald fall—which could be anytime after mid-August.

Many of today's visitors, however, are developing a taste for "off-seasoning" with their tours, and for a lower cost.

FALL FUN IN ALASKA

Alaskans spend the light, short summers working hard, making hay for the long nights ahead. In the fall they continue such favorite and vital activities as hunting and fishing, and not just for sport—a moose in the locker is money in the bank. Bear, deer, birds, fish, and food such as berries to be had for the gathering, are both tasty and a boost to family budgets. And Alaskans also take time to hike, canoe, tackle rivers by kayak and raft, and otherwise explore and enjoy their vast wilderness state.

Those who vacation in Alaska during early autumn can share in some special fall bonuses. Above the brilliant foliage, skies may be unbelievably blue, and the mountains and glaciers, always sensational, may be enhanced by fresh dustings of snow.

If you are serious about "going Alaskan," you'll find that fall will give you the opportunity to mingle with Alaskans in the outdoors. Daytime temperatures can be delightful still, though evenings get progressively nippier. Dress properly and take the morning skim of ice on the water bucket in stride. The bugs will have given up and so will the majority of campers. There'll be space in the campgrounds and in the motels and hotels for those who prefer a roof. An extra bonus is the lower price on tours, transportation, and accommodations.

Fall's most important celebration commemorates an event that took place over a century ago at Sitka, on the west side of big Baranof Island, in the northern part of the Southeast Panhandle. On October 18, 1867, Russia transferred all its holdings in "Russian America" to the United States. The ceremony took place overlooking Sitka's beautiful, busy, island-dotted harbor. On *Alaska Day* the townspeople, in period dress (including some vintage Russian-American soldier uniforms), climb Castle Hill for the ceremonies. The festivities in Sitka last for three days and feature contests, a parade, a pageant, and a costume ball.

If you get to Palmer during the ten days before Labor Day, you'll find everyone going all out for the annual *State Fair*, where they display vegetables of amazing size grown under the midnight sun.

As for regions like Kotzebue, above the Arctic Circle, early fall visitors will find the Eskimos winding up for preparation of winter food delicacies. If you are interested, someone is likely to show you what they have stashed away in their natural freezer, a deep hole dug into the permanently frozen ground—perhaps caribou, or reindeer, fish, seal, walrus, or whale meat, along with succulent Arctic berries still being picked and preserved.

Alaskans slide smoothly from fall into the holidays, celebrated with fervor even in the smallest villages. But they are just a prelude to the fun and games of winter: dogsled races, snowmobile competitions, winter carnivals. People play in the snow as long as it lasts.

FUN IN WINTER?

It's not news that the birds and the bikini set head south for winter. But how about flying north for an out-of-the-ordinary winter vacation spiced with that special Alaskan off-seasoning?

Alaskans look forward to winter, when they feel they have earned the right to unwind and play, with gusto. And the hardy residents are masters at coming up with guaranteed antidotes for "cabin fever" or other winter doldrums.

You can have a ball in Anchorage, especially if you come for the annual *Fur Rendezvous,* the "Rondy" in February. They hold a bang-up *Miner's and Trapper's Costume Ball* during the action-packed 10-day celebration and even a fur auction, which started it all in the first place.

There'll be skiing, sledding, ice skating, ice fishing and other outdoor winter fun in communities wherever there is snow and terrain to support the action. The classic dog sled competition, the *Iditarod Dog Sled Race,* takes place in March. Covering over a thousand miles, it starts at Knik, near Anchorage, ending on Nome's Front St., along the frozen Bering Sea. When the tomcod are running you're welcome to try ice fishing along with the Eskimos. "Play clothes" will include warm parkas and full cold-weather gear, of course.

Some swear there's no place like Nome to celebrate New Year's Eve. But watch out for those mid-winter nights on the town. While bar-hopping and elbow-bending in the notorious Front St. saloons, it's hard to know when to call it a night, because it hardly ever gets light in mid-winter.

If you have the time and the inclination, don't give up on sailing to Alaska, just because the luxury cruise ships have gone south for the winter. Though Arctic seas freeze, the milder, protected Inside Passage remains open. The big, sturdy Alaska State super-ferries make their runs, on a reduced schedule and at reduced prices. The scenery along this route can be awesome, with loads of fresh snow on the mountains and seaside glaciers. They say the fishing is good even in winter in the ice-free saltwater lapping at port towns from Ketchikan to Sitka.

Throughout the state, communities line up a full, action-packed winter schedule for themselves, and Alaskans are quick to recognize kindred souls from "outside." Cheechakos (newcomers) are urged to join in the fun and games. For sure, anyone who participates in these winter happenings will be exposed to Alaska's warmest side—its people.

 SEASONAL EVENTS. Alaskans are prone to celebrations year-round, and for almost any reason, iceworms to whales. Visitors are always welcome to join in. In the summer season, roughly May through September, you can count on being entertained by assorted continuous community specials:

Native dancing; dramas and melodramas; and salmon derbies galore in southeast Alaska.

All summer in Arctic towns Kotzebue and Barrow, and in Nome in western Alaska, Eskimos perform age-old, story-telling dances in parka and mukluks for visiting tour groups, and for fun. Near Haines, at Port Chilkoot, home of Alaska Indian Arts, Inc., the *Chilkoot Indian Dancers* put on a fine show, in authentic costumes they have made. Ketchikan romps through the melodrama *Fish Pirate's Daughter* at the Frontier Saloon periodically. In fact, most communities, at one time or another, will come up with entertainment based on local history, often a light-hearted spoof.

Here are a few annual, typically Alaskan events for starters. For many more events and festivals and exact dates, write the area chamber of commerce, convention and visitors bureau, or consult the *Alaska Vacation Planner*. It's available from the Alaska State Division of Tourism, Pouch E-400, Juneau, AK 99811.

January: In its landmark old Russian Orthodox church overlooking an arm of Kachemak Bay on southwestern Kenai Peninsula, Seldovia leads off with a *Russian New Year* celebration. The 3rd is *Statehood Day,* when President Eisenhower signed the act proclaiming Alaska the 49th state. It's also the anniversary of the first Russian settlement in Alaska, and the anniversary of the appointment of the first territorial governor. Tok is the major highway regrouping point after entering Alaska, and also is noted as the "Dog Capital." They rev up and rally at the *Dog Musher Association* grounds and track, continuing into February. When the races are over elsewhere, Tok holds the convivial *Race of Champions,* open to all who want to compete on their 20-mile racing trail.

February: To banish winter doldrums Cordova holds its *Iceworm Festival* complete with a 100-foot iceworm winding through the streets. Homer holds a *Winter Carnival,* and plays a *baseball game on snowshoes* during the first weekend in February. Kenai needs at least ten days for its *Winter Carnival* and *Petroleum-150,* a 150-mile snow machine race that begins and ends at the Kenai Mall. Gold fever rages in Wrangell during *Tent City Festival Days.* The *Anchorage Fur Rendezvous* features *World Championship Sled Dog Races, sportscar races (on ice),* and a *Miner's and Trapper's Ball.* In Whitehorse, Yukon Territory, Canada, the *Yukon Sourdough Rendezvous* is held at the end of February and features dog team races.

March: Racing continues with the *Fairbanks Winter Carnival* and *North American Dog Sled Championships,* also in Fairbanks. Nome sponsors the 1,000-mile *Iditarod Sled Dog Race.* This one takes time and stamina. Racing buffs gather in Nome and wait convivially in bars along the Front Street finish line, for as long as it takes for the teams to mush in—sometimes up to a month. The race commemorates an early mail route mercy-run when diphtheria serum was rushed by relays to isolated, stricken Nome in 1925.

April: A *Spring Carnival* at Mt. Alyeska and *ski races* at Juneau's Eaglecrest herald spring, and Juneau holds a *Folk Festival* with music ringing through the State Museum and the Armory. There are *Salmon Derbies* in Ketchikan, Haines, and Sitka. A *Walrus Carnival* at Savoonga, on St. Lawrence Island off the Bering Sea Coast, celebrates the end of the season for hunting the ivory-tusked marine mammals.

May: Highlight is Petersburg's *Little Norway Festival,* celebrating the first halibut landings and *Norwegian Independence Day,* May 17. In Kodiak, *King Crab Festival* with crab races.

June: The *Midsummer and Midnight Sun Festivals* (June 21): Nome has a raft race down the Nome River, starting at midnight; Fairbanks's Gold Panners play a *Midnight Sun Baseball Game* during the *Fairbanks Summer Solstice Festival;* Anchorage holds a 2-week *Festival of Music,* and an *Alaska Festival of Native Arts* at the Historical and Fine Arts Museum; starting at Fairbanks, the *Yukon "800" Marathon* winds through a grueling, 3-river, round-trip boat race; Palmer goes mad with its *Midsummer Festival* featuring *Woronzoff Horse Show,* papier-mâché *"Grotto Lunkers,"* and *Scottish Games.* There are *whaling festivals* at Barrow and Point Hope. Not too serious is the *Great Buskin River Raft Race* in Kodiak, with 5 beer breaks as part of the rules.

July: The 4th is a bang-up celebration all over Alaska, that might well run into the 5th or 6th! Small towns are choice places to be, with clan get-togethers, and competitions for prizes: a *Timber Carnival* with *Loggers Rodeo,* Ketchikan; *horse races,* Palmer; *foot race up Mt. Marathon,* Seward; and at Kotzebue, they celebrate with *Eskimo fun and games* and hold a *Northwest Alaska trade fair.*

Fairbanks Golden Days, which commemorate the discovery of gold at Fairbanks in 1902, is the biggest summer celebration; the *World Eskimo, Indian, Aleut Olympics* is probably the most unusual event. The Natives play their old games that take strength and endurance—the ear pull, knuckle hop, and high kick—and also demonstrate skills like seal-skinning (a woman's contest, record time, 60 seconds); they also choose a Native Queen.

August–September: *Gold Rush Days,* at Valdez; *Silver Salmon Derbies* at Valdez, Seward, and Whittier. A fair in southeast Alaska at Haines; *state fairs* at Tanana Valley, Fairbanks, or Palmer, near Anchorage; *Deltana Fair* with Buffalo Barbecue, Delta; spectacular drama *Cry of the Wild Ram* based on Russian-Alaska history in Kodiak's outdoor amphitheater; and Kodiak's *Jaycee Rodeo and State Fair.*

October: *Alaska Day Festival* (Oct. 18) at Sitka, where, in costume, they reenact the ceremony of transfer of Alaska from Russia to the United States. As you can tell by the spelling, *Oktoberfests* in Anchorage and Fairbanks offer real German beer and pretzels, good German food, dancing, music.

November–December: Alaskans are busy with typical Alaskan holiday celebrations, including bar-hopping in Nome. If you are there, join in.

 CLIMATE. You've probably gleaned some climate clues from "When to Go"; now for a few specifics. (Also see specific *Practical Information* sections.)

Within a vast land mass with such diverse physical features, "diverse" describes the weather as well.

Generally, "mild" fits the southeastern and southcentral coastal regions, which are tempered by the warm Japan Current. Expect rain, though. Southeast

Alaska is especially prone to precipitation. Average annual inches of rain have ranged from 29 inches in Skagway to 164 inches in Ketchikan, with Sitka and Wrangell tied halfway with 82 inches each. Temperatures range from July highs in the mid-60° F, to January lows in the low 20° F. In Juneau and Petersburg, over a hundred inches of snow have fallen mid-November to mid-April; other communities have had little or none. Southcentral areas are colder in winter being farther north; still, the temperature usually stays well above 0° F in winter and under 70° F in the warmest month, July. They count on an annual 60-inch snowfall, the better to pursue their winter sports, October–April.

The Interior prepares for severe winters, with winds that may add a chill factor sending the temperature well below 0° F. As if to compensate, the temperature may soar as high as 95° F during midsummer. Mostly it's comfortable the rest of the year, and dry compared to coastal regions to the south.

Weather is not the main attraction in the Fringes, the areas in the rim of wilderness above the Arctic Circle and along the southwestern, western and northern coasts. Out on the Alaska Peninsula, the Aleutian Island Chain, and islands to the north in the southern Bering Sea, rain, fog, and brisk winds predominate, but with some improvement in summer.

In the far north and far west regions, even the Arctic Ocean and the Bering Sea freeze solid for two thirds of the year. In contrast, when the tundra has thawed a few inches and blooms in summer (anytime it's above 50° F), it's shirt-sleeve weather for the Natives.

 PACKING. Make a packing list for each member of the family. Then check off items as you pack them. It will save time, reduce confusion. Almost any item you may need will be available in Alaskan stores and supermarkets, but the price will be higher. Always carry an extra pair of glasses, including sunglasses, particularly if they're prescription ones. A travel iron is always a good tote-along, as are some plastic bags (small and large) for wet suits, socks, etc. They are also excellent for packing shoes, cosmetics, and other easily damaged items. Don't minimize the importance of bringing sunglasses and lotion, too. Contrary to the early-day polar image of Alaska, that midnight sun burns bright and long in summer. In winter, the sun-and-snow combination can be brilliant. An Alaskan tan, or burn, can be achieved in short order when you spend time out-of-doors.

As for insect repellent, you'll do well to keep some handy. Even the most avid Alaska boosters admit to periodic plagues of mosquitoes, no-see-um's, and gnats in the "bush" (which comes right up to city thresholds). The mosquitoes peak after breakup, breeding in the soggy land through June, tapering off in July and August. Though the land is fairly insect free by September and through the winter, fishermen and other wilderness fans should carry a bug bomb and wipe-on repellent the rest of the year.

In addition to the essentials such as a camera and plenty of film, some extras that could be useful are binoculars for spotting shy animals across the tundra and Dall sheep and mountain goats in high rocky mountain pastures, a compass, and a magnifying glass to help read fine-print maps. If you fly, remember that despite signs to the contrary, airport security X-ray machines do in fact damage your films in many cases. Have them inspected by hand.

All members of the family should have sturdy, comfortable shoes with non-slip soles. Keep them handy in the back of the car. You never know when you may want to stop and clamber along a rocky trail to some site. Carry the family rain gear in a separate bag, in the back of the car (so no one will have to get out and hunt for it in a downpour en route).

"Naturism" or nudism has barely taken hold in Alaska and will probably never spread to the extent it has in such sunny states as Florida, California, and Hawaii. This is most likely due to climate; other reasons could include the aforementioned insects. However, bring a swimsuit. Many hotels have pools and health clubs. Communities have their own swimming pools, plus beaches in many recreational areas. There are saunas in surprising places—at Kachemak Bay Lodge on China Poot Bay across from the Homer Spit on the Kenai Peninsula, and at Kulik Lodge in Angler's Paradise in the Katmai. It's located so you can plunge right into icy Nonvianuk Lake. But Alaska is so big and so sparsely populated, it's safe to wager that anyone with a back-to-nature yearning will not have to go far to find a suitable spot to disrobe—while keeping an eye out for bears, and for flightseers in small planes or helicopters.

Don't be formal. Alaskans take people at face value, and if it's bearded it's in good company, along with governor, legislator, or professional. Everything is very casual, including dress. The accent is on comfort, though it's always a good idea to carry one outfit that can be appropriate for "dress up."

Whatever style you travel, travel light (even on tours, when baggage transfers are usually included). You may have to tote your own bags. Quick dry cleaning, laundry service, and laundromats are in all larger cities and most small ones.

In winter and the "shoulder seasons" the layer method of keeping warm is practical. Take some extra sweaters to add as needed under a down jacket or winter coat. When it's *really* cold, in Interior, Western, or Arctic, be prepared with warm gloves, winter boots, cap, even earmuffs. It won't hurt to have long johns underneath all of that—and watch out for frostbite!

In summer, the snow and ice will be only part of the scenery, in glaciers or on mountain peaks. Generally, the climate will be mild and pleasant. Bring something warmer for cooler evenings, a sweater or jacket, but you won't need Arctic gear. A warm parka comes with the Arctic tours, for the duration, if needed. But even in the Arctic, in summer, you'll have to dig down a few inches to find permafrost, and the ice pack will be lurking far out at sea.

 WHAT WILL IT COST? The Division of Tourism has been as anxious to change Alaska's "high price tag" label as they have been to refute the "all-snow-and-ice" image left over from Purchase debates in Congress over a century ago. Now they can claim that the rest of the world is catching up. In fact, Alaska is considered a travel bargain by many Europeans.

You'll find higher prices that in some of the other 49 states, depending on the length of the supply line and the cost of air freight. A hamburger costs more in the Arctic or in the Pribilof Islands than in southeast Alaska, for example.

Lodging choices have been improving. Budget sleeping includes camping out or reserving a remote wilderness Forest Service cabin, though the latter *doubled* in price recently. It's now $10 per party per night, and the cost of getting there by plane, boat, or afoot is up to you. Otherwise, there are wilderness resorts, motels, motor inns, trailer parks, or hotels. Some of them are high rise and high priced and may be $100 or so a night, double, and more. The quality will be fine, and some are "Alaska Deluxe." It may, however, be hard to find hotels that offer all the comforts of a major city's "Super Deluxe" establishments.

Eating possibilities are limited, even nonexistent, in some small villages, and infinite in the larger cities. You can purchase snacks to dinner makings from supermarkets, and there are chain eateries from the "Colonel" to "Mr. Salt," penthouse restaurants in hotels, and specialty restaurants featuring international dishes.

Sooner or later, however, you will wind up eating in a restaurant, and even here there are a number of things you can do to cut costs. (1) Always stop at the cash register and look over the menu *before* you sit down. (2) Have a few standard items like coffee, fruit juice, dessert, side dishes, to test the price range. (3) Look around to see what other people are actually receiving. Are the portions big or small? (Generally, they serve Alaska-sized portions in our biggest state!) How much of the meal is padded with coleslaw? Is there more than one piece of tomato in the salad? How generous, or stingy, is the supply of bread and butter? (4) Order a complete dinner; a la carte *always* adds up to more. (5) If there is a salad bar, or any kind of smorgasbord arrangement, you can fill up there and save on dessert and extras. (6) Ask about smaller portions, at reduced prices, for children. More and more places are providing them now. (7) Go to a Chinese restaurant and order *one less* main dish than the number of people in your group. You'll still come away pleasantly full. (8) Ask for the Day's Special, House Special, Chef's Special, or whatever it's called. Chances are that it will be better and more abundant than the other things on the menu. (9) Remember that in better restaurants lunch may be more of a bargain than dinner.

If you like a drink before dinner or bed, it might be a good idea to bring your own bottle. Most hotels and motels supply ice free or for very little, but the markup on alcoholic beverages in restaurants, bars, lounges and dining rooms is enormous. Confine your public drinking to the "happy hours" advertised by many Alaskan bars, and save. The price is drastically lowered on some drinks. However, learn the local drinking laws; they vary throughout the state. You may have to bring your own or go thirsty if you are in a village that has voted to be "dry" in the last election.

Another travel tip: plan ahead and buy ahead. Your flight from home can be calculated on "tour-basing fares," a great saving over point-to-point prices— perhaps, 30 to 60%. Buying an overall package tour and adding, ahead of time, optional tours out of main cities is a thrifty way to see a lot of Alaska in a limited time. Meals usually are not included on prepaid package tours, but it is good to know the basic cost, what it includes, and that it is inflation-proof for the duration of the trip.

Timing is important, too. Instead of aiming for Alaska's busy midsummer days, think "thrift season." During early spring and autumn, prices may be 10 or 15% lower, with no skimping on what the tour offers. Those who travel at these times often get more individual treatment, as may those who arrive in winter, when native hosts are less busy.

Actually, dollar for dollar, prices in Alaska compare favorably with those around the world. Regardless of how they travel, and considering what Alaska has to offer, most people return home feeling they have gotten a lot for their money.

 HOW TO GET THERE. The only way you *can't* get there is by train. Although there are trains *in* Alaska, there are no trains *to* Alaska. The nearest stations for making connections with other means of transportation are Seattle, Washington—served by Amtrak—Vancouver, B.C., and Prince Rupert, B.C., Via Rail Canada's west coast terminals along the Alaska Ferry Route. Otherwise, the choices are many, by land, by sea, and by air. Getting to and traveling around Alaska is dealt with in the *Practical Information* sections.

In general, the southeast Panhandle's myriad islands and extensive coastline are approached only by sea and air. Only Haines and Skagway, at the upper end of the Inside Passage, have overland access routes to the Interior and north. The other towns and cities are connected only by the cruise ships and Alaska ferries that travel the southeast "Marine Highway" and mainly by *Alaska, Western,* and smaller local airlines. There are no overland connecting highways.

Interior and Gulf of Alaska regions, with Anchorage and Fairbanks as the hubs, contain most of the highway system. These and many other points are also served by air, and some of them by the southwest Marine Highway system.

Except for freighters and barges making deliveries during the limited period in summer when the seas are unfrozen and friendly, areas around the Fringes of Alaska are reached only by bush plane and jet.

 HINTS TO MOTORISTS. Driving in Alaska is probably more unpredictable and challenging than in any other part of the nation. Despite generally good conditions, special precautions and preparations are needed. A mile-by-mile guide such as *The Milepost* (see "Recommended Reading," later in this section) will answer most specific questions about the pleasures and perils, and will also alert you to upcoming points of interest. For example, don't leave food lying around in your parked car. The bear, one of the strongest of mammals, has been known to tear a car apart looking for tidbits. Another animal, the huge moose, is being reported quite frequently as a driving hazard, especially along the Alaska Highway. These animals, although in the East notoriously shy of people, have become sufficiently confident and inquisitive to stray onto the less traveled highways of the Northwest. A moose usually measures an ungainly seven feet from its hooves to its humped shoulders and weighs between 1,000 pounds and a ton. The best thing to do if you come across one while driving is to stop your car and wait. If the moose doesn't move off by itself, which it will nine times out of ten, try honking your horn.

A second hazard to watch for along the Alaska Highway, especially in summer, is flying gravel. Rubber matting can protect the gas tank. A bug screen will help keep gravel off the windshield. Use clear, hard plastic guards to cover your headlights. (These are inexpensive and available from almost any garage or service station along the access routes to the Alaska and Mackenzie highways.) Don't cover headlights with cardboard or plywood because you'll need your lights often, even in daytime, when dust is thrown up by cars passing in both directions. Windshield washers are a help. If you've encountered a lot of dust, be sure to have your carburetor and air cleaner serviced frequently. Remember too, if you enter Alaska by way of the Alaska Highway, that the Canadian parts of the highway through which you must travel are, for the most part, unpaved. The speed limit is 50 mph in Canada and 55 mph in Alaska, except where posted otherwise. However, loose gravel is hazardous, and freeze and thaw also affect paving. Wise drivers assess conditions and usually stay under the limit, sometimes well under it. Seat belts are mandatory in Canada; you can be fined if stopped and you don't have them fastened.

If you get stuck on any kind of road be careful about pulling off on the shoulder; it could be soft. In summer it stays light late, and though traffic is also light, Alaska is full of Good Samaritans. It's part of the code to stop and query if someone appears to be in trouble. If they can't help you on the spot, they'll send aid from the nearest point, which could be miles away. In winter there are checkpoints for keeping track of motorists, and roads are patrolled. When traveling in winter, bring some high-energy food, such as nuts or chocolate, flasks of hot beverages, extra warm clothing and blankets, in addition to emergency equipment for your car.

 PULLING A TRAILER. If you plan to pull a *trailer* —boat or house—on your holiday trip, and have never before done so, don't just hook up and set out. You need a whole new set of driving skills—starting, stopping, cornering, passing, *being* passed, and, most tricky of all, backing. Reading about it will help a little, but not much. Try to practice in an open field, but if this is not possible, take your maiden trip in light traffic. A few useful hints: in starting and stopping, do everything more slowly and gradually than you would normally; in cornering, swing wider than usual since the trailer won't follow exactly the rear wheels of the towing car. Too sharp a right turn will put your trailer wheels over the curb. Too sharp a left turn will squash a car waiting to let you make the turn. In passing, remember you're longer than usual. Allow more safe distance ahead to pull back into the right lane. A slight bit of extra steering will help if you're *being* passed by a large truck or bus. In these situations, the trailer is inclined to sway from air currents. Don't make it worse by slowing down. It's better to speed up slightly. In backing, the basic technique is to turn the steering wheel opposite to the way you would want the car to go if you were driving it alone. From there on, it's practice, practice, practice. Most states have special safety regulations for trailers, and these change frequently. If you plan to operate your trailer in several states, check with your motor club, the police, or the state motor vehicle department about the rules. Also talk it over with the dealer from whom you buy or lease your trailer. Generally, speed limits for cars hauling trailers are lower, parking of trailers (and automobiles) is prohibited on expressways and freeways, and tunnels often ban trailers equipped with cooking units which use propane gas. In Alaska, be prepared for having to drive yourself off and on the ferries and railroad flat cars.

The condition of the Alaska Highway is generally so good that there are few problems in trailer towing, provided both the trailer and tow vehicle are in proper shape. Usually, no difficulty is encountered in towing trailers of up to 15 feet. Trailers of 16 to 30 feet must be towed by a standard-size car. Trailers of more than 30 feet must be towed by a vehicle with a rating at least equal to that of a ¼-ton truck. For trailers of more than 60 feet in length, 8 feet in width, or 14 feet in height, permits must be obtained from *Yukon Department of Highways,* 302 Steel St. Whitehorse, Yukon Territory, Canada Y1A 2C6. Weight limits are 18,000 pounds for single axle, 32,000 pounds for tandem axle, and 73,500 for wheel base 55 feet and over. One-wheel luggage trailers are not suitable for the long gravel highway. Bottled gas is available at most towns and many of the smaller stops along the highway. Most of Alaska's many fine roadside campgrounds accommodate trailers, but there are few hookups. Water is available at most stopping spots, but may be limited for trailer use. Other supplies are available at regular intervals along the highway, making it unwise to overload your car and trailer with food and other items. Trailer towing along the highway should be avoided during the spring thaw, when the roadbed is often rough. At Customs, officials may require the listing of all contents. Most small household items carried on trailers may be carried on the regular Tourist Permit. Modern, well-equipped mobile-home camps are located in all major cities, and many accommodate transient or overnight trailers.

 CRUISE SHIPS. Cruise-ship travel appeals to those who like their magnificent vistas served in comfort and luxury without the hassle of packing and unpacking. In Alaska, shipboard fun and games have stiff competition. Almost round-the-clock daylight in summer and southeast Alaska's marine and mountain grandeur encourage healthful deck sightseeing and photography. There are "shore leaves" in the towns—all different, but with typical Alaskan flavor—for exploring and shopping. Over a dozen different cruise ships sail from Vancouver, B.C., Canada; Los Angeles; San Francisco, and Seattle. The "regulars" plus some newcomers offer a wide choice of many sailings along this traditional "invasion" route to Alaska, used by Indians, explorers, fur traders, gold seekers, adventurers, and now tourists. Names and addresses of cruise ship companies to contact for information and prices are listed in the Southeast *Practical Information* section. Often the cruise is the "sea leg" of a tour that covers other sections of Alaska by assorted transportation on land and by air.

TOURS. Package tours have been proliferating in the last few years, and there are many fine ones. Pick a package that highlights places that exude "Alaska," if you are a cheechako (newcomer) and your vacation time is limited. It's possible to see much of big Alaska in only a week if you fly a lot. Most tours aim toward 2 or 3 weeks, though the trend is toward shorter, even "minitours," to particular areas. Tours use assorted modes of transportation and allow for some optional tours along the way. If you buy a prepaid, pre-packaged tour with definite word on what's covered and what isn't, your budget won't be shot during the trip, due to inflation, currently a world-wide travel worry.

Give or take a few adjectives and glowing terms, and you can believe the brochures put out by airlines, cruise ships, and tour operators pushing escorted and independent tours by land, sea, and air. Invariably, the promotion is liberally laced with colorful photographs, but Alaska's grand-scale scenery does not need any touching up. What's included is spelled out. With great distances to cover, round-trip transportation is a big item. Tours to far out places like the Pribilof Fur Seal Islands, for example, are priced to include a 2,000-mile round-trip flight via Reeve Aleutian Airways, from Anchorage. Generally, hotels, transfers, tips, guide services, and all sightseeing features outlined and described in the itinerary are conscientiously delivered. Meals are not included. Usually, there will be a choice of prices and places to eat. Meals could cost over $25 a day per person; more if you frequent the fanciest places (and drink, too), depending on current inflation rate, of course.

The big question is how to choose among the assorted general tours, plus intriguing "optional tours" off the beaten tour trails. They come in varying lengths with a wide range of prices. Compare; sometimes the lowest price is not the best value, considering what is included and what is extra. Most tours leave room in larger cities, Anchorage, Fairbanks, and Juneau, to add some optionals. It is advantageous to include them when you plan your trip. Your best friend can be your local travel agent, especially those knowledgeable about Alaska, and with the letters CTC following their names. It stands for Certified Travel Counselor, the designation awarded by the Institute of Certified Travel Agents to those who have five years or more experience and have mastered a tough 2-year course, and passed four 4-hour exams. A good travel agent is hardworking and will know all the time- and money-savers for getting you to Alaska and home again. Using their service won't add to your costs. They may well have been on a "fam" (familiarization) trip to the Great Land, and be able to steer you in the right directions. Or they will know where to get the information.

To start you planning, here are some active firms majoring in Alaska tours. They are known and respected for giving top value and performance. Some firms have "grown up" with Alaska tourism, and are now reinforced by the second generation. They support DOT (Division of Tourism) and belong to AVA (Alaska Visitors Association), where they socialize in hearty Alaskan style, and also talk over their mutual problems and successes. They work closely with airlines that will get you from home to Alaska direct or from West Coast tour departure points, and with cruise ships, ferries, motorcoaches, railroads, and local Alaskans interested in promoting tourism in their communities.

Alaska Tour & Marketing Services, Inc., 1500 Metropolitan Park Bldg., Olive Way and Boren Ave., Seattle, WA 98101, keeps a finger on the pulse of all Alaska travel and majors in the most diversified optionals. ATMS is the parent company of Exploration Holidays and Cruises. Here, the "parents" are Robert Giersdorf, president of ATMS, and his wife Lori, senior vice president. Daughter Debbie is executive vice president of *Exploration Cruise Lines;* her husband Ed Ritchie is the cruise division personnel director. *Travel Holiday* magazine's 1983 National Travel Poll gave "Special Kudos" to ECL ships for scoring "particularly high in courtesy of staff." Some 93% of passengers graded them "excellent." Son David is executive vice president of *Alaska Exploration Holidays and Cruises;* (800)–426–0600. "Working teams," from a string of huskies to husbands and wives and whole families, are common throughout the Alaskan scene, as you'll discover as you travel there.

Alaska Exploration Holidays and Cruises round up adventures that accent wilderness, Russian-American history, gold rush, Native cultures, fishing, natural history, photography; there's something to pique the special interests of almost everyone. Explorer Class ships feature a new cruising concept with three of their uniquely designed ships summering in Alaska: the 32-stateroom, 64-passenger *Glacier Bay Explorer,* the 44-stateroom, 88-passenger *Majestic Alaska Explorer,* and the 46-stateroom, 92-passenger *Great Rivers Explorer.* All have a shallow draft and a bow-landing facility that allow exploring in unusual places up icy fjords and port-calling at small villages along the Inside Passage. The 158-passenger M/S *North Star,* roundtripping from Prince Rupert, B.C., Canada, joined the Explorer Class fleet in the summer of 1985.

ATMS packages tours throughout Alaska, specializing in the more unusual destinations described in the *Fringes of Alaska* chapter. Arctic packages offer the choice of overnighting at Barrow, at the top of the continent, or Kotzebue, above the Arctic Circle, or gold-rush-founded Nome on the Bering Sea. The 3-day "Great Arctic Adventure" overnights at both Kotzebue and Nome. One-day Arctic jaunts are a special for travelers who can spare only a day for wandering off their general tour itinerary.

Tours may be combined with Inside Passage cruises. Especially popular are the first and last "positioning" cruises of the ships to and from Seattle. "Alaskan Odysseys," operated by *Special Expeditions,* a division of Lindblad Travel, (133 E. 55 St., New York, NY 10022), are longer *Explorer* voyages, cherished by nature lovers and photographers. More good contacts for Alaska packages:

Alaska Northwest Travel Service, 130 2nd Ave. So., Edmonds, WA 98020; (206) 775–4504. (At the Seattle Center, in 1984, to honor 25 years of Alaska Statehood and 50 years of their popular *Alaska* magazine, the company sponsored a lively 4-day *Alaska Northwest Trade & Travel Fair* that may be an annual event.)

Alaska Travel Bureau, Logan Bldg; 1411 4th Ave., Seattle, WA 98101. (206) 624–1477.

Atlas Tours, Ltd. (Gray Line), Sheffield Hotel, Box 4340, Whitehorse, Y.T., Canada Y1A 3T5, (403) 668-3161, handles Yukon Territory.

Royal Hyway Tours, 2121 4th Ave., Suite 1340, Seattle, WA 98121, (206) 467–6644. New, well-equiped, spacious motorcoaches for comfortable, personalized highway and city touring and sightseeing.

Kneisel Travel, Inc., 345 N.E. 8th Ave., Portland, OR 97232. Norm Kneisel, "Mr. K" himself, led the first motorcoach tour to travel the full length of the Alaska Highway. Today his galaxy of deluxe tours are classic. "Mr. K's Alaska Treasure Chest" has air/sea tours for independent travelers. The "Green Carpet" programs are for those who want to travel in an escorted group. The Kneisel tours, from their founding, are based on Mr. K's philosophy of "the finest in carefree travel arrangements." They allow choices in ferries and cruise ships, but they make a point of including worthwhile extras in the initial tour price, such as upgraded cabins rather than the simplest ones on cruise ships, shore excursions, and complete sightseeing throughout rather than pay-as-you-go. Clients always know where they are going and where they've been. Departure morning they receive a "Travel Log" of their itinerary and interesting sights to watch for, with space to add their own notes and observations.

Knightly Travel Service Inc., 1200 Westlake Ave. N., Suite 503, Seattle, WA 98109.

Maupintour, Box 807, Lawrence, KS 66044. Top-quality escorted tours.

Princess Tours, Fourth & Blanchard Building, Suite 1800, Seattle, WA 98121, (206) 382–4205, promotes their image as "The Vacation Company." Their tours include sailings on the *Sun Princess, Island Princess* and the *Royal Princess.* Princess offers well-planned Alaska vacations that combine air/sea/land travel. They have appropriate, descriptive names for the things you'll see the most of: "Wilderness Route," "Klondike Adventure," and "Gold Rush Country" are examples. Leaning toward the trend to shorter tours, they have some that take a week or so: "Southeast Sampler," "Glacier Bay Grandeur," and "Alaska Voyager." These are designed so that it is simple to add special-interest optional tours. The longest and most comprehensive Alaska vacation in Princess's book is "The Best of Alaska, Escorted." They promise travelers (who may be nervous about traveling independently in big Alaska) an intrepid leader, sworn to reveal all things best and beautiful along the way. The trip extends from Vancouver, B.C., to Kotzebue above the Arctic Circle, including such high points on the way as Denali National Park and the excursion to mammoth Columbia Glacier.

TravAlaska Tours, 4th & Battery Building, Suite 555, Seattle, WA 98121, is headed by "Mr. Alaska," a veteran in the tour game and Alaska travel since 1946. Among President Chuck West's many "firsts" in the industry is flying the first tourists to the Arctic in the early 1950s. TravAlaska offers low-cost, all-season tours of a week or two that take in Chuck's favorite places on an independent basis, tailored to individuals. These custom tours allow travelers to match varied transportation with their budget—luxury cruise or more economical ferryliner, for example. TravAlaska personnel meet and expedite tourists at each transfer point. *Alaska Yukon Motorcoaches,* an associate company, covers most Alaska roads and many in Canada, over scenic routes. *Alaska Sightseeing Company,* a division of AYM, has bases in Anchorage, Fairbanks, Haines, Juneau, and Ketchikan. In the Alaska tradition, the vice president and general manager is Dick West, Chuck's son. A popular innovation are the 10- to 16-passenger "Cub Coach" sightseeing vans. If you are 65 or over, be sure to ask your travel agent about TravAlaska's "Senior Citizen Spring Special."

Westours, 300 Elliott Ave. W., Seattle, WA 98119. Long on experience in Alaska travel, this tour company has at their disposal *Holland America Cruise ships* and their own *Fairweather* mini-cruiser between Juneau and Skagway, described in the Southeast chapter. They also have Gray Line motorcoaches for their "Hyway Tours" through Alaska and Canada, including the Canadian Rockies, and for city sightseeing. Their *Sightseeing Alaska* brochure, available at regional Westours travel desks or from the above address, features diverse excursions, such as a 6-hour "Eagle River Float Trip" (from Anchorage) and an informative "End of the Pipeline" tour (in Valdez). Westours hotels, in strategic places for housing their tour groups, are some of the finest. The company works closely with major airlines. The staff, augmented by Alaska enthusiasts in summer, goes all out to look after Westourists at all key points. The motorcoach driver/tour guides are exceptional, and include natives, such as members of a homesteading family, who know the area well. Westours offers a comprehensive collection of cruises, cruise/tours, and flightours, plus optional tours, covering thousands of miles to and from and within Alaska. They swear that their "Basic Alaska Tour" has never been equaled.

Airlines flying to and within Alaska offer promotions that include air travel bargains. Travel agents stay alert for such, and the airlines advertise them boldly. Inquire at your nearest airline regional office, or the following addresses.

Alaska Airlines, Vacation Dept., P.O. Box 68900, Seattle-Tacoma International Airport, Seattle, WA 98168. Ask about their "Buy Alaska" fare. $10 each to stop over in Ketchikan, Sitka, Juneau, Wrangell, Petersburg, Yakutat, Cordova, or Anchorage, if you buy a round-trip ticket Seattle to Fairbanks. They also fly tours to Glacier Bay and to the Arctic including Prudhoe Bay.

Northwest Orient Airlines, Minneapolis-St. Paul International Airport, St. Paul, MN 55111, or your regional sales office. They offer special air tour fares in connection with independent tour routings.

Western Airlines, 3830 International Airport Road, Anchorage, AK 99502, offers "Magic Weeks" in Alaska and service between gateway cities Seattle, Portland, and Honolulu, and Alaska.

Wien Airlines, Tour Office, 4797 Business Park Blvd., Building G, Anchorage, AK 99503; toll free for tour information in the continental U.S. call (800) 562–5222. They claim they can "take you to more cities in Alaska than any other airline." Ask about their "Passport" fare covering many, and about senior citizen fare promotions.

SPECIAL INTEREST TOURS. The Division of Tourism's comprehensive *Alaska Yukon Vacation Planner* devotes pages to operations that cater to people who want to pan for gold, go on photo safaris, run rivers, fish, hunt (over a hundred licensed big game guides), backpack, trail ride, go dogsledding, mountaineering, skiing, and flightseeing. The following outfits majoring in Alaska wilderness expeditions might have what you are seeking: *Alaska Discovery,* P.O. Box 26, Bustavus, AK 99826; (907) 697–2257. One-day to two-week adventure trips head into seven unique regions, among them Glacier Bay and Admiralty Island. Instructed by expert guides, sharing camp chores, even novices take to outdoor living and travel. *Alaska Sportfishing Packages,* Suite 1320, 4th & Blanchard Bldg., Seattle, WA 98121; (800) 426–0603. They feature the best fishing throughout the state, described in their "Fish Our Alaska." *Alaska Travel Adventures,* 200 N. Franklin St., Juneau, AK 99801; (907) 586–6245 or toll free (800) 227–8480, aim their wilderness adventures, graded according to difficulty, to small groups and families. A popular first rafting experience for all ages is the Mendenhall River Float Trip starting in the shadow of the face of the giant Mendenhall Glacier near Juneau.

Mountain Travel, 1398 Solano Ave., Albany, CA 94706, (415) 527–8100, toll-free (800) 227–2384, emphasizes remote areas in their hiking, climbing, and rafting expeditions.

Nature Expeditions International, Box 11496, Eugene, OR 97440; (503) 484–6529. 17-day expeditions feature Alaska's natural history, with college credit.

Outdoor Alaska, Box 7814, Ketchikan, AK 99901, (907) 247–8444 or 225–3498, features Misty Fjords National Monument Tours.

Questers Tours & Travel, 257 Park Ave. S. New York, N.Y. 10010, (212) 673–3120, concentrates on bird and plant life.

Sobeck Expeditions, Angels Camp, CA 95222, (209) 736–4524, and *Western River Expeditions,* 7528 Racquet Club Drive, Salt Lake City, UT 84121, toll-free (800) 453–7450, in Utah call (801) 942–6669, are also good bets for the unusual.

Keep in mind that when you come to the end of the road in Alaska, it is often the start of more adventure. Optional tours to more remote places around Alaska can be purchased by travelers "on their own," in car or camper, or tied in with a package tour for substantial savings using tour-basing air fares.

Ask about local sightseeing possibilities at information desks in hotel lobbies, and visitor information centers. They'll tell you and sell you what's available, gold dredges to nightlife tours.

If you are traveling on your own, what do you do with your camper and gear? There are safe places to leave them at departure points. Look in the yellow pages of directories in Anchorage, Fairbanks, and Juneau, if you are wondering what to do with your pet. There are many listings.

To sum up the tour situation:

Over a century ago, Russia sold Alaska to the U.S. in one big bargain package. Now it's being resold in smaller packages, to tourists. Alaska-covering tours, in general, travel in the best of—but similar—circles around the state. The optionals are planned out of the main cities on the itinerary. However, if you have a yen to see some special place—even Siberia—chances are there's a way. When in Nome, check bush airline *Ryan Air Service,* at the airport. Besides their scheduled milk runs to deliver people and goods to small far west coastal communities, they flightsee near the International Boundary and Date Line, where you can peek into the Soviet Union—and "tomorrow."

 **HOTELS AND MOTELS.** As you might expect, accommodations in Alaska frequently carry the tang of the frontier, but there is actually no lack of modern conveniences. You'll recognize some familiar chain names: Great Western, Hilton, Holiday Inn, Sheraton, and the recurring Sheffield Houses—an Alaskan chain that has hotels in Anchorage, Fairbanks, Juneau, Kenai, Kodiak, Sitka, Valdez, Dawson City, Beaver Creek, and Whitehorse, Y.T., Canada. (These were started by William Sheffield, present Governor of Alaska.)

Knowledgeable tour operators and travel agents candidly point out that the accommodations and service may seem rather basic in some places in the "last frontier." Those open only seasonally might have a transient, young, inexperienced staff, which is not expecting to cater to deluxe-minded clientele. What's lacking in expertise, though, is usually offset by enthusiasm and a genuine eagerness to see that guests are comfortable while they enjoy the best of the area.

Throughout Alaska, there'll be intriguing choices ranging from high-rise and tower suites to wilderness lodges and cabins. The most sophisticated accommodations in amenities and service are, naturally, in the larger cities. Some hotels have athletic clubs, swimming pools, plus other facilities for handling large parties, meetings, and conventions. Along the highways and in towns there'll be comfortable smaller lodgings available, more than likely exuding hospitality distinctly Alaskan.

Prices are generally a notch higher than in the "lower 48's" northwestern states. But, as almost everywhere else in the world, prices are hard to predict because of inflation. In smaller cities, especially in southeast Alaska, prices will be lower—and places to stay fewer. While the larger cities have many hotels and motels, summer travel is heavy in our 49th state and you should reserve ahead. Space is blocked in advance by tour groups; the price of rooms included in a package tour will be an overall saving because rooms are based on group rates. There are lower rates during "thrift season"—early spring, late fall, and winter. Hotel and motel chains usually have toll-free WATS (800) lines; call (800) 555–1212 to see if there is an 800 number for the Alaska hotel you want to reach. Or stop by visitor information centers and chambers of commerce, wherever you are, for local lodging leads, and prices.

Although the names of the various hotel and motel categories are standard throughout this book—*deluxe, expensive, moderate, inexpensive*—the prices listed under each category may vary from area to area. This variance is meant to reflect local price standards, and take into account that what might be considered a *moderate* price in a large, urban area might be quite *expensive* in a rural region. In every case, however, the dollar ranges for each category are clearly stated before each listing of establishments in the appropriate *Practical Information* sections.

Free parking is assumed at all motels and motor hotels; you must pay for parking at most city hotels, though certain establishments have free parking, frequently for occupants of higher-than-minimum-rate rooms. *Baby sitter* lists are always available in good hotels and motels, and *cribs* for the children are always on hand—sometimes at no cost, but more frequently at a cost of $1 or $2 per night. The cost of a *cot* in your room, supplementing the beds, will also be around $3 per night, but moving an *extra single bed* into a room will cost from $7 in better hotels and motels.

Senior citizens may in some cases receive special discounts on lodgings and in restaurants—it doesn't hurt to ask. Holiday Inns give a 10% discount year-round to members of the NRTA (National Retired Teachers Association) and the AARP (American Association of Retired Persons), both headquartered at 215 Long Beach Blvd., Long Beach, CA 90802. The ITT Sheraton chain gives 25% off (call [800] 325–3535) to members of the AARP, the NRTA, the National Association of Retired Persons, The Catholic Golden Age of United Societies of U.S.A., and the Old Age Security Pensioners of Canada. A price break for senior visitors may come in unexpected places. In the window of the Fairbanks Inn Beauty Shop (and others) they may offer senior citizen shampoos and sets for less than the going rate. Take your I.D. along to Alaska.

Bed-and breakfast has come to Alaska. It's a great way to meet Alaskans, and they're willing to share not only their facilities, but also their knowledge of their home town. Styles and standards vary widely, of course; generally private baths are less common and rates are pleasingly low. Prices may range from $25 to $50 per night, including breakfast. In many small towns such guest houses are excellent examples of the best a region has to offer of its own special atmosphere. Each one will be different, so that their advantage is precisely the opposite of that "no surprise" uniformity which motel chains pride themselves on. Few, if any, guest houses have heated pools, wall-to-wall carpeting, or exposed styrofoam-wooden beams in the bar. Few if any even have bars. What you do get, in addition to economy, is the personal flavor of a family atmosphere in a private home. In popular tourist areas, state or local tourist information offices or chambers of commerce usually have lists of homes that let out spare rooms to paying guests, and such a listing usually means that the places on it have been inspected and meet some reliable standard of cleanliness, comfort, and reasonable pricing.

Youth hostels are another housing alternative. The Alaska Council, AYH, P.O. Box 4-1461, Anchorage, AK 99509, has information. Or contact the National Offices, American Youth Hostels, 1332 I St. N.W., Suite 800, Washington, DC 20005. Alaska has 13 youth hostels where travelers—not always in their youth, and even groups and families—may stay for under $10 a night. The Anchorage Youth Hostel, P.O. Box 4–1226, Anchorage 99509; phone (907) 276–3635, is open year round. Others, for the most part operating summer seasons only, are located in Delta Junction, Haines, Homer, Juneau, Ketchikan, Kodiak, Sitka, Soldotna, Sutton, Tok, Nome, and Fairbanks.

The facilities are varied and so are the rates. Some offer meals and there may or may not be kitchen facilities available. Local visitor centers also have information and can point hostel-seeking travelers in the right direction.

 CAMPING. Almost every town has a public campground, and there are many commercial campgrounds, as well. No fees are charged at *Alaska state campgrounds* and *waysides*. (See "State Parks" section, below.) Contact *Alaska Department of Natural Resources,* Division of Parks, 619 Warehouse Ave., Suite 210, Anchorage, AK 99501. Camping in the *Chugach* and *Tongass national forests* will probably require payment of a $4–6 fee; there is a 14-day limit at most of these campgrounds. Contact *U.S. Forest Service,* Box 1628, Juneau, AK 99802, or 2221 E. Northern Lights Blvd., Suite 230, Anchorage, AK 99504. You can also stop in personally at Bldg. C, Huffman Business Plaza, 12101 Industry Way, Anchorage. The *Bureau of Land Management* operates about 25 camping areas for no charge. (An exception to this is the *Delta BLM campground* on the Alaska Hwy.) Contact Bureau of Land Management, 701 C St., Box 13, Anchorage, AK 99513. For camping in *national parks and preserves,* including *Denali, Glacier Bay,* and *Katmai,* contact *National Park Service,* 2525 Gambell St., Anchorage, AK 99503. Some are free; some are $6 a night. *Camping in the National Park System,* Stock #024–005–00853–5 tells all; send $1.50 to Superintendent of Documents, U.S. Government Printing Office, Washington, D.C. 20402. The *Fish & Wildlife Service* maintains primitive campgrounds in the *Kenai National Wildlife Refuge.* No reservations, but information is available from the Refuge Manager, Box 2139, Soldotna, AK 99669.

National park campgrounds in Canada usually have a nightly fee of $5–8. In addition, a license sticker is required for motorists staying overnight: $2 for a 4-day permit; $10 for an annual permit. *Territorial campgrounds* in the Yukon Territory charge $25 for nonresidents per season; $5 a night.

 DINING OUT in Alaska means a wide variety of exciting and unusual foods for the traveler. Reindeer steak or stew, sourdough bread and sourdough pancakes, and sheefish are only a few Alaskan specialties that visitors like to try. Not to be missed here, of course, is seafood—the king crab, fresh salmon, halibut, or tiny Alaskan shrimp, and scallops. You may be offered "moose milk," but unless you see it produced from the animal before your very eyes, it will probably be ordinary milk laced with cinnamon and (likely) some whiskey. Check the hotel listings for the city you are visiting. Often hotel or inn dining rooms are the best in town, or the only ones.

For evening meals, the best advice is to make reservations in advance whenever possible. For motel stayers, life is simpler if the motel has a restaurant. If it hasn't, try and stay at one that is near a restaurant.

Few places in Alaska are very fussy about customers' dress, but you'll see signs requiring shoes and shirts. Shorts are almost always frowned on for both men and women. Standards of dress are becoming more relaxed, so a neatly dressed customer will usually experience no problem. If in doubt about accepted dress at a particular establishment, call ahead.

Roadside stands, fast food restaurants, and cafeterias have no fixed standards of dress.

If you're traveling with children, you may want to find out if a restaurant has a children's menu and commensurate prices (many do).

When figuring the tip on your check, base it on the total charges for the meal, not on the grand total, if that total includes a state sales tax. Don't tip on tax.

Restaurants are divided into price categories as follows: *deluxe, expensive, moderate,* and *inexpensive.* Restaurant meals will cost more in Alaska, and as a general rule, expect restaurants in metropolitan areas to be higher in price, although many restaurants that feature foreign cuisine are often surprisingly inexpensive. We should also point out that limitations of space make it impossible to include every establishment. We have, therefore, included those which we consider the best within each price range.

Although the names of the various restaurant categories are standard throughout this book, the prices listed under each category may vary from area to area. This variation is meant to reflect local price standards, and take into account that what might be considered a *moderate* price in a large urban area might be quite *expensive* in a rural region. In every case, however, the dollar ranges for each category are clearly stated before each listing of establishments.

Chains: There are now several chains of restaurants, some of them nationwide, that offer reliable eating at excellent budget prices. Look for them as you travel, and check local telephone directories in cities where you stop.

TIPPING. Tipping is supposed to be a personal thing, your way of expressing your appreciation of someone who has taken pleasure and pride in giving you attentive, efficient, and personal service. Because standards of personal service in the United States are highly uneven, you should, when you get genuinely good service, feel secure in rewarding it, and when you feel that the service you got was slovenly, indifferent, or surly, don't hesitate to show this by the size, or the withholding, of your tip. Remember that in many places, especially seasonal resorts, the staff are paid very little and depend on tips for the better part of their income. This is supposed to give them incentive to serve you well.

In Alaska, on a *tour,* it is often specified that tips and baggage handling are included. On some *cruise ship* lines you may see signs stating "tips are not required." However, you'll get the message that tips are not unwelcome (but voluntary), and they'll share the "formula." It varies according to amount of service, such as use of wine stewards, or other special treatment that you require. Generally, $6 or $7 a day, per person, is expected. Some cruise ship lines say to allow 5% of your fare. Smaller cruise ships (like the Explorer Class™) suggest $4 per day, per person, and tips are pooled among all the crew. On excursions where the motorcoach driver and/or tour guide has been exceptionally informative and helpful (and they usually are), the passengers may be inclined to take up a kitty, or to tip individually. Throughout Alaska people often go out of their way to help visitors, obviously with no thought of a tip. Use your good judgment and try not to insult a new-found "friend" who was just being hospitable and helpful as a matter of course. The following may be helpful guidelines. These days, the going rate on *restaurant* service is 15% on the amount *before* taxes. Tipping at counters is not universal, but many people leave 25¢ on anything up to $1, and 10% on anything over that. For *bellboys*, 25¢ per bag is usual. However, if you load him down with all manner of bags, hatboxes, cameras, coats, etc., you might consider giving an extra quarter or two. For one-night stays in most *hotels* and *motels* you leave nothing. If you stay longer, at the end of your stay leave the maid $1–1.25 per day, or $5 per person, per week, for multiple occupancy. If you are staying at an *American Plan* hostelry (meals included) $1.50 per day, per person, for the waiter or waitress is considered sufficient and is left at the end of your stay. However, if you have been surrounded by an army of servants (one bringing relishes, another rolls, etc.), add a few extra dollars and give the lump sum to the captain or *maitre d'hotel* when you leave, asking him to allocate it.

For the many other serivces you may encounter in a big hotel or resort (though probably not frequently in Alaska), figure roughly as follows: doorman, 25¢ for taxi handling, 50¢ for help with baggage; parking attendant, 50¢; bartender, 15%; room service, 10–15% of that bill; laundry or valet service, 15%; pool attendant, 50¢ per day; snackbar waiter at pool, beach, or golf club, 50¢ per person for food and 15% of the beverage check; locker attendant, 50¢ per person per day, or $2.50 per week; masseurs and masseuses, 20%; golf caddies, $1 per bag, or 15% of the greens fee for an 18-hole course, or $3 on a free course; barbers, 50¢; shoeshine attendants, 25¢; hairdressers, $1; manicurists, 50¢.

Transportation: Give 25¢ for any taxi fare under $1 and 15% for any above. Limousine service, 20%. Car rental agencies, nothing. Bus porters are tipped 25¢ per bag, drivers nothing. On charters and package tours, conductors and drivers usually get $5–10 per day from the group as a whole, but be sure to ask whether this has already been figured into the package cost. On short, local sightseeing runs, the driver-guide may get 25¢ per person, more if you think he has been especially helpful or personable. Airport bus drivers, nothing. Redcaps, in resort areas, 35¢ per suitcase, elsewhere, 25¢. Tipping at curbside check-ins is unofficial, but same as above. On the plane, no tipping.

Railroads suggest you leave 10–15% per meal for dining car waiters, but the steward who seats you is not tipped. Sleeping-car porters get about $1 per person, per night. The 25¢ or 35¢ you pay a railway station baggage porter is not a tip but the set fee that he must hand in at the end of the day along with the ticket stubs he has used. Therefore his tip is anything you give him above that, 25¢ to 50¢ per bag, depending on how heavy your luggage is.

DRINKING LAWS. Twenty-one is the age at which you may start. Communities vote on whether they want to be dry or wet, and they may vacillate. Check before you go to places in far-flung areas, if you are concerned. There'll be a wide choice of taverns in most towns and cities in the populated areas. Some are highly colorful. Seek—and ye shall find. Be forewarned that many bars close only between 5 A.M. and 8 A.M. If you're lodging near one—and it's hard not to in this well-salooned land—it may get a bit noisy outside around six in the morning, as bartenders clean up with a bottle-breaking symphony.

BUSINESS HOURS AND LOCAL TIME. Business hours for banks, shops, offices, cinemas, etc., are pretty much the same as for the rest of the country, except that those somehow related to tourism may be open longer in the summer. They celebrate the usual holidays on schedule, plus some special Alaskan ones: *Seward Day* (the Purchase), March 30; *Alaska Day* (the Transfer), October 18; and *Admission (Statehood) Day,* January 3.

Recently the state legislature has simplified things by putting Alaska on two time zones instead of four. Most of the state is on *Yukon Time,* an hour earlier than Pacific Standard Time. Only four far-west Aleutian Island communities are on *Alaska-Hawaii Time,* an hour earlier than the rest of Alaska's Yukon Time; two hours earlier than Pacific Time. Daylight savings time is observed in summer. As of this writing, the Yukon Territory and most of British Columbia, Canada, are on Pacific Time, with a few exceptions in eastern British Columbia, on Mountain Time.

SPECTATOR SPORTS. Anchorage, Palmer, and Kenai field good independent *baseball* teams. The *Fairbanks Gold Panners* are one of the top nonprofessional teams in the country. A highlight of the summer is the *Midnight Sun Baseball Game,* played at the Growden Memorial Stadium without artificial light.

Basketball is popular, too. The *University of Alaska* takes on college cagers from other states, and a 6-day *Gold Medal Basketball Tournament* livens up Juneau in mid-February.

Curling is an old Scottish favorite, played and watched avidly in winter in Anchorage, Fairbanks, and Whitehorse, Y.T., Canada.

During Christmas week in Kotzebue, the Eskimos compete in *dog team racing, snowshoeing, snowmachine races, wrestling,* and *finger and ear pulling contests,* and other Native, and not-so-Native, sports. That's good practice for the late-July, 3-day *World Eskimo Indian Aleut Olympic Games* staged in Fairbanks.

Footracing is a possibility for fun when the snow is gone. Seward's grueling *Mt. Marathon Footrace* each July 4 sends the hardy and the hopeful up the 3,022-foot peak behind the city and back, with the best racers completing the run in less than an hour. Long-distance runners vie in the over-26-mile *University of Alaska Equinox Marathon* at Fairbanks in the fall.

Probably only experts (and the hardy) will compete in a race like the mid-January, 200-mile cross-country *snowmachine race,* Kenai to Homer and back. Spectators may opt for beginnings and endings only, considering the problems they might have following the participants throughout.

RECREATION ALASKA STYLE. In summer: Yes, you *can pan for gold* (but don't count on striking it rich). Some tour packages provide the opportunity, and there are private concessions where, for a fee, you can try your hand. "Recreational mining"—for the fun and adventure of it—is open to all on certain public lands. Be sure to read the leaflets on the dos and don'ts and locations issued by the Bureau of Land Management, P.O. Box 13, 701 C St., Anchorage, AK 99513; Box 1150, Gaffney and Marks Rd., Ft. Wainright, Fairbanks, AK 99707. The main thing to check on before dipping your gold pan into a promising stream is that you are not on someone else's grubstake.

It's possible to tee off for *golf* almost to midnight, in Fairbanks, for example. The "greens" (which may not be that color up north) sometimes sport another kind of "game"—glimpses of wildlife—and spectacular scenery as well.

The state and federal governments have cleared miles of *hiking* trails in forest and mountain areas. *Mountain climbing* ranges from afternoon rock ascents to tackling the highest peak in North America. But be prepared in every respect, and have guides on any extended climb.

Rivers and lakes abound for *canoeing, kayaking,* and *rafting* expeditions with wilderness-wise leaders. Food and gear are usually furnished with the package price; or there'll be local charters and rentals available.

Underwater, *diving,* both *scuba* and *skin,* is popular along the southeast and Gulf of Alaska coasts. Sitka, Ketchikan, Juneau, Kodiak, and Anchorage all have places that rent equipment. Alaska divers wear no less than quarter-inch wet suits.

There is wonderful *fishing* and *hunting* throughout the state. For information on regulations write *Department of Fish and Game,* Box 3–2000, Juneau, AK 99802. They will provide statewide information, but suggest you seek local advice. (See "Tourist Information" in *Practical Information* for local Fish & Game Dept. addresses.) Fishing licenses are needed for those over 16 and can be acquired at most sporting goods stores and wilderness lodges. A special $5 permit is needed for king salmon and steelhead trout. Nonresidents pay $36 for a year's license, $20 for a 14-day license; $10 for a 3-day license. *Spearfishing* is fair, but the principal trophy is the king crab.

All nonresidents regardless of age must have a valid hunting license and tags in their possession while taking or attempting to take game. These are considerably more expensive than fishing licenses: $60 for a hunting license; $90 for a hunting and fishing license; $200 for hunting and trapping. Locking tags or "trophy fees" are $150 for wolf and wolverine; $135 for deer; $200 for black bear; $250 for elk and goat; $300 for moose or caribou; $250 for brown/grizzly bear; $400 for sheep; and $1100 for musk ox. The Alaska Dept. of Fish and Game puts out a quarterly magazine (free to Alaskans; $5 to nonresidents) that features news and trends. Write to the department at the address given above.

Don't leave your swim suit home when you pack for your Alaska vacation. Coastal waters are chilly, but lakes are warm enough in summer for *waterskiing* and *swimming,* thanks to nearly 24 hours of daylight. Some towns have community swimming pools; there are resorts with hot-spring-filled pools, and hotels and motels in cities are leaning toward putting in pools for their guests.

In winter: Alaska's powder snow offers an exciting challenge, accepted by the *skiing* residents of many communities. At Juneau, *Eaglecrest* ski area is across from the city on the slopes of Douglas Island. It has a chairlift, rope tows, and a day lodge. There is also skiing on glaciers of the *Juneau Ice Field,* reached by helicopter. There are accessible ski slopes near Fairbanks and on the Kenai Peninsula. *Turnagain Pass,* 59 miles from Anchorage on the Seward Highway, is popular with cross-country skiers and snowmobilers. The snowfall here is often over 12 feet. Skiers from all over the world gather at *Mt. Alyeska,* to take advantage of ski packages, and national and international competitions held there. Multiple rope tows and chairlifts hoist enthusiasts to higher elevations for spectacular vistas of Turnagain Arm.

Besides the snow for *dogsledding* and *snowmobiling,* the ice on frozen lakes is popular for *skating* and *ice-fishing* during the winter months.

 WHAT TO DO WITH THE CHILDREN. *Around and about Anchorage with Children,* by the *Anchorage Volunteer Service League,* is full of ideas for family fun. $6.50 brings it postpaid from P.O. Box 3762-S, Downtown Station, Anchorage, AK 99510. Or, if you are in Anchorage, ask at the Log Cabin where it's available for $5.95. *Denali National Park,* with its wildlife, birds, and flora, will amaze, excite, and instruct. At various places the children will see animals in the open; for animals for close-up viewing there is the *Alaska Children's Zoo,* 7 miles from Anchorage. The theme historic park *Alaskaland,* at Fairbanks, seems designed for children of all ages. A ride on the sternwheeler *Discovery* out of Fairbanks will be a trip long remembered; so will a trip on the *Alaska Railroad.* Fishing streams, especially those with *salmon spawning,* draw interest. *Indians,* and all the products they craft, will leave indelible impressions. *Skagway,* a living page out of the past, will appeal to kids with a taste for history and color. Local shows: the *Chilkat Dancers* at Port Chilkoot; the melodrama *Fish Pirate's Daughter* in a bar at Ketchikan; Skagway's *In the Days of '98;* Kodiak's drama, *Cry of the Wild Ram;* and Juneau's *Gold Creek Salmon Bake* may be highlights of a vacation for some youngsters. Gold mines, gold panning, ghost towns, old forts, museums, gift shops, sled dogs, totem poles, sawdust-floor saloons where popcorn and soda pop are served, ferry boats, glaciers, fishing boats, baseball games at night without lights, nights without darkness, chair lifts to high places, riverboat races, sourdough breakfasts—these and a list that could extend for pages more will keep kids alert, cheerful, and responsive to the environment.

 STATE PARKS. Write to *State of Alaska Dept. of Natural Resources,* Division of Parks, 619 Warehouse Ave., Suite 210, Anchorage, AK 99501, for an informative folder and map of Alaska's State Park System, America's largest (and youngest). The system includes campgrounds, recreation areas, waysides and historic sites. The largest park is *Wood-Tikchik State Park,* reached by air from Dillingham. Others are next-largest *Chugach State Park,* near Anchorage; *Chilkat State Park,* south of Haines; *Sitka National Historical Park* (one acre), *Denali State Park,* about 140 miles north of Anchorage; and *Kachemak Bay State Park* and *Kachemak Wildnerness Park* on the Kenai Peninsula. Plentiful campgrounds throughout the state offer fishing, hunting, hiking, bird watching, and other outdoor activities. Following are a number of such typical campgrounds: *Bird Creek,* on Seward Highway 26 miles south of Anchorage, is one of Alaska's most popular recreation areas. There is spectacular scenery along Turnagain Arm and an inspiring view across the Arm to Hope and Chugach Range from Bird Creek. *Hope,* a once-booming gold rush city, is now a small village. Abandoned gold mines can be found up Resurrection Creek Valley. Rainshelter, picnic units, camping sites. Excellent salmon fishing in Bird Creek. *Eklutna* is nestled in an Alpine canyon, 23 miles north on Glenn Highway, 8 miles east on gravel road; it has a 1,200-foot air strip. Freshwater glacial streams with waterfalls. Toe of Eklutna Glacier at far end of canyon. Spruce and cottonwood. Dall sheep and mountain goats often visible on canyon walls. Bear, moose, fox, coyote, ptarmigan, grouse also seen. Picnic area, campsites. *Chatanika River,* Fairbanks, is 39 miles north on Steese Highway. Located in area of extensive mining operations, here visitors can see where huge gold dredges separated gold from gravel. Even beginners can pan and come up with gold from the streams. Good hunting and fishing in area. Some picnic tables.

Stariski is 22 miles north of Homer, at Mile 154 on Sterling Highway. Attractive grounds, with grassy areas framed by spruce trees. Bluebells and fireweed bloom in June and July. Excellent views of Mt. Iliamna and other peaks on Alaska Peninsula across Cook Inlet. Rainshelter, picnic area, campsites. *Bernice Lake* lies 10 miles north of Kenai on North Kenai Rd. Small, lovely lake, popular for swimming, boating, and picnicking. Restful site with superior scenery. Picnic area, campsites.

The rules and regulations are standard and insure your maximum pleasure. Follow fire rules; no firearms; leash pets; protect the facilities and natural features; no off-road driving; dispose of waste in the proper places. There's no fee attached for staying in Alaska's state parks and waysides at present. Many of them offer facilities such as boat-launching ramps, and there are trails to hike. Space may be scarce and your stay limited in some of the more popular areas such as Eagle River and Bird Creek in the Chugach district, and Fort Abercrombie on Kodiak Island.

NATIONAL PARKLANDS. The conflict is an old one: environmentalists at odds with the industries—oil, mining, and timber. Those whose priority is to preserve in its natural state as much land as possible; those whose priority is to develop the land in order to keep active the industries and the jobs they provide. Finally, the decisions have been made on how much land to preserve, how much to develop, and how to classify it all.

The two national forests—the *Chugach* and the *Tongass*—comprise a total of more than 23 million acres, more national forest land than in any other state. *Denali National Park and Preserve* is a remote and unspoiled wilderness dominated by Mount McKinley. More spectacular scenery can be found at *Glacier Bay National Park and Preserve,* 40 miles northwest of Juneau, with 16 active glaciers touching tidewater. *Katmai National Park and Preserve* is on the Alaska Peninsula across from Kodiak Island: ocean bays, fjords, lagoons, volcanic crater lakes, and glacier-covered peaks. *Klondike Gold Rush National Historical Park* commemorates the gold rush, extending from Pioneer Square in Seattle to Skagway and beyond, following the route of the gold seekers. *Sitka National Historical Park* is the place to see totem poles. *Pribilof Islands,* in the Bering Sea, is a seal and otter reserve. *Clarence Rhode Wildlife Refuge,* to the northwest of Bethel, encompasses one of the world's largest waterfowl breeding grounds. Nunivak Island, site of *Nunivak National Wildlife Refuge,* is noted especially for its herds of reindeer and musk ox. And there are more: for general information on parks, preserves and monuments, contact the National Park Service at 2525 Gambell St., Anchorage, AK 99503; and U.S. Forest Service, Information Center at Centennial Hall, 101 Egan Drive, Juneau, AK 99802. For wildlife refuges, contact the U.S. Fish and Wildlife Service, 1011 E. Tudor, Anchorage, AK 99503.

CONVENTION SITES. Alaska handles about 6–700,-000 tourists and conventioneers annually. Because of this the Alaskan cities are well-equipped to offer a variety of activities suitable for programs for spouses. These include local sightseeing tours, ranging from wildlife viewing to nightclub visits —even health clubs! It is characteristic for hospitable Alaskans to arrange special treats, such as visits in Alaskan homes, champagne brunches, and fur fashion shows. Most conventions, especially those of an international or national character, go to Anchorage. They are now making good use of the new 100,000 square foot *Convention Center,* expected to attract a majority of the world's meetings. It's on W. 5th between E and F Streets, across from the even larger *Performing Arts Complex,* under construction. The state's second most popular convention city is Fairbanks. Juneau has been for long a noted regional convention site, as has Ketchikan, the city closest to Seattle. It would be hard to surpass the scenery and fine facilities of the *Sitka* and the *Valdez Convention Centers.* Kodiak boasts one of the busiest and most picturesque fishing ports in the U.S.A. Kenai is a favorite convention center for oil-related or technical groups.

Denali Park Hotel, Chalets, Alyeska Resort, and *Glacier Bay Lodge* all have convention and meeting facilities. (For further convention information, write the local Convention and Visitors Bureau.)

TELEPHONES. The *area code* for all points in Alaska is 907. The area code for the Yukon Territory, Canada, is 403.

HINTS TO HANDICAPPED TRAVELERS. One of the newest, and largest, groups to enter the travel scene is the handicapped, literally millions of people who are in fact physically able to travel and who do so enthusiastically when they know that they can move about in safety and comfort. Generally their tours parallel those of the non-handicapped traveler, but at a more leisurely pace, and with all the logistics carefully checked out in advance. It's essential that handicapped persons who need special help inform cruise companies and tour operators when they start to plan their trip. Some companies require a medical O.K.—for their protection, as well as for the handicapped person's. Several important sources of information in this field are: *Access to the World: A Travel Guide for the Handicapped* by Louise Weiss, available from Facts on File, 460 Park Ave. S., New York, NY 10016. This book covers travel by air, ship, train, bus, car and recreational vehicle; hotels and motels; travel agents and tour operators; destinations; access guides; health and medical problems; and travel organizations. *Easter Seal Society for Crippled Children and Adults,* Director of Education and Information Service, 2023 West Ogden Ave., Chicago, IL 60612. The *President's Committee on Employment of the Handicapped,* Washington, DC 20210, has issued a list for handicapped travelers that tells where to write for guidebooks to nearly 100 U.S. cities. The Committee also has a guide to *Highway Rest Area Facilities* that are designed to be accessible to the handicapped. For a list of tour operators who arrange travel for the handicapped, write to *Society for the Advancement of Travel for the Handicapped,* 26 Court St., Brooklyn, NY 11242.

In addition, many of the nation's national parks have special facilities for the handicapped. These are described in *National Park Guide for the Handicapped,* available from the U.S. Government Printing Office, Washington, DC 20402. TWA publishes a free 12-page pamphlet entitled *Consumer Information about Air Travel for the Handicapped* to explain available various arrangements and how to get them.

Travel in Alaska is no tougher than elsewhere for a handicapped person. Those who have been there vow it's worth any extra effort expended—and they say they come home with a real sense of achievement! Visitor information centers in many Alaskan cities and some small towns will help the handicapped, no matter what the problem. In Anchorage they are developing aids for the deaf and blind.

The *Evergreen Travel Service* near Seattle has long been interested in travel for the handicapped. They claim that it is harder to imagine a cheerier, tougher bunch, and organize and expedite individual and group travel to Alaska, among other destinations in the world, including a wheelchair cruise through Alaska's Inside Passage in 1983. For information, write Betty Hoffman or her son Jack at Evergreen Travel Service, Inc., 19505-L 44th Ave. West, Lynnwood, WA 98036; phone (206) 776–1184. Another competent source of handicapped travel information is Douglass Annand, author of *The Wheelchair Traveler,* Ball Hill Rd., Milford, NH 03055.

LIBRARIES. The *Alaska Historical Library,* Juneau, contains more than 15,000 volumes of Alaskana, many of them rare. Included is the famous Wickersham Collection, the most extensive collection of books, documents, and manuscripts relating to Alaska. In Fairbanks, the five-level *University of Alaska Archives and Noel Wien Library* house outstanding Alaskana. The repository of government documents is a key resource source; they receive 11,000 periodicals. In Anchorage, both the *National Bank of Alaska's Heritage Library* and the *Alaska Pacific University Library* have extensive Alaskana collections. Virtually every town and city maintains a public library, many with volumes of historical importance. *Sheldon Jackson College,* Sitka, has an excellent collection of Pacific Northwest exploration.

RECOMMENDED READING. Maybe it's due to those long winter nights that Alaskans are well educated and avid readers. Book stores, all dealing in Alaskana, are rampant, with most always an airport branch; all great for browsing. Some favorites are the *Book Cache* in Anchorage; the *Baranof Book Store* in Juneau. Highway and other independent travelers would do well to invest in one of the almost mile-by-mile guides like *The Milepost,* Alaska Northwest Publishing Co., Box 4 EEE, Anchorage, AK 99503 ($12.95, in Canada $14.95, plus $1 postage—or plus $3 postage if you want it sent first class); it's long revered and useful. Ask also about their new *Wilderness Milepost.* The same company publishes *Alaska* magazine and a wealth of books about the state, including the Alaska Geographic series, and a fact-filled *Almanac* for $5.95; $7.50 in Canada. For cooks: long-time Alaskan Ruth Allman's handwritten *Alaska Sourdough* recipes ($6.95); and *Lowbush Moose,* a collection of retired Alaska State Trooper Gordon Nelson's favorite recipes and anecdotes ($6.95) and the *Alaska Wild Berry Guide and Cookbook,* $13.95; Canada, $16.95. Larry Lake's *Alaska Travel Guide,* Box 15889, Salt Lake City, UT 84115, ($9.95 plus $1 postage) includes a hotel directory and it's glove-compartment size. *Alaska Travel Publications, Inc.,* Box 4–2031, Anchorage, AK 99509 has books on specific wilderness areas: the *Katmai, Mount McKinley, Prince William Sound.* They sell for $12.00, postpaid. *Alaska, the Complete Travel Book,* by Norma Spring, with color and black-and-white photographs by Bob and Ira Spring, Collier Books, 866 Third Ave., New York, NY 10022 ($7.95). State legislator Mike Miller's *Alaskabooks,* Box 1494, Juneau, AK 99802, are small, inexpensive, but full of accurate, useful information—particularly *Camp-*

ing and Trailering and *Off the Beaten Path.* Each sells for $2. His newest local guide, on Juneau, sells for $3.95. It is most useful to have in hand while you are in the capital city. The official, free *Alaska and Canada's Yukon Vacation Planner* is updated annually. It's available by writing Alaska State Division of Tourism, Pouch E, Juneau, AK 99811. It lists current guidebooks, maps, and charts. Among the guides on specific areas are *Alaska's Parklands, The Complete Guide* $14.95; *55 Ways to the Wilderness in Southcentral Alaska,* $8.95; and *Mt. McKinley, a Climber's Guide,* $4.95—all three published by The Mountaineers, 300 3rd Ave. W., Seattle, WA 98119. A handbook on Glacier Bay can be bought for $3 plus $1 handling through Alaska Natural History Assoc., Glacier Bay Nat'l Park, Gustavus, AK 99826.

AN INTRODUCTION TO
ALASKA

Bigger than Life

Ask an Alaskan enthusiast what's so "great" about the Great Land
in the northwest corner of our continent, and stand back for an earful.
Just the name "Alaska" is enough to trigger a torrent of prose (or
poetry) comparable to the unleashing of the state's mighty rivers during
the annual spring ice breakup.

You may be sorry you asked, unless you are serious about wanting
to know, and you are planning to travel to Alaska. First come the
generalities: the soul-satisfying wilderness where birds, animals, and
sea life are confronted on their home grounds; the rugged natural
beauty of the land—fresh, unspoiled as yet; lots of elbow room for
recreation, with skiing, hiking, climbing, snowmobiling, fishing, hunt-

ing, beachcombing, river rafting, rock-hounding, and bird-watching, for starters.

Next, some specific Alaskan superlatives: the most western state; the most northern, its tip almost at the top of the world; and the tallest, thanks to Mt. McKinley, highest point on the North American continent. And you'll hear boasts about what Alaska has the most of: shoreline; time zones; daylight (in summer); darkness (in winter); wildlife; and size—being two-and-a-half times bigger than runner-up Texas.

In truth, the enthusiasm is justified. Alaska is a unique and fascinating travel destination: the nature of the land, what it's like to travel there—including cost, and the nature of the people.

The History

The First Visitors

Alaska, over the centuries, can be compared to a sleeping giant, periodically aroused by those who would like to share the treasures hoarded in vast virgin forests, mountains, and seas. Scientists estimate that the first visitors came 25,000 to 35,000 years ago, probably following their food supply—meat on the hoof and paw—which was heading for then-greener pastures. Animals and people used a land bridge lasting about 3,000 years, which spanned the Bering Sea, connecting the Asian and North American continents. When it was drowned again by the melting of ice-age glaciers, seafarers continued to paddle across.

In waves of different ethnic backgrounds, some early "tourists" stayed to settle, making up the basic aboriginals of Alaska: the Aleuts in the Aleutian Island chain; the Eskimos in the Arctic; various Indian tribes in the milder coastal regions of southeast Alaska and the Interior. Other tribes migrated southward to people the rest of the continent.

Russian America

The Russians, close neighbors on the west, came to call in the 18th century. They met native Aleuts as they island-hopped along the volcanic island chain. In 1741, they sighted the mainland. The Aleuts had been calling Alaska a similar-sounding name meaning "the great land." The Russians chose to claim and colonize their discovery as "Russian America" for the rest of the 18th and over half of the 19th century.

Their first settlement was on Kodiak Island in the Gulf of Alaska, but in a few years, Governor Baranof moved the capital to Sitka. It was more on the traveled path, had a milder climate, and was better sheltered.

Trade flourished west to Hawaii and down the western coast to Fort Ross, California. The Russians built ships with the abundant Sitka spruce. Sitka-cast iron bells for missions and ice for San Francisco bars were part of the southbound cargo. Northbound ships brought back food for the colonies. Furs were in demand in the courts of Europe and Asia, especially the lovely, soft seal fur. Russian fur traders had found the annual breeding rookeries in the Pribilof Islands—tiny dots in the Bering Sea—and they harvested the fur seal almost to extinction.

History Repeats Itself

The Russian colonies in "Russian America," far removed from their capital (then St. Petersburg), were proving too expensive to maintain. Russia preferred to relinquish its holdings to the United States rather than to the more aggressive British and Spanish, both busily exploring and trading along the northwest coast. Negotiating with William H. Seward, U.S. Secretary of State, the Russians came up with a bargain offer.

In 1867, after much debate in Congress, the United States reluctantly paid 2½¢ an acre for this white elephant, far removed from the heart of the U.S. For most of the next century, the treasures stored in "Uncle Sam's attic" lay unnoticed, except for sporadic gold bonanzas. Sensational at the time, these were inclined to peter out, or else were controversial, or hard to reach.

The circa-1900 flurry of gold rushes drew thousands, but relatively few stayed on. The panicky recognition that Alaska's position was strategic for national defense in World War II brought in military installations, people, and a federal government-based economy. Searches for metals and other vital raw materials caused off-again, on-again excitement. The development of the oil discoveries on the North Slope had to wait for the green light in the form of Native Land Claim settlements and proven ecology-protection measures.

The achievement of statehood in 1959 was sensational, but mainly in Alaska. For several years thereafter, people from "outside" (everywhere else but Alaska) were still asking how to get there from the United States, wondering if English was spoken, and what kind of foreign postage was required.

The 1964 earthquake hit the most densely populated area, Anchorage, hard. In 1967, the year that Alaskans held a year-long party to celebrate the Centennial of Purchase, floods inundated Fairbanks, second largest city. These catastrophes helped to pinpoint Alaska on the map. Based on necessity, disaster triggered a wave of new buildings and modernization.

The events which started Alaska's latest boom—heard round the world—were the settlement of the Native Land Claims and the building of the oil pipeline. There are yet many problems to be resolved, among them tax structures, use of land, and whether to build more roads into underdeveloped areas. But Alaskans are optimists. They believe the prosperity with them now will continue—around the corner, maybe forever. The potentials are tremendous, and free enterprise flourishes in newly formed Native corporations. Somewhat stumbling, these corporations are dedicated to administering their lands and the income from them for the good of all the natives.

In the Arctic, too, tourism appears to be a natural. The Eskimos are hospitable by nature and accustomed to entertaining transient visitors. Over the years they've practiced on explorers, adventurers, Arctic researchers, and the military. They are investing their dollars in the "creature comforts" they think visitors need, like modern hotels, and in housing, stores, and utilities for themselves.

The Alaskans

Alaskans today are a convivial mix of native (about a sixth of the population) Indians, including Eskimos and Aleuts; born-in Alaskans; immigrants from all over the continental "South-48" states and Hawaii; and descendants of foreign explorers and settlers, including Russians.

Native Alaskans

Descendants of the prewhite inhabitants of Alaska now number about 70,000. Some live in widely separated villages scattered along the 25,000-mile coastline and the great rivers of the 49th state, and many others have moved to the larger cities, such as Anchorage and Fairbanks; some have gone as far as the "Lower 48." The villages, some 200 of them, rather than the tribes, are, as a rule, considered to be the basic social units. Population of villages ranges from about 30 to 500. The so-called tribe name usually denotes the language group, not the nation.

The Native Land Claims Settlement Act was passed in 1971. This allowed for $900 million in cash plus 44 million acres of land to be paid to the Natives for their rightful historic lands—a landmark settlement. To administer this, 12 Native Regional Corporations have been formed in Alaska; the 13th is for all Alaska Natives residing "outside." The Native Alaskans—Indians, Eskimos and Aleuts—are citizens of the United States, naturalized collectively by the Citizenship Act of 1924. They are not wards of the government, though the Bureau of Indian Affairs and other federal agencies do perform functions aimed at meeting the special needs of these first families of the largest state. That there have been and remain bitter feelings causing disputes is no secret.

On the western and northern coasts are the Eskimos—famed in photograph and travel brochure. This harsh habitat, generally treeless with short summers and long, cold winters, was able to sustain a rich culture, which evidence indicates flourished 2,000 years ago. Even today, in remote places, while the Eskimo moves more and more into the money-economy of the white man, the Eskimo male still hunts walrus, whale, and seal, and his wife retains her fur-sewing skills. His boat, powered by an outboard engine, is covered with walrus skin. Visitors are sometimes surprised to learn that there are no reservations and that Alaskan Eskimos never did live in igloos, as did their Canadian cousins. In the remote north, where building material is scarce and freight high, houses are usually built from driftwood and salvage. Modest frame homes predominate elsewhere. Native clothing is still seen, but store-bought jackets and boots are gradually taking over from the famed fur parkas and mukluks. The ubiquitous tennis shoes and sweatshirts are now making appearances on the smaller set. On the surface, the smiling Eskimos appear happy in their changed way of life, but serious social studies indicate the transition has been traumatic and has left deep scars. But they are still exceptionally friendly with visitors and appear to enjoy putting on an entertaining show, built around their cultural past, for expectant tourists.

In the interior of Alaska are the formerly nomadic northern Athapascans, closely related to the Navajos, Apaches, and Hopi of the southwestern states. They live along wide river valleys bordered by high mountains—a land of short summers and severe winters.

On the Alaska Peninsula, extending down the Aleutian Chain, are the Aleuts, related to the Eskimos. Some of the finest basketry in the world was formerly produced by the Aleut women of Attu Island. Today the Aleuts generally live in well-constructed frame houses. Many are members of the Russian Orthodox Church.

To visit some Natives on their home (ancestral) grounds—the Pribilof islands, home of the Aleuts, and Arctic Eskimo towns—it is necessary to fly. Nome, turn-of-the-century gold rush city, is now the home of the King Island Eskimos, who used to live on a large rocky island in the Bering Sea.

It's possible to arrange a visit to smaller, more remote villages around the coast and along the Yukon and Kuskokwim rivers by bush planes on their daily rounds. If you want to stay longer, the pilot usually knows someone who would be willing to take in a guest for overnight, or a few days. You pay for lodging, and can either bring your own food or pay a little more and take pot-luck with the family.

Indian groups that are more accessible live along the southeast seacoast, among islands of the Alexander Archipelago. The Tsimpshians migrated from British Columbia in the late 1800s and settled Metlakatla on Annette Island, just south of Ketchikan. The Haidas came from Canada's Queen Charlotte Islands in the 1700s to live at the village of Hydaburg on Prince of Wales Island. The Tlingits left Canada to spread out to the north and dominate trade long before the first Europeans came to call. Thanks to the mild climate and the bounty of forest and sea, the Tlingits lived an affluent life. They had time to be sociable and to develop their arts, especially woodcarving.

The art of carving tall totem poles is being perpetuated. North and south of Ketchikan are stands of authentically reproduced totems. The Sitka National Historical Park has totems outside the Visitors' Center, and carved housepoles inside. Near the head of Lynn Canal, at Haines-Port Chilkoot, Alaska Indian Arts, Inc., has been studying, preserving, and reproducing Tlingit Indian arts and crafts from totem carving to Indian dancing.

Human Nature

There are few noticeable language or racial barriers among the still-small population of stubborn, independent, hardworking residents. A visitor may notice some general "Alaskan" qualities: their vigor and their youth (average age mid-twenties) and that they seem well educated.

Alaskans are individualists. Probably having lots of elbow room has something to do with it. They revel in their wide-open spaces and freedom for infinite outdoor recreation. Debates are still rampant over how much land should be saved and how much used. The recent reckoning sets aside more acreage in national parks and preserves, monuments, forests, and game refuges than in the other 49 states combined; most of it is undeveloped, so far.

Alaskans fish and hunt for subsistence, for food in the locker, and a boost to the family budget. Whole families work together at what needs doing, especially during the long, light summer months. They are experts at work, often handling more than one job at a time. If they seem to work hard, you should see them play! The calendar is full of games and festivals celebrating everything from ice worms (Cordova in February) to whales (Point Hope in June). Almost any excuse puts them in a festive mood.

The original sourdough miners, those who panned during the gold rush, have found their eternal golden reward. It's been over 80 years since that big bonanza. There are still original Alaskan homesteaders, who earned their property by "proving up": building a cabin and living off the land. A recent state homesteading bill opened up some land by lottery for homesteading again, but with strict rules.

The *real* Alaskans now are the ones who live there, sticking it out through boom and bust, forever enthusiastic about their raw, rarely mild, sometimes violent land. They accept the unexpected and cope with what they have to. The happiest visitors adopt their philosophy.

Alaskans know it takes time to get around and savor their big state. Moreover, everything written or rumored has probably been true at some time or place. The key is to stay flexible. Take possible (inevitable) delays or change of plans with an open mind. They may not necessarily refer to disaster, but the saying among Alaskans is that if something *can* happen, it will.

If there is something you want to know, never be afraid to ask. Alaskans will point you toward their favorite things: a colorful bar, museum, children's zoo, local entertainment, or the top rock group currently playing in town.

Sorting Out the Geography

The grand-scale peninsula jutting into two great oceans and two seas has multiple personalities and many faces. Geographically, there are several Alaskas; glaciers, snow, ice, and permafrost are balanced by smoking volcanoes, desert sand, grassy plains, and rain forests. Though some areas grow trees thick as fur on a husky pup, there are infinite stretches of tundra, from the Russian meaning "where the trees are not."

The weather is dry, and the weather is dank, with record rainfalls and fog in some areas. An outdoor thermometer on a bank in Fairbanks, in the interior, can register minus 60° F. in winter and soar to 98° F. in summer. The seasons are unequal: long dark winters, offset by short light summers. Fall and spring are fleeting, pronounced, and beautiful. These contrasts are contained in Alaska's six, varied geographical regions that shape up into a big dipper, which is the state's chosen symbol and the inspiration for its flag.

A young native, Benny Benson, designed the flag that won a school contest sponsored by the American Legion in 1926. He had good reasons for choosing the Big Dipper's 7 stars and the North Star in gold, against a deep blue background: "The blue field is for the Alaska sky and the forget-me-not, Alaska's state flower. The North Star is for the future State of Alaska, the most northerly of the Union. The Dipper is for the Great Bear—symbolizing strength."

Think of the Dipper tilted so its handle stretches down from the bowl south and east. Southeast Alaska, also called the Panhandle, is a substantial string of lush, green, timbered islands plus a narrow coastal strip, separated from Canada by mountains. No connecting conventional highways here. Between the archipelago and mainland Alaska winds the famous Inside Passage water route to Alaska, well-used even before its gold rush heyday at the turn of the century. Indians, explorers, traders, and adventurers plied it in the past. Today's "Marine Highway" traffic includes freighters, yachts, barges, ferries, and cruise ships.

The rest of the Alaskas are contained in the cup. The bulkiest Alaska is the interior, a vast basin bordered on the east by Canada and defined by giant mountain ranges and mighty rivers. Here, and bordering the Gulf of Alaska area, including the Kenai Peninusla, are most of Alaska's still-scanty roads, including the end of the Alaska Highway in Fairbanks. About one fifth of the state is accessible by road.

More Alaskas, set off by natural barriers, stretch around the coastal fringes, washed by the Pacific and Arctic oceans and the Bering and Chukchi seas. No roads lead to western and southwestern Alaska. Travel via the Dalton Highway, formerly the North Slope Haul Road to Prudhoe Bay on the Arctic Coast, is restricted beyond Disaster Creek. However, these regions are served by planes, bush size to jet. Some of the best of Alaska adventuring lies in the far-out places.

FISHING AND HUNTING IN ALASKA

Where Wildlife Abound

You can believe those boasts about Alaska's wildlilfe. Just as the brochures describe it, the state is a hunter's and fisherman's paradise. It contains as many big game species as do all the rest of the states combined. With the small game, marine mammals, fur animals and other unclassified creatures as well, this is a state teeming with animal life. Those contributing to game harvests—i.e., those huntable under specific regulations—range in habitat from the beluga whales in coastal seas to the Dall sheep in high mountain crags and pastures. In size, they range from mighty moose to small red squirrels.

And you can swallow those fish tales. They're mostly true, whatever is said about quantity, quality, variety, and size—including "the ones that got away."

There'll be some kind of fishing or hunting going on almost year-round. But be aware that areas do close. Closings are announced by the Alaska Department of Fish and Game, as needed for preservation purposes. Visitors will need to check the current regulations before they hunt or fish.

Fish Alaska!

Thousands of streams, rivers, lakes, ponds, and the saltchuck surrounding 34,000 miles of shoreline provide an exciting variety of both salt- and freshwater fishing. Within almost every Alaskan dwells a fisherman (or woman), full of advice about how, when, and where he or she likes to catch them. Opinions will vary and if you get into such topics as bait, lures, flies, and other equipment, it can be a long conversation.

Southeast's superb fishing is said to be due to migrating masses of fish swimming through the island maze. Having to swim around points and squeeze through narrow waterways creates an amazing number of fishing "hot spots," such as Behm Canal, near Ketchikan.

In the southeast Panhandle salmon is king—and also red (sockeye), pink (humpback), chum (calico), and silver (coho). It's generally agreed that the best time of year varies with the species of fish you're angling for. Salmon haunt most coastal waters and some streams, as well.

June and July are the best months for hooking the fighting king, considered the most prized salmon. They average twenty pounds. Trophy-size kings weigh in at 45 pounds or more. You can still see the largest one caught to date; this 126½ pounder is stuffed and lying in state in the museum at Petersburg.

Most of the other kinds of salmon are caught during the summer months and into September. For steelhead, the ultimate challenge, hardy fishermen aim for March–April and October–November. Huge Pacific halibut, red snapper, ling cod, and rockfish are caught almost any time.

Some of the best trophy trout fishing awaits in freshwater west of Anchorage, in lakes, streams, and rivers of southcentral and southwestern Alaska, including the Kenai Peninsula. These remote areas are reached mostly by float plane. Fly-in trips for a day or more offer a variety of action-packed angling for Dolly Varden, lake trout, northern pike, Arctic grayling and rainbow trout.

Bristol Bay, less than an hour's flight time southwest of Anchorage, is renowned. Most of the world's sockeye—or red salmon—come out of Bristol Bay waters and are processed there, with fishermen and canneries working round the clock to "make the pack." The best time to witness this feverish activity is in July. Make reservations, for aircraft may be booked solid carrying cannery crews. In addition to salmon, Bristol Bay region is famous for grayling, Arctic char, Dolly Varden, northern pike, and rainbow trout. Fishermen who have thrown out their lines around the world say that some of the top sport fishing anywhere is in the major rivers and lakes of the Bristol Bay region.

Alaskans use small planes like taxis for reaching fishing hot spots. During only a few-hours stopover, visitors can do the same, or take a fishboat charter. Avid fisherman-cruisers have been known to stop in at a sporting goods store, buy (or rent) equipment and a 3-day license, then beetle off to fish a remote mountain lake, or try their luck in the saltchuck. Back at the ship, renewed, they have their own fish stories—and proof—to show and tell at dinner.

Along the Alaska Highway and other major routes there are many fine fishing spots. If you are traveling with tent or trailer, you'll want the list from the Fish and Game Department so you can plan to stop overnight and also get in some fishing.

Around the northern and western fringes of Alaska there are special treats. At some spots you may be able to fish through the ice for tomcod and tanner crab along with the Eskimos in late spring before the ice pack moves out. Dress for it. If you're with a tour, they'll lend you warm clothing: parkas, insulated pants and boots. Another Arctic challenge is the sheefish, a cousin to the salmon, and delicious!

If you are over sixteen, you'll need a fishing license to show to diligent wardens patroling their beat. As for equipment, facilities in saltwater areas generally provide it; those in freshwater may expect you to bring your own. Bring your pet lure, of course.

Hunt Alaska!

Alaska's vastness and isolation make it necessary to plan ahead for whatever type of hunting a visitor has in mind. There are unequaled opportunities in all regions of Alaska, whether you think big (game) or small (game)—or both.

Some of the most spectacular trophy hunting is provided in western Alaska, where many of the best-known guides and outfitters accommodate visiting shooters. The most-prized Kodiak, or Alaska brown bear, the largest land carnivore, is taken on Kodiak Island and on the Alaska Peninsula.

Grizzly bears are most often taken in the interior, where the forest and mountains also provide shelter—diminishing as civilization marches on—for black and brown bears, moose, caribou, and Dall sheep. Deer, black bears, brown bears, moose, and mountain goats are found in southeast Alaska.

August through November is considered the open season on most game—but dates are not rigorous. There is also some hunting in the spring. Seasons and bag limits vary considerably between the game management units, so it's best to contact Fish and Game Department Offices. (See the *Practical Information* sections later in this book for the appropriate addresses.) There are many closed areas and restricted species, such as the Arctic's polar bear and walrus and the musk ox. To hunt some protected species, you may have to draw for it, paying an additional fee of $5 or $10.

Togetherness is encouraged when hunting brown bears, grizzly bears, and Dall sheep. Nonresidents are required to have guides for these. The guide can be a relative living in Alaska, but only parents, children over 19, grandparents, sisters, or brothers of the nonresident hunter are eligible to act as his or her guide.

Though Alaska's big game take gets most of the attention, it's outnumbered in quantity, if not in bulk, by the small game harvest. Widely distributed, the small game are hunted in "outings" rather than "safaris," which evolve for stalking the big ones. The small game include hares and rabbits, beavers and mink, minor fur animals trapped for profit by part-time Alaskan trappers, and some marine mammals.

Game birds native to Alaska include three species of ptarmigan and four species of grouse. They're found in all sections of the state. Ruffed grouse and sharp-tailed grouse like some open land along with plenty of hardwood trees and shrubs for cover. They live in valleys around main rivers and tributaries, especially the Yukon and the Kuskokwim rivers. The willow ptarmigan, Alaska's state bird, is the biggest and most abundant game bird. It and the rock ptarmigan show up almost everywhere in the state. The smaller white-tailed ptarmigan likes the higher parts of the Kenai Mountains and the Alaska Range and some areas of the Panhandle's Coast Range. Spruce grouse opt for southcentral and interior forests, which are not as densly timbered as southeast forests, preferred by blue grouse. Some hunters swear that the finest waterfowl shooting is on the Stikine River flats near Wrangell in southeast Alaska. They also vouch for moose and bear along the Stikine, plus mountain goat in the upper elevations.

Of the migratory birds, the majority of over 25 species that nest and are hunted in Alaska are ducks: mallard, pintail, American widgeon, green-winged teal, and shoveler. Canadian geese, white-fronted geese, and black brant are the migratory birds most sought.

The Alaska Lands Act set aside 10 national preserves where sport hunting and trapping are allowed. The conditions are still under review and being hotly debated: conservationists vs. harvesters. The act also allows continued subsistence use—the gathering of wild renewable resources for food by rural Alaskans who have always relied on it to live. Twenty-five years of Fish and Game management have evolved laws and regulations, both state and federal, bag limits and seasons, and the effect of the take is regularly and carefully monitored. The intention is to assure protection and preservation, for a sustained yield of this valuable wildlife resource.

Your best bet if you are serious about hunting is to sign on with an expert. A list of registered Alaska guides is available from the Department of Commerce, Guide Licensing & Control Board, Pouch D, Juneau, AK 99811. Also write the Alaska Department of Fish and Game, Box 3–2000, Juneau, AK 99802 for current regulations. Fish and Game offices don't sell licenses; these are issued by designated agents, or write the Licensing Section, Alaska Department of Revenue, 1107 W. 8th St., Juneau, AK 99801.

Fishing and Hunting Accommodations

Adventure-type camping expeditions, with guides, aim to keep you as comfortable as possible while hiking or kayaking or canoeing to hunting or fishing grounds, and there may be a base camp set up. Wilderness lodges offer complete hunting and fishing package stays ranging from moderate to deluxe. Some come with practically everything furnished including guides who know their way around. Two notable examples of lodges, both with spectacular fishing, are located in fascinating and contrasting wilderness areas, molded by opposing forces of nature. Brooks Lodge, on Naknek Lake in the Katmai National Park, features the "Valley of Ten Thousand Smokes," sculpted by a violent volcanic eruption in 1912. Far different is Glacier Bay National Park. From the beautifully designed Glacier Bay Lodge, a trip up-Bay some forty miles will allow the visitor to hobnob with the wildlife and inspect the faces of retreating glaciers, which developed and then melted to fill the spectacular bay.

Prices usually include lodging, airfare from the Alaska gateway (Anchorage, Juneau, or Ketchikan); meals in most cases; guide service; and other services, varying somewhat with the lodge packages. Count on spending at least $255 to $325 a day (per 1985 prices), depending on length of stay and location of the lodge or fishing yacht.

Try not to figure your fish's or game meat's cost per pound in the light of what it cost you to get it. Whether packed in ice for eating later, or stuffed for a wall trophy, it may seem like it cost a mint of money.

Instead, consider the excitement, the grand-scale scenery, and the soul-renewing adventures that were an intrinsic part of taking it in Alaska. True sportsmen consider all that *worth* a mint.

Wildlife Watching

Keep in mind that wildlife *watching*—not shooting or catching—is the engrossing activity for the majority of Alaska visitors. They're alert to everything from bald eagles to Arctic lemmings, and close encounters with moose aren't rare. Sometimes they dispute the right-of-way on highways; road signs include "Moose Crossing." And on St. Paul Island of the Pribilof group, there's even a "Seal Crossing" posted. The best opportunity to spot Alaskan wildlife is probably found in Denali National Park.

Low-flying planes and cruise ships often afford travelers a look at whales—usually finbacks or humpbacks—and the antics of smaller mammals, such as porpoises.

And would you believe *fish watching?* It can be fascinating in streams near cities or far out in the wilderness. Salmon often leap formidable barriers like 8-foot Brooks Falls in the Katmai, as they swim upstream to return to their spawning grounds. Often when salmon run in spawning streams, they are joined by bears who wade into the water and snatch out all the fish they can eat. Anan Creek, not far from Wrangell, is just one of the good places to spot fishing black bears and occasional grizzlies. (Grizzlies deserve their reputation: they're unpredictable and can be quite dangerous.) Other good places to watch bear fishing are Pack Creek on Admiralty Island and at the McNeal River on the Alaska Peninsula.

Be aware that the "biggest" and "the most" boasts also include mosquitoes and no-see-ums. Once in the bush, whether hunter, fisher, or watcher, *you* are fair game. Be prepared with repellent, and in the worst season—roughly May into early July—keep covered.

TOURING ALASKA

How to See It All

A "grand circle route" has evolved with the development and improvement of transportation and roads. It's expandable and reversible, and as personal as you want to make it, and, depending on your style of travel, as rugged or as comfortable as you choose. Typically, if you go one way by land (Alaska Highway), you return by water (Inside Passage) several thousand miles and days, or weeks, later. Or vice versa. In between, when you come to the end of marine and land routes, you take a plane. No roads lead to the fringes of Alaska: the Arctic Coast, Far West Alaska, and out onto the Alaska Peninsula and the Aleutian Island Chain.

Cruise ships and tour operators offer combination land/sea/air tours for varying lengths of time and assorted prices. They follow this circular route in general, spelling out the variations and embellishments.

They usually allow opportunities to add optional tours, preferably when you sign up for the basic tour.

Roughing It (More or Less)

If roughing it is your longsuit, there's no better place than vast, largely untamed Alaska to hone your outdoor living skills. Even those who consider themselves camping veterans admit to facing challenges unequaled elsewhere. But in the same breath they are likely to hail the rewards of living close to nature and traveling at an individual pace. You can take time to photograph and appreciate wildlife and scenic surroundings or follow a trail deep into the wilderness.

Where and How to Really Rough It

This means either traveling on foot, with all survival gear on your back, or by raft, canoe, or kayak, following river trails. If by canoe, be prepared for numerous portages around shallows or rapids. But, as you glide through the backcountry you'll gain a unique perspective of little-seen wilderness. Those who crave more action can take to the bays and fjords of coastal Alaska for "bluewater" touring, or the excitement of running a wild whitewater river in kayak or raft.

If you want to take your wilderness one step at a time, all the rules for hiking and climbing anywhere apply to Alaska—and then some. No one is more anxious that both residents and visitors have successful, safe, and meaningful experiences than the agencies that steward Alaska's abundance of forests, mountains, and rivers: the National Park Service, Forest Service, State Parks Department, the Bureau of Land Management, and the Coast Guard. They want people to enjoy, but also to cherish, the Great Land while using it. To this end, they make available pamphlets with information on all aspects of outdoor recreation—even recreational gold panning—and they go to great lengths to spell out possible hazards.

Besides these government services, there are also private enterprises that are interested in preserving the wilderness where they do business. These include hunting and fishing guides and guides who lead wilderness adventure treks on foot or by canoe or kayak. Even the large tour companies are aware that much depends on conserving the wilderness image of our "last frontier." Cheechakos (newcomers) might do well to investigate where the Alaska entrepreneurs go and how they travel, and perhaps sign up with them for a group roughing-it trip, led by someone well experienced in the wilderness. They'll advise you on equipment you need, or perhaps furnish it, and will know how to handle or alleviate possible threats to experiencing complete pleasure in their particular area. Of course, roughing it, you can expect some lumps. . . . but along with any miseries, you'll have good company!

Hikers should contact the Forest Service Headquarters for information and maps and plan with care and with an awareness of possible hazards lurking off the beaten paths.

Alaska's two national forests, the Chugach and the Tongass, between them cover most of southeast Alaska and much of the coastal area of Southcentral. They border or are near most of the major coastal cities, and offer magnificent, natural recreational areas within easy reach. There are perhaps 500 miles of maintained trails—not many, considering the vast primitive expanse that beckons.

Hikers seem to be especially fond of the Resurrection Pass Trail, one of the most popular in the Chugach National Forest. Gold miners walked it first, and there are still claims being worked in the vicinity.

The primitive flavor of the state is further preserved by the fact that there are fewer campgrounds (most undeveloped) than in any of the western states. Most wilderness enthusiasts feel this adds to the overall experience. They enjoy the challenge of setting up camp in backcountry and undeveloped roadside areas when dictated by convenience or need. However, that wilderness rule "pack it in, pack it out" always applies. It's an obligation to dispose of litter, human waste, and garbage in such a way that the site is left in mint condition.

Katmai National Park and Preserve is an unusual wilderness on the Alaska Peninsula across from Kodiak Island. There is no highway access; visitors get there only by air or private boat. The Katmai consists of over 4,200 square miles of ocean bays, fjords, and lagoons, backed by a range of glacier-covered peaks and volcanic crater lakes. Behind these lies an interior wilderness of forest, lake chains, and the volcanic Valley of Ten Thousand Smokes. The area was established in 1918 as a national monument, only six years after one of the most violent volcanic eruptions in recorded history gave the valley its name. Most people are content to take the package tour from Anchorage and sightsee out of Brooks Lodge on Naknek Lake. Adventuresome and rugged souls opt to travel in the Park and through the valley in the style of the early-day visitors—on foot and with backpacks. They start from the campground at Brooks River, where the ranger station dispenses regulations and advice about dealing with the wildlife, including abundant fish and waterfowl, moose, and the Alaska brown bear, largest land carnivore.

Denali National Park and Preserve is certainly one of the continent's outstanding wilderness areas, dominated by the highest peak in North America, 20,320-foot Mt. McKinley. This jagged, bulky mountain with two principal peaks rises some 17,000 feet above the surrounding parkland. It's an ice-and-snow-covered spectacle from afar or at the closest approach, which is about 26 miles away unless you hike in. Many do, with the goal of climbing the mountain, but only under the strictest regulations and painstaking preparation. Mountaineering expeditions are required to register with the superintendent at Denali; at least two months prior notice is recommended.

The Park, expanded on three sides to encompass more than 6 million acres, straddles the Alaska Range southwest of Fairbanks. Although the mountain dominates, other attractions of this giant natural history museum of tundra and wildlife are not overshadowed. Anyone visiting the park should first stop at the Riley Creek visitor center, near the park entrance for information on campgrounds and hiking areas (there are few established trails but lots of land for cross-country hiking), maps, and other tips on what to see and do.

Less accessible than Denali, Glacier Bay National Park and Preserve has its own fascinating attractions for the roughing-it crowd. Located 40 miles northwest of Juneau in the Fairweather Range of the towering St. Elias Mountains, visitors, including tour groups, get there by sea and air. The recent legislation which changed this former monument to park status also extended its boundaries. Deep fjords, tidewater glaciers, jutting icebergs, and ice-capped mountains add up to some of Alaska's most spectacular scenery and make a home for a myriad of rare species of wildlife.

The geologically inclined will be impressed by the examples of early stages of postglacial and interglacial forests. But the "hottest" attractions are those icy glaciers, grown bigger and better in Glacier Bay than anywhere else in the world. Many glaciers terminate their downward journey at tidewater, which makes the area a great laboratory for observing them.

There's a campground at Barlett Cove, near park headquarters, and camping is allowed in many sites (unimproved) along the several hundred miles of coastline and among islands. The staff at the Glacier Bay Lodge where tour groups stay is mostly wilderness addicted. Often these are young people on summer vacation from college, and they vie for positions at Glacier Bay for the opportunities to rough it during their time off. They canoe or kayak up-Bay, or hitch a boat ride, to hike and camp in choice locations. Sandy Cove is popular; so is Wild Goose; and one called Blue Mouse Cove. Campers there swear they've seen the odd little creatures.

"Roughing it" explorers of Glacier Bay, especially boaters, even if they are with a well-guided group, should be aware of icy dangers. A wave caused by falling ice from a glacier face can swamp a small boat, and survival time in those chilly waters is short. "Know before you go" is the motto here and in other bluewater areas. Charts, tide tables, maps, and local information, including the current whale situation are essential.

The possibilities for "roughing-it" wilderness exploring are limited only by one's desire and stamina. Besides the national parks and forests, there are opportunities in national monuments, wildlife refuges, and state parks. Admiralty Island National Monument, just south of capital Juneau, had an Indian name first which meant "Fortress of Bears." That's a clue to what is still there. There are also descendants of Indians who settled there and lived on the island's bounty over a thousand years ago. Of historic interest are things left by past visitors: miners, fish cannery workers, even whalers, but even more important is the fact that Admiralty exists today as a natural, balanced ecosystem —a special place.

There are many special places on the Kenai Peninsula, spacious and wonderful wilderness south of Anchorage, a favorite of Alaskans. Canoe routes in the Kenai Wildlife Refuge connect lakes named for the wildlife likely to be seen there, e.g., Junco, Eider, Nuthatch, Redpoll, Kinglet, Swan, Cygnet, Teal, Duckbill, Grebe, and Loon lakes.

However you rough it, and whether you take the high routes or the low ones to fulfill your particular wilderness longings, the message is: take care. Be aware that the hazards are there, from insect or animal bite (or worse) to frostbite. Even in summer, be prepared for temperature changes above timberline. It can drop from 90° F to below freezing after the sun disappears. You'd better believe those bear facts and cautions about all animals. Watch the water, too; when in doubt, boil it first. Carry a good map and compass and know how to use them.

Above all, before striking out, file your plan of travel with someone who cares—relative or ranger—and give your expected date of return. Then, if anything beyond your control *does* occur, they'll know where to start looking if you don't show up on schedule. (See *Facts at Your Fingertips* for addresses of parks departments to contact for specific information.)

Roughing It a Little Less

There's no question, considering the cost of transient housing and possible scarcity of rooms in summer, that camping gear with warm sleeping bags is top-priority equipment for budget-conscious travelers. The state, federal, and territorial (Canadian) campgrounds are a boon to people trying to travel north inexpensively while circuiting Alaska.

The Alaska Highway is still an achievement that appeals to pioneer spirits. Sometime, everyone should drive it (or go by motorcoach) at least one way, if just for perspective. The Alcan, a historic and monumental Canada–United States joint venture during World War II, was pushed through mountain and muskeg in a few months. It set a record for the building of military highways.

You'll find adequately spaced campgrounds while driving the Alaska Highway. From Mile 0 at Dawson Creek, Canada, through the over 1,500 miles to the official highway end in Fairbanks, there'll be facilities and supplies. The longest distance without some "civilization" may be 40 or 50 miles.

Touring by car, self sufficient with tent and commissary, or even by well-equipped recreational vehicle offers some challenges along with the rewards. (See "Hints to Motorists" in *Facts at Your Fingertips.*)

You won't be lonesome as you travel the circuit route. Families, retired couples, and young people will be sharing the strategically placed and scenic campgrounds. Except at the height of the camping season, you should find space in the roomy recreation areas, though the Alaska State Park System is on a first-come, first-serve basis; no reservations needed for the present. Not all campgrounds are in the wilds. Many are in or quite close to populated areas. Almost every town has a public campground. There are also commercial campgrounds with all the conveniences available.

In Yukon Territory the fee is $25 per season, or $5 per night for use of all territorial government campgrounds, and they are exceptionally pleasant. Campground stickers are sold at visitor information centers and by campground maintenance offices.

As a do-it-yourself, independent traveler your schedule is flexible. It allows you to blend into a friendly community for a few days of sightseeing, fishing, a trip into more remote wilderness areas, or a visit to areas in the fringes of Alaska.

A great do-it-yourself sport is following roads to their endings. Only a few miles out of cities and towns and you are in wilderness. Even on main roads, you are likely to see wild animals. Watch for warning signs posted where moose are likely to amble across. South of Anchorage, one branch of the Kenai Peninsula Highway terminates at Seward on lovely Resurrection Bay. The other, the Sterling Highway, ends at Kachemak Bay near the tip of the peninsula. The Richardson Highway terminates in oil-busy Valdez, southern terminal of the pipeline. It traverses gorgeous mountain scenery and winds down a narrow canyon. The route has evolved from gold rush trail to wagon road, and now it is a fine paved highway to the interior, paralleled by the pipeline. Road endings are usually gateways to other areas. In this case, a ferry at Valdez crosses spectacular Prince William Sound, noted for bird and sea life and for the Columbia Glacier (one of the largest), to Whittier. From here, a railway portage connects with the highway to Anchorage.

Touring in Comfort

There are plenty of rugged ways to see big, beautiful Alaska, but cruising isn't one of them. Today's "floating resorts" have all the comforts of home and then some. The spacious luxury liners that ply the Inside Passage are a far cry from the motley craft the feverish gold seekers clambered onto, and even from the steamships of the cruising-to-Alaska boom, during the 1890s.

Like the birds and the humpback whales, cruise ships migrate annually from their winter cruising grounds to summer in far north Alaska. Passengers are treated to some of Alaska's grandest marine and mountain scenery and sightings of its prolific wildlife.

Cruising

Cruising is a style of travel that could be addictive, as well as fattening. Chefs definitely cater to the inner man and woman. Specialties at breakfast, lunch, dinner (and in between, such as at a midnight buffet) are likely to reflect the ship's country of origin. On Sitmar's Italian-style ships, for example, don't pass up the pasta, served with a choice of many sauces—every bit, including the dough, prepared aboard.

Chefs serve their national dishes as well as southeast Alaska's superb seafood: tiny shrimp, scallops, king crab, king salmon, halibut—and you can be sure that sometime during the voyage the dessert spectacular will be a flaming Baked Alaska. Moreover, artist-chefs can't resist sculpturing table decorations from large chunks of crystal-clear ice, calved by glaciers and snagged in nets by the ship's crew.

Lush green panoramas of timbered islands and mountain slopes lead up to formidable snowy peaks; fjords, glaciers, small fishing and logging towns can be seen; and lively bird and sea life lose nothing for being viewed in comfort from a deck chair or through a picture-window in the lounge. It's unusually smooth sailing in sheltered waters. The myriad islands on one hand and the towering peaks on the other are protection for this roomy passage "inside." And Alaska cruising can mean almost round-the-clock daylight for watching the shifting spectacular scenery and visiting friendly little ports where English is spoken.

The big question maiden voyagers ask is "Which ship shall I choose?" There is no pat answer. Each has its own personality and all have their particular charms. Old salts, knowing they can count on the amenities they became accustomed to on a previous cruise, are inclined to stick with the same ship wherever she sails. And they'll anticipate paying about $225 per day per person for a comfortable cabin on leading cruise ships (see *Practical Information for Southeast Alaska* for the companies to write for information and brochures).

Among ship possibilities for cruisers who prefer to "think big" are the *Noordam* and the *Fairsky*. World travelers include the *Royal Vikings* and the *Sagafjord*. Scholars might choose the *S.S. Universe* geared to educating passengers. Some others: the *Island Princess,* twin to TV's "Love Boat," a smaller sister, *Sun Princess,* and a new, bigger sister *Royal Princess;* the French *Rhapsody;* and the *Stardancer,* which boast's space to carry vehicles and offers motoring tourists a luxury-cruise sea leg along their route.

There's no denying that life aboard the big ships (embarking from Vancouver, B.C., Canada, and farther south) is easy to take. Between port calls in the larger cities of Ketchikan, Juneau, Sitka, or Skagway, it's sailor's choice whether to relax and do nothing, or to join in the abundant fun and games. Daily bulletins tell what's happening on and off the ship. Among the diversions are movies, bars, food, bridge tournaments, bingo, art classes, and exercise—you name it. Top professionals entertain in the lounges.

Especially for adventuresome cruisers who think that smaller is better, are the *Majestic Alaska Explorer* and *Great Rivers Explorer*. They are patterned after earlier "explorer" sister ships, such as the somewhat smaller *Glacier Bay Explorer* (see discussion of Glacier Bay in Southeast section). They can put into small harbors and penetrate glacial fjords where the big cruise ships can't maneuver along the Inside Passage. Their shallow drafts and unique bow-landing features allow the ships to debark passengers in unusual places without a dock or dory. Informality, including family-style dining all at one sitting, as well as visiting on deck and in the spacious lounges, promotes a great feeling of camaraderie among the passengers and crew.

While cruising Alaska's Inside Passage, including Glacier Bay, Explorer Class ships emphasize happenings and destinations, especially those off the beaten cruiseways. In the small community of Haines, for example, passengers go ashore for a "potlatch"—Chilkat Indian dances served up with tasty fresh salmon in an authentically built tribal house.

The captain is as enthusiastic as his passengers, and maintains a flexible schedule so that interesting places and events can be pursued wherever and whenever they occur. Smooth and quiet, and totally compatible with the environment, these smaller ships can slip close to feeding whales or bears foraging ashore, or can nose up to a waterfall.

On the *Explorers,* whenever there is a lull in the lounge, entertainment is spontaneous; it might be a sing-along around the player piano, or provided by talented passengers and crew members.

On both big and small ships, cruise directors tell about the Indians, Russians, explorers, fur traders, fishermen, and gold seekers who formed the background of this vast, moist Panhandle region. Their rain advice is "Be prepared, then ignore it as the locals do." Port calls allow time for shopping, local sightseeing tours, and even for some options like flightseeing and fishing.

Smooth Touring Combinations

Package tours are a comfortable answer for visitors who have two or three weeks to give to their travel agent for planning. They usually combine an Inside Passage sea leg with extensive travel by air and/or highway. These can be set up as group travel experiences, or you can go it on your own.

They are still talking about what has to be the ultimate—so far—in individualized, deluxe touring in Alaska. A travel agent from Texas called a travel agent in Ketchikan, Leisure Corporation, which has a reputation for fulfilling the more unusual requests. It seems the Texas agent's two female clients wanted to tour Alaska, but in the style to which they had long been accustomed: by limousine, with chauffeur.

The ladies and their chauffeur-driven limo raised eyebrows as they traveled the highways and rode the ferries during the 18-day itinerary. They covered territory from the Gulf of Alaska to the interior and Mount McKinley, delved into Canada's Klondike to amaze the gold rush town of Dawson City, made the news in capital Juneau, and caught the fancy of everyone in Ketchikan. Deluxe all the way, this tour (in utmost comfort) cost them almost $1,000 a day each to take in all the sights and stay in the best places.

From all reports, everyone had a ball, and the ladies loved Alaska "even though it's bigger than Texas!" They hinted that if they were younger they might even make Alaska their home . . . and vowed that this maiden limo swing around Alaska and the Yukon Territory would not be their last.

If cost is a consideration, you might better settle for an independent fly-drive tour package or a cruise/tour package (see "Tours" in *Practical Information for Southeast Alaska* and in *Facts at Your Fingertips*).

Group tours cover the circuit routes and avoid duplication of travel. They use motorcoaches with personable, knowledgeable drivers and escorts for the land portions, and take to ferries and cruise ships for the sea legs. They usually allow time for optional air tours farther afield out of main cities. First-time visitors to Alaska especially appreciate the advantages of a well expedited cruise/tour, where reservations and baggage handling are all taken care of and there is someone standing by to give advice or help solve problems, if necessary.

Out of the Past

A particular delight of sightseeing in almost overwhelmingly large Alaska is taking to varied, sometimes ingenious, or historic modes of transportation as needed, or just for fun or photos. They may be included in some packages or are available as options.

Many still mourn the "mothballed" narrow-gauge White Pass & Yukon Route railroad, engineered to switchback through the mountains between Skagway and Whitehorse during the turn-of-the century gold rush. However, since the state purchased the Alaska Railroad from the federal government in 1984, it's increasingly popular as an alternate to the highway connecting Anchorage and Fairbanks. Local and express runs provide passenger, vehicle, and freight service. (See *Practical Information* sections for Anchorage, Fairbanks, Southcentral, and Interior Alaska.)

Out of Fairbanks is another delightful sample of early-day transportation, a riverboat. The sternwheeler *Discovery* churns up the Chena River, reminiscent of the days when the Yukon was the "marine highway" to the Klondike. During a 4-hour trip, paddle into Fairbanks's golden past. The captain and hostesses, often local students from the University of Alaska, describe and point out many phases of far north life: vintage and modern log homes, trapper's camp, dog teams, float planes, and rich gold streams.

You'll see some sled dogs, unemployed in summer, staked out in Eskimo towns while the pups roam and scrounge freely. With the accent on saving energy, "working" dog teams may come back in full force. Meanwhile, dog sleds are still considered most practical for patrolling beats like Denali National Park in winter, and fine looking teams are groomed for myriad sled-dog races. To keep their dogs in shape and competitive, "mushers" may offer dog sled rides to visitors, even in summer. They put the sleds on wheels and run them on the tundra, even pitting them against a tour bus when a road parallels a promising stretch.

Just for contrast, sightseeing options in Anchorage include hot air balloons, and there's another very popular mode of transportation forty miles down Turnagain Arm from Anchorage. Would you believe a chair-lift? At Mount Alyeska, Alaska's largest year-round see and ski resort, Alaskans and visitors take a leisurely ride up 2,000 feet to grand picture-taking viewpoints. The sundeck overlooks mountain-bordered reaches that Captain Cook named. He thought there was a through passage to Prince William Sound, but found the way blocked by mountains and the magnificent Portage Glacier. So he had to "Turn again" (and go back).

Other than Jets

Besides commercial jets, there are many small air services listed in cities and towns. Small planes are fine for picture-taking and sightseeing in the bush country, and the pilots are some of the most skillful. As they say, "There are old pilots and bold pilots, but no old bold pilots."

A record number of Alaskans own and fly planes. Note the number of small planes lining Anchorage's Hood Lake next to the International Airport. Out of town, you may see a plane parked next to the house. Because of the distances and limited number of highways, air travel is necessary, and popular.

And in the Future

Now that the controversial Alaska pipeline is completed, some see the working "haul" road as a new travel-corridor to the far north. As an extension of the Alaska Highway, it would add additional recreational road-miles.

The North Slope could become a major tourist attraction, perhaps even an Arctic museum of oil exploration. Those who have already been there, as workers or visitors, have been impressed with the effort put into preserving the Arctic's fragile ecology. Today, great numbers and varieties of birds continue to nest in ice-melt lakes among the permafrost mounds called "pingos." The caribou have continued to migrate, in spite of pump stations, gathering lines, drill pads, wells and "Christmas trees" (capped wells).

And there are barely touched destinations to explore around the coastal fringes: islands like Shishmaref, historic World War II sites out in the Aleutian Island Chain, and the Bristol Bay fishing banks.

Coastal western Alaska boasts a "Window on the East" as intriguing as Russian Peter the Great's "Window on the West," near Leningrad. Flightseeing planes go within the very shadow of Siberia. Though poles apart in politics, the mainlands of the U.S.S.R. and the U.S. are separated by 55 miles at the narrowest point in the Bering Sea. Every once in a while someone talks of rebuilding that landbridge, or constructing an underwater tube. Think of the tourism possibilities! Except for the problem of bridging the Atlantic, and some complexities of connecting roads across the continents, it could be the start of a "Trans-World Highway."

Travel promotion experts and marketing specialists are kept busy trying to predict the trends. Surveys show that travel north continues to increase and that Denali National Park is still the top tourist attrac-

tion. They've determined that the "typical tourist" is somewhat younger now, and inclined to be independent. Fine, all-inclusive package
tours, attractive in scope and price, continue to draw individuals and
groups, including many senior citizens. This means increasing the food
and lodging facilities and expanding the travel possibilities—the places
a traveler can reach and those that appeal to special interests.

Some main pattern changes have to do with season and length of
stay. Innovators in the travel industry see Alaska as more than a
summer-only destination. They are fashioning attractive tours and happenings for every season, even the dead of winter.

Because of improved travel, especially by air, and competitive
(cheaper) fares, the trend is toward shorter and more frequent trips to
the Great Land. Visitors with only a few days for vacation can jet to
and explore one area at a time, or in little more than a week touch
on more than one remote area. For example, an 11-day "Athapascan"
Cruise/Tour (through *Exploration Holidays & Cruises)* jetted to Anchorage for two days before jetting to the Arctic. It overnighted in
Kotzebue then toured Nome on the way back to Anchorage. Next, the
tour went by rail to Mt. McKinley, overnighting in Denali Park. It
continued by rail to Fairbanks, then by plane to Whitehorse. From
there, motorcoaches toured through spectacular mountains to goldrush
Skagway's port, start of a southbound Inside Passage cruise that includes port calls at small communities and cruising glacial fjords,
before the flight home from Ketchikan. The price, from $2,365 in 1985,
included almost everything but meals (other than those aboard ship).

Anchorage and Fairbanks are already world air-crossroads with a
rapidly developing cultural climate and potential wealth to support fine
arts. They may be on the way to take their place among the world's
great cities. Future travelers may flock there to enjoy the very best
music, art, drama, and sports.

If this introduction has titillated your adventuresome spirit, read on.
The essays and the more specific *Practical Information* sections, will
help you to decide your style of travel in Alaska and will point you in
some right directions.

SOUTHEAST ALASKA

Few Roads Lead to the Panhandle

The best place for island-hopping in Alaska is in the southeast Panhandle region, where an almost-drowned mountain range makes up the Alexander Archipelago. It parallels a strip of the United States Northwest coast, set off from Canada by mountains that are well over a mile and a half high. This narrow mainland strip, plus the mountain-top island chain, make up Alaska's five-hundred-mile-long "Panhandle." Actually it's a dipper handle which extends south and east from the main body of the peninsula state. The cup holds the other diverse areas of Alaska: the Gulf and Interior, and the far northern and far western coastal fringes.

Thinking in terms of a grand circle tour of Alaska, the time-proven sea approach is a winner. On the other hand, if you choose to reverse the circle, the same marine- and mountainscapes and multiple evergreen islands of the southeast Panhandle add up to a grand finale—they are the very essence of Alaska.

Either way, the scene, on a grand scale and gorgeous, continues to remain much as it was when earlier visitors admired it—canoe-paddling Indians, explorers of assorted nationalities in sailing ships, gold rushers who crowded onto almost anything that would float, and a wave of hardy tourists who came to sightsee the Great Land by steamship, before 1900.

For today's travelers, the choice is town-hopping with Alaska Airlines jets or by local air taxi services; port-calling via Alaska State Ferries or private boat; and by cruise ship. Sailing under many flags, a flotilla of cruise ships summer in southeast Alaska waters, granting shore leaves to their passengers in assorted ports.

The towns along the Inside Passage are all different, each with its distinctive flavor, from first port Ketchikan, dedicated to fish and wood chips, to Sitka, with a Russian dressing. Place names—of towns and of myriad waterways—give clues of earlier visitors, who left their mark around southeast Alaska. There's little mistaking nationalities among such labels as Baranof, Kupreanof, Prince of Wales, and Petersburg. Klawock and Ketchikan are derived from similar-sounding Indian names.

No Roads Lead to Ketchikan

Twenty years ago, Ketchikan and other similarly isolated Panhandle towns came as close to being connected by a "road" as they are likely to, with the inauguration of the state's extensive Marine Highway System. It was an instant hit with Alaskans, who have been happily riding and singing "The Ferryboat Song" ever since.

Though there is periodic talk of a connecting combination ferry and over-island highway, it's not likely to happen very soon (if at all). The barriers are formidable for road building in the usual sense, paved or unpaved.

Ketchikan is perched on a large mountainous island underneath 3,000-foot Deer Mountain. The island's name is a jaw-breaker, Revillagigedo, named by English mariner George Vancouver who was exploring the Inside Passage in 1793. He often named things for his crew and friends, in this case the Viceroy of Mexico.

Locals say Ketchikan's name was inspired by the local Indians, who were referring to a nearby waterfall that reminded them of an eagle with its wings spread out. However, it's apt for the appearance of the town as well. Imagine that you have hiked the 5-mile trail to the top of Deer Mountain and are looking out over the town and surrounding area. Ketchikan appears squeezed onto a narrow shelf. Actually, it's

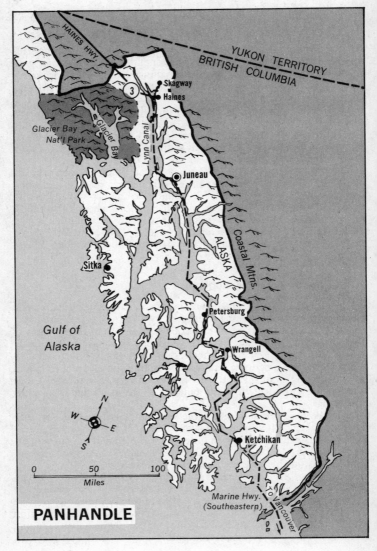

HAINES HWY.

YUKON TERRITORY
BRITISH COLUMBIA

③

Skagway
Haines

Glacier Bay
Nat'l Park

Glacier Bay

Lynn Canal

Juneau

ALASKA

Coastal Mtns.

Sitka

Gulf of
Alaska

Petersburg

Wrangell

N
W   E
S

0   50   100
Miles

Ketchikan

Marine Hwy.
(Southeastern)

To Vancouver

PANHANDLE

more like an overhang, considering that much of the 3-mile-long waterfront section is built out over the water. The docks are on pilings, and
with no place to grow but north and south from its center, the town
has a spread-eagle shape. There is plenty of waterfront action, with
ships coming and going, and small float planes and air taxis skimming
off and swishing down like big insects.

It's obvious that Ketchikan's skyline hasn't been static. Some high-
rises mark the two up-and-coming shopping centers at both ends of
town. The large pulp mill is a standout, and there are schools, including
a community college, small boat harbors, parks, and many attractive
homes valiantly climbing the steep backdrop.

Ketchikan's Past

A capsulized history of Ketchikan starts with the Indian fishing
camp at the mouth of Ketchikan Creek, long before white miners and
fishermen came to settle in 1885. Shortly before 1900, however, the new
town's future was brightened by gold discoveries and the establishment
of a cannery and sawmill. Fishing industries peaked in the 1930s, but
declined in the 1940s. Thick, fast-growing forests fed the growing
timber industry and the mill of the Louisiana-Pacific Pulp Company.
Today, along with timber, fish, and pulp, the town is banking on
tourism, a molybdenum mine, and a hydroelectric project.

Ketchikan ranks fourth in Alaska city size. Population is 7,200, over
11,000 counting the surrounding communities it serves, mostly based
on fishing and logging. Many of these small villages such as Klawock,
Metlakatla, Hydaburg, and Craig, on neighbor islands reached by
smaller ferries and smaller planes are also leaning toward tourism.

Alaska Sightseeing Company, Gray Line of Ketchikan, and new,
deluxe Royal Highway Tours motorcoaches offer 1- to 3-hour tours
that provide a valuable orientation to the town and environs. On your
own you'll find lots of atmosphere and exercise hiking the steep streets
that give way to wooden staircases leading to homes and sweeping
views of Tongass Narrows and islands. As they say in Ketchikan, all
that's needed are "a pair of sneakers and an hour or two" to cover the
high points at your own pace. Well-placed signs put up by the chamber
of commerce lead you onward from the visitor center, located next to
the attractive waterfront park downtown by the City Pier, where the
cruise ships dock. Whether exploring by car or afoot, the Ketchikan
Visitors Bureau is a good place to start.

There is interesting browsing in the Tongass Historical Society Museum in the Centennial Building, built in 1967, the 100th anniversary
of the purchase of Alaska from Russia. The museum shares the building with the public library. Seasonal displays feature the arts and crafts.

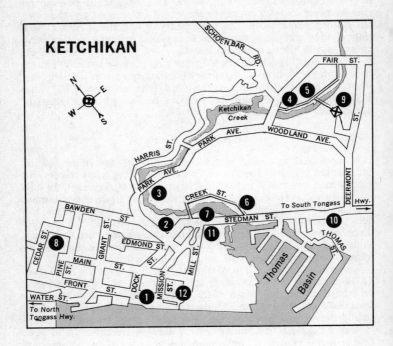

Points of Interest

1) Visitor Center
2) Tongass Historical Society Museum
3) Fish Ladder-Salmon Carving
4) Deer Mountain Hatchery
5) World's Largest Gold Nugget (a spoof!)
6) Dolly's House
7) Chief Johnson Totem
8) Kyan Totem
9) Totem Heritage Center
10) Ketchikan Mural painted by 21 Native artists
11) Federal Building and Tongass National Forest Visitors Center
12) Post Office

Permanent exhibits in the museum include pioneer relics, minerals, Indian items and artifacts. Outside, Ketchikan Creek tumbles in rapids fought each season by salmon on their way upstream to spawn. Wooden Creek Street, on pilings, is across the stream from the museum. It marks what's left of a notorious part of town, including some of the infamous "houses of ill repute." Dolly's House is also a museum, but quite a contrast to its staid neighbor, the Tongass Museum. This restored house of prostitution retains the furnishings and decor picked by Dolly herself. Nearby, the Deer Mountain Hatchery in City Park offers year-round viewing of prized king and coho salmon reared for release in Ketchikan Creek.

One facet of tourism involves both trees and Indians, the art of totem carving. In Ketchikan you won't have to look far to see these "monuments in cedar." Some are downtown near the docks. Chief Johnson's totem was set in the heart of town in 1901. Chief Kyan's totem at the top of Main Street lures visitors. You'll get money within 24 hours after touching it, so they say. More are within walking distance, at the Totem Heritage Cultural Center, near the fish hatchery. This was started as a Bicentennial project for preserving the Tlingit and Haida poles from nearby Indian villages. You'll find authentic information here on the types of totems: Heraldic, depicting social standing; Memorial, usually for a dead chief; and Mortuary, with a section for ashes; devastating Ridicule, or "shame poles" for putting down an enemy; Potlatch poles for festivals; and—most common and important—House Poles, used in constructing community tribal houses.

At Totem Bight, on a point north of Ketchikan, overlooking Tongass Narrows, a stand of authentically reproduced totem poles guards a fine hand-crafted tribal house. It is a 16-minute drive and a short walk through the forest from the parking lot to the totem park.

Saxman Totem Park is about 2 miles south of Ketchikan at the Indian village of Saxman, named for a missionary who helped the Tlingit Indians who moved there before 1900. Natives can "read" the poles depicting birds, animals, and water dwellers. They (or a tour guide) can also identify the big chiefs portrayed including Abraham Lincoln, whose tall-hat makes him quite identifiable. He was honored for abolishing slavery in the U.S., which included the newly acquired Territory of Alaska. Until then, the souvenirs that warfaring tribes had been bringing home were often people, to serve as slaves. In case you wonder why the President is cut off at the knees, they say it is because the grateful Indians were working from a postcard photo, and that's where it ended. The time-rotted original of the Lincoln totem is encased in glass in the state museum at Juneau.

From town, you won't go far in either direction before running out of road. The North Tongass Highway starts at the Federal Building where area information is on display and ends about 18 miles later at Settler's Cove Campground. The South Tongass road ends at a power plant. Side roads soon terminate at campgrounds and trail beginnings, viewpoints, lakes, boat launching ramps, or private property. There are also several trails in the environs of Ketchikan that are not too difficult. Less than a mile from downtown, near the city landfill, the 3-mile Deer Mountain Trail takes off. Other favorites are the 2-mile Perseverance Trail near Ward Lake and the mile-long nature trail, with signs, leading around the lake.

If you switch to sea and air transportation, sightseeing possibilities in the Ketchikan area are expanded.

Local air services offer the unfeathered fine bird's-eye views of spectacular granite and snowfield-draped mountains in high wilderness behind the city. Float planes often put down in a deep clear mountain lake for picture-taking.

Visitors with longer time to spend can reserve one of more than 50 Forest Service cabins in the Ketchikan area. Some are accessible by hiking, or boat; most are fly-ins. There are also more luxurious accommodations.

The active Visitor Center and the Chamber of Commerce steer visitors toward what's going on. For example, visitors are welcome to fish in the community-sponsored April-to-September salmon derbies. Winning fish are usually well over 50 pounds and the prizes add up to thousands of dollars. Nearby Behm Canal is one of Southeast's fishing hot spots. You can drive to Clover Pass Resort, 15 paved miles north of Ketchikan, a headquarters for the salmon derby. Hopeful fishermen strike out from here for hooking fighting king salmon. Yes Bay is 45 miles to the northwest, and besides fishing, features hiking, beachcombing, and birdwatching (see "Wilderness Lodges" in *Practical Information for Southeast Alaska*).

Wrangell

Next up the line is Wrangell (rang'gull), also on an island near the mouth of the Stikine (stick-een') River, but not a cliffhanger like Ketchikan. It's a waterfront town, though with a different emphasis. Here, it's the shipping point for timber processed in the town's big sawmills, a port for logging tugs, and for Japanese lumber ships.

The town might well have developed a split personality, having been exposed to motley influences over the years: soldiers, Indians, fur and gold seekers, fishermen, loggers, rivermen. With a past that goes back to the Russians, Wrangell existed under three successive flags: first Russian, then British, and finally American, accompanied by as many name changes. First it was called Redoubt Saint Dionysius. Next the

British named it Fort Stikine. Then the Americans settled for the simpler name Wrangell, almost the same as the name the Russians had given to the whole island, when they named it for an early governor, Baron von Wrangel.

Don't count on much road travel while in Wrangell. Besides the two-mile loop to the airport, there is only the Zimovia Highway. It passes through town from the ferry dock and gives up at Pat's Creek campground, just over 11 miles. In between there is a short trail off the highway that goes to woodsy Rainbow Falls.

The Stikine River, however, shows possibilities of again becoming a "marine highway." In the past, the Stikine gave access to interior gold fields and was important as a mining supply route. History may be repeated, with copper the prize. Meanwhile, the Stikine has been discovered by river runners, who traverse part of its length in assorted craft. They get around its impassable Grand Canyon by making an air portage to Telegraph Creek, then running the rest of the 160 miles to Wrangell.

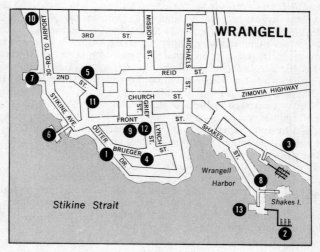

Points of Interest

1) Visitor Information
   A-Frame
2) Boat Harbor
3) Chief Shakes Gravesite
4) City Hall—Totem

5) City Museum
6) Cruiseship Dock
7) State Ferry Terminal
8) Marine Bar (Fort
   Dionysius)
9) Petroglyph—Natl. Bank
   of Alaska

10) "Our Collections"
    Museum
11) Post Office
12) Stikine Native
    Organization totem
    carvers
13) Seaplane Float

Tourism and services are very informal in smaller, waterfront-dominated Wrangell, still off the beaten big cruise ship path. Ferries dock just north of the pier-side Stikine Inn. Smaller cruise ships, such as the *Majestic Alaska Explorer,* tie up at the closest dock, only a short walk to the Inn and "downtown."

The town appreciates the regularly scheduled ferries, and everyone loves having the cruise ships call. In fact, they greet them with music and dance—the dancers, ranging from young tots to the young-at-heart, may turn out for a lively cancan, in costume. They may be joined by some local Stikine Indians, who dance in costume in the tribal house on special occasions.

The Wrangell Chamber of Commerce Visitor Information center is conveniently located close to the docks in a small A-frame building at Front Street and Outer Drive. It's usually open when ships are in port. On request, the center will arrange a guided tour, often led by an enthusiastic student. However, all you'll need is a free, current *Visitor Guide* put out by the *Wrangell Sentinel,* Alaska's oldest continuously published newspaper (from 1902). It tells all, with map.

The Wrangell Museum, on Second Street, north of the Visitor Information A-frame, across from the federal building, has petroglyph carvings in its Indian section, and many local historical items. Farther north, at the end of town, a private collection of artifacts and 19th- and 20th-century memorabilia is displayed in Bigelow's Museum and Gift Shop. When traveling in the other direction stop in for a refresher at the Marine Bar, near Shakes Island. It's on the site of Fort Dionysius, established when the Russians settled there in 1834, to keep the Hudson Bay Company from fur trading up the Stikine River.

If you're interested in the archaic, be sure to look along the beach for petroglyphs, carvings on the rocks believed to have been doodled long ago by Indians waiting out hunting and fishing sessions. One is near the ferry terminal; more are reached by a boardwalk trail taking off from the Airport Road.

More recent Indian art—many fine totem poles—decorate the streets, and a choice collection is on an island just offshore, reached by a foot bridge. Little mid-harbor Chief Shakes Island honors the Indian chief with a replica of his community house under the watchful eyes of superbly carved totem faces. Inside the house are more examples of Indian art, and some of their working tools.

Petersburg

Getting to Petersburg is an experience, whether you take the "high road" or the "low road." Alaska Airlines claims the "shortest jet flight in the world" from takeoff at Wrangell to put down at Petersburg. The schedule allows 20 minutes, but it's usually more like 11. At eye level, the Marine Highway route squeaks through Wrangell Narrows, full of markers and other aids to help navigate the reefs and currents in the ticklish 23-mile stretch between Kupreanof and Mitkof Islands. It is sensationally narrow in places.

At first sight of Petersburg you might think that you are in the old country. Neat and cheery white Scandinavian-style houses and store-fronts, decked with bright-colored swirls of leaf and flower designs, and a sizeable fishing fleet adorn the waterfront.

The healthy looking people will sport fishing garb, most likely from hip boots to Norwegian knits. If you happen to land there near the 17th of May, they may be wearing old-country costumes and dancing schot-tisches on the docks. You may even hear Norwegian spoken. But don't worry about a language barrier; visitors can get by very well with "Skol!" Every year on the weekend closest to "Syttende Mai" these descendants of Norwegian fishermen, who settled Peter Buschmann's town in 1897, go all out to celebrate Norwegian Independence Day and the fame of their halibut. Though the town is devoted to fish of all kinds, scaly and shell, it's best known for having Alaska's largest home-based halibut fleet.

The Norwegians turn out to greet arriving visitors and summer cruise ships that are able to call now since the new, bigger dock is completed. Greeters may be a bold band of "Vikings" accompanied by a kitchen band playing a fishy tune like "I Like Hooked-nose Salmon." If your name is Norwegian, you'll have it made.

It seems that everything has a fish flavor. Eat some, for sure, in the restaurants, or if you are there during the Festival, take in a local "fish feed." And don't miss the Clausen Museum, 2nd & Fram streets. In front is a large bronze sculpture, called "Fisk," (fish) in honor of them all. Inside you'll see a king salmon, the record-breaker, at 126½ pounds.

Visitors can find out what they want to know about Petersburg at the museum, or at the Chamber of Commerce, Harbor Master Bldg. on Harbor Way. How about a hot tub, sauna, or shower? Ask Viking Travel, on Main Street, or phone 772–4266. Though travel, especially Alaska Marine Highway and airline ticketing is their long suit, they are also home base for Petersburg's only "spa"—a bathhouse, open even-ings.

The flatter, sea level terrain in the vicinity has created some sloughs. One of them is a photographers' delight. Because of the tides, the houses bordering Hammer Slough are built on stilts. Along with ware-houses and boats reflected in the still water, they make a picture-worthy scene.

You can drive a couple of miles to Sandy Beach picnic and recreation area. Drive the 34-mile Mitkof Highway for campgrounds and a fish ladder at Falls Creek. The ladder helps migrating coho and pink salmon bypass the Falls on the way to spawning grounds; it's at Mile 10.9 of the highway and can be observed just off the roadside. Best time is late summer and early fall. Also on Mitkof Highway is the Crystal Lake Fish Hatchery. The fish hatchery is open to visitors who want to learn about this state operation which involves coho, king, and chum salmon and steelhead trout. Near the end of the highway is the Stikine River Delta; at low tide the mud flats are exposed.

Petersburg's biggest attraction, literally, is about 25 miles east of town. The LeConte Glacier is the continent's southernmost tidewater glacier. It's very active, "calving" ice chunks so big that they are far from melted down by the time they reach the main channels. The new *Explorer* ships pay weekly calls, and sightseeing charter flights and day cruises out of Petersburg are popular. Viking Travel on Main Street will have up-to-date listings of available tours. Sightings of whales, porpoises, and seals are almost guaranteed.

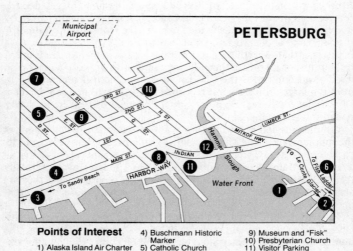

Points of Interest

1) Alaska Island Air Charter
2) Beachcomber Inn
3) To eagle observation point
4) Buschmann Historic Marker
5) Catholic Church
6) King Salmon Hotel
7) Lutheran Church
8) C of C Info.
9) Museum and "Fisk"
10) Presbyterian Church
11) Visitor Parking
12) Sons of Norway Hall

Tlingit/Russian Sitka

For centuries before the Russians came at the turn of the 18th century, Sitka had been the ancestral home of the Tlingit Indian nation. Isolated on the far west side of their large island, they cherished their affluent life, living off the land and sea. And the living was easy, with plenty of game in the forests and a wealth of seafood. It was small wonder that the Indians took a dim view of Russian intrusion.

Governor Baranof, guiding light for the settlement of Sitka, second capital of Russian America, left his name and mark. Sitka's island is named Baranof, and it is situated in the northern part of the large Alexander Archipelago. The Governor coveted the Sitka site for some of the same reasons the Tlingits did: beauty of setting, milder climate, and the forests. However, the Russians needed the wood for building craft larger than war canoes. Their ships traded far west to Hawaii and the Orient, and south along the west coast as far as Fort Ross, California. Baranof was well aware of the convenience of Sitka's location. Eventually the city grew and became so lively that it was called the "Paris of the Pacific." But not without a notable setback.

The *first* settlement site a few miles north of today's Sitka was called Fort Archangel Michael. It was established in 1799 and destroyed by the Tlingits in 1802. "I shall return," vowed Baranof, and did, in 1804, bent on building his next capital on the Tlingit's choice village property. The final "Battle for Alaska" began with the attack on their stronghold atop the hill. It ended at the Tlingit fort a few miles down the beach, when the Indians withdrew to the other side of the island and stayed there for the next twenty years. The battle site is now the 105-acre Sitka National Historical Park.

The Sitka Visitor Bureau headquarters is conveniently located in the beautifully designed Centennial Building on Harbor Drive. A big Tlingit Indian war canoe is displayed in front. Inside the building you'll find a museum, auditorium, art gallery, Convention and Visitor Center offices, and lots of friendly people with advice on what to see and how to do it. They'll know if the peppy New Archangel Russian Dancers are performing, if the annual Salmon Derby is in progress, and if there is a festival or contest, such as the logging championship competitions. They'll start you on your own walking tour, or direct you to a guided bus tour. The staff is enthusiastic, from students to "Double O's" ("Older Ones"). Many of the latter are retired Alaskans living in the Pioneer Home, the big building dominating the downtown square and marked by a flourishing hedge of Sitka roses. On the lawn, a two-ton bronze statue of a grizzled prospector honors all "sourdoughs." Some of the Double O's are history buffs who lived through much of Alaska's lively early-20th-century history.

In the Centennial Building, there is also an accurate model of "New Archangel," as the Russians called the colony they built on the ruins of Indian Sitka. It shows where the Russians built boats, milled flour, cast bells for California missions, and cut ice from Swan Lake to ship to gold rush-booming San Francisco bars.

For almost ten years, Sitka's town jewel, St. Michael's Cathedral, dating from 1844, was missing. Russian-built with onion dome and carrot spire, the building burned in 1966, leaving a heart-breaking void smack in the middle of the main street. During the fire, everyone turned out. Through superhuman effort (maybe a miracle), most of the religious objects that could be carried, or that weren't fastened down, were saved.

St. Michael's Bishop Gregory was born in Kiev. He has a special affinity for the charming church. The ceremonies making him the first bishop of Sitka and Alaska to be consecrated in the Alaska diocese were

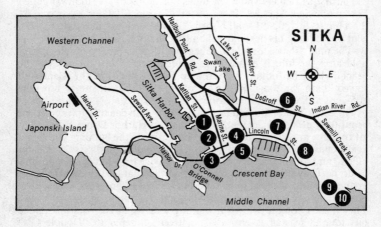

Points of Interest

1) Russian Cemetery
2) Block House
3) Castle Hill
4) Saint Michael's Cathedral
5) Centennial Bldg., Visitor Bureau
6) Sitka National Cemetery
7) Sheldon Jackson College
8) Sheldon Jackson Museum
9) Sitka National Historical Park
10) Tlingit Fort

celebrated in the replica of the church, even before it was completely rebuilt.

The new cathedral stands downtown in the center of Lincoln Street. The Bishop stewards the lovely old treasures with TLC. Among them are ornate gospel books, including one from Fort Ross, chalices, crucifixes, some much-used wedding crowns, and an altar cloth said to have been worked by Princess Maksoutoff herself. There are many priceless icons, religious portraits in oil with only faces and hands exposed, the rest covered with ornate silver and gold-wrought frames. The Sitka Madonna icon was presented to the church by Russian American Company workers. Nearby, the Russian Bishop's House dates from 1842. It is now being restored as a National Historic Landmark by the National Park Service.

For photos, atmosphere, and orientation, the best spot is up some steps to the top of "Castle Hill," west of Saint Michael's. This promontory in downtown Sitka was the site of many major historical happenings. The "castle" of first Governor Alexander Baranof is long gone now, of course. What's left are some venerable cannons, a number with Russian markings. They point west to the Pacific Ocean past the lovely, island-flecked harbor and Mt. Edgecumbe, an extinct volcano that looks like a mini-Fujiyama.

Note the only other furnishing—a flagpole. Every October 18, everyone gathers around it, many wearing period costumes, the men with beards and the ladies with bonnets. Then they reenact the same ceremonies, lowering the Russian Double Eagle flag and raising the American flag that in 1867 marked the transfer of Russian America to the United States. Congress promptly renamed the new territory "Alaska." Here, too, on January 3, 1959, was raised the first 49-star American flag, signifying Alaska statehood.

From Castle Hill, the newer landmarks are obvious, such as modern hotels that contrast with the distinctive vintage buildings, and the John O'Connell Bridge. It connects Sitka's island with Japonski Island, where the Mt. Edgecumbe Alaska Native boarding high school, hospital and jet airport are located.

North of Castle Hill you can visit a crumbling old cemetery where a Russian princess is buried. She is said to have cried as she stood beside her husband, Governor Maksoutoff, during the transfer ceremonies.

Sitka's Indian side is well represented at Sitka National Historical Park, beginning with totem poles in front of the building and along a shady lane that leads to the old fort site. The Park is across town from Castle Hill and the Russian Cemetery. Inside the attractive Visitor Center, The Battle for Alaska is replayed in audio-visual, and there is a magnificent display of original totemic art. In the Indian Cultural

Workshop rooms, artisans revive old crafts from wood carving to the difficult, almost lost, art of Chilkat blanket weaving.

Sitka's Russian past is reflected in the Russian Bishop's House on Lincoln Street, near Crescent Harbor. Built in 1842 for Alaska's first Russian Orthodox Bishop, it's one of the few Russian log structures remaining in Alaska.

At the nearby Sheldon Jackson College campus, the museum collection started by this early day missionary and educator also displays prized items, both Russian and Indian, including a detailed diorama of the original Indian Village. The museum, enlarged during 1985, is now owned by the State of Alaska. Take a walking tour of the campus and you'll see historic buildings. The original school started in 1878 and evolved into a high school and now a college.

Before the bridge, a small ferry carried everyone back and forth for a few cents. All luggage and freight went to town aboard army "ducks," the amphibian craft developed during World War II. No one denies the convenience of the graceful-looking bridge, but visitor-wise the little ferry was a gem. Rubbing shoulders and talking with residents while crossing the harbor and admiring Sitka's marvelous setting made a captivating introduction. And it was a great unwinder after the jet speed arrival at the airport.

Over the years, Sitka's fortune has fluctuated with fishing and sea-food processing plants, a Japanese-owned pulp mill, and federal government agencies. Just as the residents were adapting to sea invasion by the state ferries and a growing number of cruise ships, they were propelled into the jet set. Alaska Airlines inaugurated the Sitka air gateway to Alaska in 1967. Altogether, this has led to a fast-developing new industry, tourism, and in one way or another most of the residents are involved. There are evening cruises out of Crescent Harbor near the Centennial Building. Leaving at 6 P.M. in the summer, they explore Silver Bay, touching on the scenic, the wild, the historical and even the industrial facets of Sitka as the ship sails by the pulpmill waterfront. (Call 747-8941.)

Juneau, the Capital

Although the state capital is on the mainland, getting there by road is out of the question. Access is only by sea and air.

The Juneau office for Alaska Exploration Holidays and Cruises, 76 Egan Drive, #110 (586-6883), has brochures and a travel counselor with information on available optional tour packages. Gray Line, in the Baranof Hotel, and Alaska Sight-Seeing Co., Cape Fox Sheffield House, offer local motorcoach tours daily in summer.

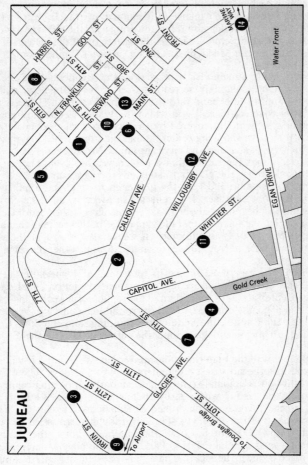

Points of Interest

1) Four Story Totem
2) Governor's Mansion
3) Grave of Joe Juneau and Dick Harris
4) Harris & Juneau Monument
5) House of Wickersham
6) Memorial Library and Totem
7) Native Crafts Exhibit (Federal Bldg.)
8) Old Russian Church
9) Plaque to Chief Kowee
10) State Capitol Bldg.
11) State Museum
12) State Office Bldg.
13) Log Cabin Visitor Center
14) Marine Park with Visitor Info.

JUNEAU

This northerly part of the Panhandle is set off by mountain barriers, including a formidable expanse of ice and snow, the Juneau Icefield. Lurking just beyond the mountains towering over the city, the approximately 4,000 square mile icefield is the source of all the glaciers in the area, including the Mendenhall Glacier, about 13 miles from downtown Juneau.

Besides being a main visitor attraction, the Mendenhall has been a good neighbor, obligingly retreating over some years now, making room for Juneau to expand into the suburbs. Less than 50 years ago, the glacier covered the rocks on which the Visitor Center now stands. Now the area formerly covered by the glacier is taken over by a jet airport, a modern shopping center, homes built on property with some very fine views, and camp and picnic grounds. No one seems particularly worried about the rumor that a cooler weather cycle may be due which could cause the glacier to start advancing again.

You can drive up and look the glacier in its mile-and-a-half wide, 100- to 200-foot high face. It is reflected in Mendenhall Lake, formed by melting ice, beginning about 1900. The displays in the Visitor Center tell about the plant and animal life supported in this recreational area. It's open 9 to 6 daily in summer; on weekends the rest of the year. Hiking trails take off from the center and also many other places in and around Juneau.

In 1980, the capital celebrated its centennial with special events all year. Some of the projects are now permanent attractions, such as the Visitor Center at Third and Main. This replica of an early log cabin church is a quaint contrast to the surrounding modern government buildings, the Capitol, the State Office Building, and the State Court Building, all metal and glass, and the tallest structure, the Federal Building.

Pick up a walking map (most businesses have them) and it will also lead you to some surprises, remainders from earlier days. The Governor's Mansion is colonial-style, its tall, smooth supporting pillars on the porch contrasting with nearby Indian totem poles. At Fifth and Gold streets, the tiny onion-domed St. Nicholas Russian Orthodox Church, dating from 1894, is a standout, though surrounded by other buildings now. It's not far from the landmark hotel, the Baranof. Juneau's award-winning Marine Park along the busy waterfront is a great place to meet the locals. There may be swinging entertainment, such as the "Natural Gas Jazz Band" livening up an occasion, perhaps the Fourth of July. There is also an information kiosk by the seaplane docks and Merchant's Wharf shopping mall, manned by volunteers in summer. Start from here and follow the map from the waterfront on up as high as you want to climb. Once you head away from Gastineau Channel, the route is increasingly verticle, up narrow streets and wooden stairways, past homes clinging to town-confining Mt. Juneau and Mt. Roberts.

The Alaska State Museum in the subport area houses excellent Indian displays, rocks and minerals, and mounted wildlife specimens. Ramps instead of stairs, a boon to the handicapped, lead to upper levels. High on a slanty street overlooking Juneau is a small house-museum. James Wickersham, a judge, historian, and collector of Alaskan treasures lived here early in the century. For many years, the Judge's niece, Ruth Allman, hosted popular narrated tours of the house and its intriguing memorabilia, and served guests her delicious "Flaming Sourdough Treat." In 1984, the State bought the home and closed it for a period of preservation and restoration. (See "Museums" in *Practical Information* at the end of this chapter.)

A ghost of Juneau's golden past haunts the slopes of Mount Roberts. Some ruins of buildings of the Alaska-Juneau Mine that produced over $80 million in gold before it was closed in 1944 are reminders that, before government, gold was a bigger business. Rich strikes by Joe Juneau and Dick Harris were made here in 1880, before the mad rushes elsewhere. The stampede that followed their discoveries settled Juneau, the first "Alaska" town, following the Purchase. Across the Douglas Bridge and south from Sandy Beach, there are remains of the Treadwell Mine. Old pilings along the shore and rusting machinery in the woods give little hint now that here was a mine even bigger than the A–J.

By 1900, there was agitation to move the capital from Sitka to booming Juneau. The reason? Sitka was considered too isolated and far off the beaten track to be the seat of government. Legislators argued that the capital should be nearer the population center. In 1906, the deed was done.

Ironically, in 1974 the vote favored moving the capital from Juneau's 20,000 population area to a spot between the state's two largest cities. In 1976, voters approved a site near Willow, deemed within easier reach of over half of the state's residents, although it is wilderness. Since then there have been some second thoughts.

Estimates from the drawing board indicated that a lot of pipeline revenue might be consumed by rebuilding from scratch and by moving costs; the money might be used to better advantage. Then, too, many have a genuine appreciation for Juneau's capital attributes, located as it is amid Southeast Alaska's great recreational opportunities. Funding for the capital move was defeated in the 1982 election. At this writing, whether the issue is dead or dormant is anyone's guess.

Glacier Bay

Two hundred years ago, no visitors saw Glacier Bay. It was only a dent in an icy shoreline when Captain George Vancouver passed by in his ship in 1794. Over the next hundred years, due to a warming trend and some earthquakes, the ice rivers melted and retreated with amazing speed up their fjordlike inlets, forming Glacier Bay. Nature's healing touch followed, repairing the scars of the glacier-scoured shores by covering them with lush rain forests that attracted abundant wildlife. The unusual icy wilderness also attracted naturalist John Muir, in 1879. He was fascinated by the flora, fauna and sea life. The Indians called the area "Thunder Bay," because of the sound effects caused by the calving of glaciers dropping huge ice chunks into the bay. Muir's namesake glacier has now retreated miles farther up the bay from the small cabin next to its face, where the naturalist lived while taking his notes. This glacier and others have left miles of waterways for birds, seals, whales, porpoises, and adventurous visitors.

Glacier Bay National Park, where nature has stored her great collection of tidewater glaciers, continues to attract nature lovers, wildlife watchers, and fishermen. "On your owners" can contact the Park Headquarters for essential information on camping and recreation in the monument. Cruise ships bring their passengers up the Bay for closeups of glacier grandeur, the highlight of an Inside Passage voyage. Alaska Airlines schedules flights from Juneau that take only 12 minutes and air taxis fro Juneau, Skagway, and Haines fly to Gustavus Airport. From there it's ten miles by bus through mossy forest to overnight in Glacier Bay Lodge.

In 1985, the *Glacier Express,* a well-appointed, 200-passenger, high-speed catamaran began daily round-trip morning excursions between Juneau and Glacier Bay. Tour groups may be routed the "low road" via the *Express* for eye-level views of wilderness wonders, and return via the spectacular mountain-hopping "high road" by jet—or vice versa.

Gracious Living in the Ice Age

An evening cruise of the most active calving glaciers, Margerie and her neighbor Grand Pacific, and Lamplugh Glacier, is a highlight of the *Glacier Bay Explorer*'s two-day/one-night excursion to Glacier Bay, leaving daily from Juneau in summer. Her sister ships, the *Majestic Alaska Explorer* and the *Great Rivers Explorer,* cruise the length of the Inside Passage out of Ketchikan, and also include a memorable day in Glacier Bay.

No two cruises are exactly alike—that's part of the adventure—but glacier watching is spectacular, whether from the decks, the Vista View Lounge, or the dining room with picture windows. A tumbling icy-blue face of a glacier and the towering Fairweather Mountain Range behind is a wide-screen spectacular.

The captains are alerted for bow landing possibilities. At some glaciers they can nose the *Explorer* into shore and the crew extends a stair-stepped ramp through an opening in the bow. Then everyone can walk ashore to observe a surprising variety of small plants reinvading the recently (comparatively speaking) glacier-scoured terrain.

As the lush rain forests disappear and the vegetation dwindles, the up-Bay boat seems to be taking a trip back to the Ice Age. A Park Service naturalist is aboard to interpret the many facets of this most unusual national park, making the trip a learning experience. Everyone is encouraged to share what they see and it's relayed over the loudspeaker. Perhaps a black bear will amble over a talus slope. For sure there will be goats gamboling on 5,000-foot Mt. Wright. The *Explorer* quietly approaches nesting sites in the Marble Islands. Wherever food is plentiful—fish, plankton, shrimp stirred up in shallows by the tide—there'll be flocks of sea birds: puffins, scoters, oystercatchers, cormorants, phalaropes, kittiwakes, guillemots, murrelets, and assorted gulls. More than 200 species have been sighted, plus shorebirds, including the ptarmigan (the state bird) and the majestic bald eagle.

And you'll learn about ice, which is usually near at hand. It's scooped up, pure and crystal clear, as needed for the bar. Bartenders swear it lasts longer than the mundane ice cube. Their authority is the ranger who explains how snowflakes fall high in the mountains, granulize, and become highly compressed on their hundred-year trip to salt water; thus works nature's slow-motion, automatic ice machine.

The longer the time spent in the monument, the better. It's possible to combine tours and cruises and optional flightseeing and fishing packages available from the lodge.

Personnel of Glacier Bay Lodge and the adjacent Park Service Headquarters work together to see that monument visitors get the most out of their stay. Enlightening films and talks are scheduled in the lodge in the evening. Naturalists escort daily walks on nearby rain forest trails and along the living water line. One trek that is never the same twice is through the fleeting world of sea creatures and plants revealed for a short time at low tide before being claimed again by the sea.

Fjordlike Lynn Canal

Captain George Vancouver, famous British explorer (and name dropper), discovered this waterway in 1794. Assuming it connected with other seas, he called it Lynn Canal, after King's Lynn, his home in England. Actually, this fjord stretches north of Juneau and after sixty scenic miles deadends at Skagway.

Almost 200 years later, a Seattle-based travel company, Westours, in a sense rediscovered Lynn Canal. They felt that this area, bordered by snowy mountains, glaciers, steep timbered slopes, and supporting a wealth of sea and bird life, should be seen in broad daylight. And so they altered their cruise pattern along the Inside Passage and added a specially built day cruiser for the best viewing of Lynn Canal's choice assets.

Their big, world-class cruise ships sail north from Vancouver, B.C., and turn around at Juneau. From there passengers switch to the *Fairweather,* which links the longer sea leg with tour destinations throughout the heart of Alaska. Though smaller, the smooth, fast *Fairweather* has maximum creature comforts. They include a narrator and four attentive hostesses, besides the captain and crew, seats that recline, and cocktails for sale. A feast for the eyes is right outside the extra-large picture windows and is augmented by complimentary beverages and a hearty snack, served up with tidbits of local lore.

Informality is the keynote during the 5½-hour cruise. You'll learn about nature and how to identify whales, porpoises, seals, and seabirds. In season fishing boats will be netting salmon, king to sockeye. And you'll have your turn to see the view from the bridge, to scan the radar, to study the charts, to peek at the log, and to pick out some landmarks.

Most Westours comprehensive Alaska itineraries include the *Fairweather,* traveling either north or south. Northbound, after overnighting in Juneau, you are taken by motorcoach to the Yankee Cove Landing. It's several pleasant miles from the city, past green islands, quiet bays, and titillating glimpses of Juneau's most famous asset, the Mendenhall Glacier. Southbound, after overnighting at Skagway, passengers step on board at the gold rush town's famous harbor.

Explorer ships cruise the mountain-bordered upper reaches of Lynn Canal in daylight, and also schedule a port call at hospitable Haines in time for sightseeing and an evening salmon bake. Although highway and ferry travelers have long appreciated the community's high cultural levels and superb recreational opportunities, most big cruise ships pass by what looks like an old army post. Actually, the military-style buildings from the early 1900s surround a large parade ground and house a town, Port Chilkoot, and also a national historical site, home of the Chilkat Center for the Arts. After World War II, the town's founders bought the substantial but little-used Fort William H. Seward as army surplus, and moved in. Right next door is Haines, traditional in appearance and started by Presbyterian missionaries in 1881. These adjacent towns are now incorporated.

The Dalton Trail led from this area to the Klondike gold fields before the better-known Chilkoot Trail to the north. Enterprising Jack Dalton staked it out, based on a well-used Indian route to the interior. Then he got *his* gold by charging a substantial toll to use the trail.

Haines

A missionary, S. Hall Young, and famous naturalist John Muir picked the site for this town meant to bring Christianity and education to the native Indians. The location is a beautiful one, on a heavily wooded peninsula with magnificent views up the Inside Passage and of the Coastal Mountain Range. Its Lynn Canal neighbors are Skagway, 15 miles to the north, and Juneau, about 75 miles to the south.

From religious beginnings in 1881, Haines by 1897 was a gateway and supply route to the Klondike in the Yukon via the Jack Dalton Trail. It boomed in 1898 when gold was discovered nearby in Porcupine (now deserted). In 1903, an army post was started at Portage Cove, just south of town, and by 1905, Fort William H. Seward had a full garrison with two companies of soldiers. By 1918 there were four companies, and Alaskans were drafted from there for World War I. In 1923, they changed the name to Chilkoot Barracks, and for nearly 20

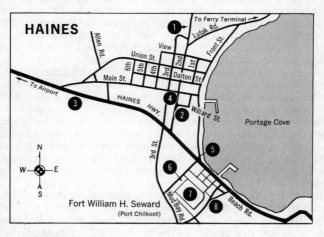

Points of Interest

1) Mt. Ripinsky Trail
2) Visitor Information
3) Fairgrounds

4) Sheldon Museum
5) Mile 0 of the Haines Highway
6) Halsingland Hotel
7) Tribal House
8) Chilkat Center for the Arts

years this was the only Army post in Alaska. World War II put all of Alaska on the map, and units from Chilkoot Barracks were the nucleus for military installations in bigger cities and places such as Cold Bay and Dutch Harbor out toward the Aleutian Islands.

After the war, the deactivated Chilkoot Barracks were sold to a group of veterans "lock, stock, and barrel," you might say. They renamed their purchase Port Chilkoot and considered developing the vast recreational possibilities of the beautiful area which so far had concentrated on such basic industries as fishing, fish processing, mining, and lumbering. The adjacent communities merged in 1970 becoming the City of Haines, combined population about 2,000.

Together, they now emphasize the hunting and fishing, and camping at Chilkoot Lake, Portage Cove, and Mosquito Lake (don't let the name deter you—it's beautiful there). They are all within easy driving distance and offer unusual bird-watching. Though eagles stay in the Chilkat Valley all year, they concentrate at about Mile 19 on the Haines Highway in the fall. Their white heads a standout against blue sky and foliage, hundreds cover the river flats and perch in the trees during November and December.

The entrance to Haines, on Haines Highway, is marked by impressive Welcome Totem Poles. The Visitors Center at Second and Willard has maps, brochures, and suggestions for sightseeing and entertainment, camping, hiking, fishing, and other recreation. There is also an information desk at the Halsingland Hotel on the quadrangle of Port Chilkoot's Fort William Seward. They'll have information on local tours, times, and prices, and on subjects from bald eagle sightings to Indian dancing, performed frequently in summer.

"Haines Is for Hikers" is the lead for a folder describing the local trail systems. One system south of town on the Chilkat Peninsula takes in areas being developed as a large state park. Trails lead to Battery Point and Mt. Riley. The more strenuous one, the Mt. Ripinski Trail System, was named for a teacher in the Presbyterian boarding school, who settled in Haines in 1896. It's a day-long hike to the trail register on the higher northwest peak, but the view from the 3,610-foot summit is a photographer's delight on clear days: the contrasting communities; Lynn Canal bordered by its snowy mountains; waterfalls and alpine meadows.

In fact there is a great deal you can photograph in the area without such effort. You can drive toward the picturesque cannery at Letnikof Cove and take photos of the Davidson Glacier and the Rainbow, a hanging glacier that glistens in the sunshine and drops chunks of ice during rainy weather. And the walking tour of historic Fort William H. Seward is mostly a level one. A map and folder describing the buildings facing the parade ground gently guides visitors from one of the first buildings, the Cable Office, which is now an art shop, past officers' quarters, the former hospital, post exchange, barracks, and many more.

Totem Village, on the parade ground, includes a replica of a pioneer trapper's cabin and cache, a reproduction of a tribal house, an Indian drying and tanning rack for pelts, and a small collection of large totems. A totem pole 132½ feet tall, heralded as the world's largest, was carved here and dedicated to "all the Indians of southeastern Alaska." Exhibited in Japan's Expo '70 at the Alaska Pavilion, this mighty totem is now in the village of Kake, Alaska. Though not part of the original post, Totem Village belongs here as part of the heritage of the Chilkat Indians, represented in this living museum, which is still under renovation and reconstruction. You can enjoy a salmon bake here—the Port Chilkoot Potlatch. The fresh Lynn Canal salmon are baked nightly over an open fire.

There's a new museum built on the site of the surveys for the original mission, now the town of Haines. Sheldon Museum and Cultural Center is on hallowed ground donated by the United Presbyterian Church, at the end of Main Street, downtown near the waterfront. Don't miss seeing the priceless collections of community treasures, including those of the museum's founder, pioneer citizen Steve Sheldon (1885–1960).

The Chilkat Indians

The Chilkat Indians, a branch of the Tlingits, were notoriously warlike a hundred years ago. Their strategic position helped them to guard mountain passes and waterways against most invaders who might have challenged them for the game-abundant forests and fish-filled fjords, lakes, and streams. They managed to keep most visitors at a distance, the better to enjoy their way of living, in which work alternated with periods of leisure when they had time for artistic pursuits, especially woodcarving, weaving, and dancing.

Since then, with the inevitable encroachment of people, ships, planes, and roads, much has changed—for better or worse, depending on your viewpoint.

Today some Chilkats still beat drums, flash spears, war dance, and perpetuate some of the old ways. They do it to help preserve some of the best of their culture, and for visitors. For a number of years now, friendly Chilkats in Haines have been reviving their arts and crafts under the direction of Carl Heinmiller, a white man from Ohio and an expert woodcarver. He started projects like totem pole carving, mask-and costume-making, and lively Indian dancing as antidotes for the lack of activities for young people—both Indian and white—in Port

Chilkoot, then newly incorporated and isolated. An Eagle Scout himself, one of his first efforts was to organize a Boy Scout troop.

He figured Indian dancing was a logical study project for the area, as a starter. But Carl came up against a blank wall and a generation gap when he went for advice to the elders of the close-by old Indian village of Klukwan. They had to be convinced that the young people and Carl were seriously interested before they would pass on traditional dances and mask designs which had been inherited and were private clan property.

Through museum research Carl carved masks the Indians couldn't distinguish from their own, and he helped the young people study and prepare intricate dance costumes, until finally the key leaders were convinced. Once the youngsters started learning the chants and dances, there was no doubt of their enthusiasm. Girls were asked to join the activities, and the project grew into Alaska Youth, Inc., which has received some financial help from the government.

Carl was rewarded by the Indians. The Eagle (Scout) became a Raven in the clan, with a high and worthy Indian name. Since then the dancers have won honors in intertribal competitions, and have been ambassadors to cities in other parts of the world. In some places they left a souvenir at city hall—a carved totem pole.

The Chilkat Dancers are not the only result of Carl's help and concern for Native Alaskans. Alaska Youth evolved into Alaska Indian Arts, Inc. (A.I.A.), now directed by Carl's son Lee, while Carl assists and also serves as town magistrate. A.I.A., besides rekindling the natives' interest in their heritage, also provides employment for fishermen in the off-season, and for the handicapped. Handicapped himself since World War II, Carl understands the problems.

Though funding has been sporadic and the number of workers fluctuates accordingly, visitors always find the school intriguing. Inside the former fort hospital, now the Alaska Indian Arts Skill Center, people will be carving Alaska soapstone, jade, ivory, and wood, or perhaps etching silver, buffing copper, carving and painting wooden plaques, or making costumes. Outside, Tlingits may be carving a totem pole or other large item.

The fort gymnasium has been nicely remodeled as a little theater and is much used for community programs and plays. The Chilkat Dancers perform there when audiences are too big for the authentically reconstructed tribal house on the parade ground.

The Canadian Connection via the Haines Highway

Haines is Mile 0 on the Haines Highway, a 159-mile road connecting the Marine Highway with the Alaska Highway at Haines Junction,

Yukon Territory. Some people who take their cars on the ferry choose to disembark here and take this route to reach Anchorage or Fairbanks. Part of the Haines Highway follows the Dalton Trail.

The Haines Highway, skirting the eastern foothills of the St. Elias Mountains, leads over 3,493-foot Chilkat Pass, past snow-bordered lakes reflecting rugged mountains. This is the domain of snowpeaks, glaciers, glacial streams, and clear-water recreation lakes. Many travelers feel that the scenery along the Chilkat River estuary, which the highway parallels for 16 miles, is comparable to the Himalayas.

If you start early enough in the morning from either end of this highway there is time to sightsee and still reach the other end—seaward it's Haines; mountainward, the Alaska Highway—without being hampered by the lack of paving or the fact that the border closes up tight at night. If you have the time, it's well worth planning to stop over at one of the not-too-numerous resorts.

At Mile 21 a side road makes a 2-mile loop to the Chilkat village of Klukwan, one of the oldest Indian settlements of the region and for centuries before the white man a center of Tlingit culture. The American bald eagle, no stranger in southeast Alaska, arrives in the Klukwan area by the thousands in the autumn to feed on the late summer salmon run.

At Mile 27, Mosquito Lake state campground is located 2½ miles off the right side of the highway. The 33 Mile Roadhouse advertises the last gas for 85 miles; better tank up. At Mile 35, the abandoned Porcupine Mine and the ghost town of Porcupine can be seen across the Klehini River from the road. The asphalt road of Alaska gives way to the gravel of British Columbia at Mile 41. Depending on your direction of travel, you must stop at either U.S. or Canada Customs, almost next door to each other. No facilities or accommodations here, and they close up at night. Twenty-three miles onward, the road, after winding headily up a mountain, crosses 3,493-foot Chilkat Pass. At Mile 87 the road crosses into Yukon Territory. At Mile 95, just before the bridge, a trail leads leftward to Million Dollar Camp and waterfall, a fine picnic area. At Mile 106, a tight, twisty, rough road leads 2½ miles to the abandoned Dalton Post, established in 1892. At Mile 110, follow a sign that will send you off the road half a mile to Klukshu Indian village, a small settlement on the river of the same name. The village is on the old Dalton Trail. Good photographic possibilities in the village include: fish traps on the river banks, meat caches, log cabins, terrain of the Dalton Trail. At Mile 117, Lake Dezedeash Resort and Lodge, at the southern end of Dezedeash Lake, has rooms, horseback riding, fishing, restaurant, cocktail lounge, store, gas, garage, and complete hookups for trailers and campers open year-round, a gateway to Kluane National Park. (Write Haines Junction, Y.T., Canada YOB

1L0; [403] 634–2315.) Skiing, dogmushing, and ice fishing in winter. At Mile 133 a side road on the left leads to Kathleen Lake Territorial Campground, with 42 campsites, kitchen, and boat launch. This lake has many grayling and rainbow trout and the rare kokanee, a land-locked salmon. Be sure to have the right license—or all three—for fishing in British Columbia, the Yukon Territory, and Alaska. Half a mile up the highway is Lake Kathleen Lodge, with rooms, restaurant, laundromat, and complete garage service (Mile 138, Haines Highway; [403] 634–2319). Haines Junction, less than 17 miles on, has tourist accommodations—rooms, store, garage. The Junction lies 98 miles west of Whitehorse on the Alaska Highway route from Dawson Creek.

Skagway

Skagway, 17 miles north of Haines, is the northernmost port on the Inside Passage. It was the end of the sea leg of a gold rusher's journey, and the jumping-off place for the arduous overland trek to reach Canada's rich Klondike gold fields. Technically, it's the same for visitors today, but they accomplish the feat in a fraction of the time, and with none of the discomforts.

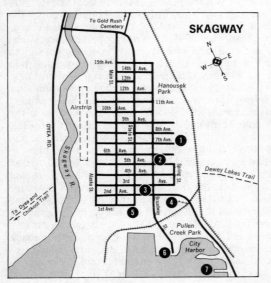

SKAGWAY

Points of Interest

1) Trail of '98 Museum
2) Eagles Hall
3) Soapy's Parlor
4) RR Depot (Nat'l. Park Service Visitors Center)
5) Milepost 0 Klondike Highway 2
6) Ferry Dock
7) Cruise Ship Dock

Most of the cruise ships and ferries turn around here. (An exception is Westours world-class ships, which turn around at Juneau, where the *Fairweather* day boat shuttles between the capital and Skagway. Both the *Cunard Princess* and the *Rhapsody* continue north to explore College Fjord and Prince William Sound of the Gulf of Alaska and turn around at rail port Whittier near Anchorage.)

In Skagway, ships dock only a short walk from downtown—near the site of the famous gold rush gun duel between infamous outlaw "Soapy" Smith and good guy Frank Reid. Cruise ship passengers are primed for excursions to the summit of White Pass, or they may be on a tour continuing to the Interior and North.

The Klondike Gold Rush National Historical Park Visitor Center in the refurbished vintage railroad depot has historical exhibits and dispenses Chilkoot Trail hiking information. The Skagway Convention & Visitors Bureau booth in the same building directs travelers to campgrounds at Prospector Park and Liarsville and to sightseeing—even by horse and buggy. Among the sights are the Gold Rush Cemetery (about a mile and a half from downtown, where you can see graves of local gold rush legends), Reid Falls (a short hike from the cemetery), flower gardens, Skyline Trail to the top of AB Mountain, and to Upper and Lower Dewey Lakes for fishing. Hotels housing tour groups dispense tour and entertainment information and tickets at desks in their lobbies.

Skagway is an important link of the developing Klondike Gold Rush National Historical Park. It follows the historic path of the turn-of-the-century gold seekers, beginning in Seattle's Pioneer Square, the departure point. In Skagway, a sizeable downtown section of business buildings and homes—all listed in the National Register of Historic Places—is being restored. Two other segments of the Historical Park commemorate the Chilkoot Trail and the White Pass Trail. The project is international, as Canada develops portions from the summits of Chilkoot Pass and White Pass (International Boundary) all the way to Skagway's Canadian counterpart, Dawson City, of Klondike fame.

Skagway had only a single cabin, still standing, when the Yukon Gold Rush began. At first the argonauts swarmed to Dyea, nine miles west, but when it was found that a dock could be built at Skagway, this town became the great gateway to the Klondike. Skagway mushroomed overnight into as rich and wild a mixture of people as Alaska ever knew. Three months after the first boat landed, in July 1897, Skagway numbered perhaps 20,000 persons, with well-laid-out streets, hotels, stores, saloons, gambling houses, and dance halls. By the spring of 1898, according to a Northwest Mounted Police report, "Skagway was little better than a hell on earth."

The exciting environs of Skagway, topped by 7,000-foot-high mountains, is matched by the flavor of the boardwalks, false-front buildings, and old stores along the dirt streets that extend from the dock. In all Alaska, there is no town to match the pioneer flavor of Skagway. "Progress," in terms of modernization, is resisted in favor of tourist appeal. However, the accommodations are not only interesting and comfortable but also most attractive, such as the lately built, modern Westours Klondike, and Alaska's oldest, the modernized Golden North Hotel. The friendly residents will keep you busy for as long as you stay with their list of things to see and do.

In this town of about 800 people, time is kept standing still. To hear the locals talk, it was only yesterday that Soapy Smith, Alaska's most notorious outlaw, and Frank Reid, representing the forces of law and order, met in mortal confrontation.

Volumes have been written about the heyday of this lively ghost town. You'll likely see them well displayed in souvenir shops, among them Mike Miller's *Soapy,* Howard Clifford's *Skagway Story,* and Archie Satterfield's *Chilkoot Pass.*

The gist of the Smith-Reid encounter was that bad guy Smith and vigilante good guy Reid met down at the dock and shot it out on a pleasant July evening in 1898. Smith died instantly; Reid passed away 12 days later. Both men are buried in the Gold Rush Cemetery.

The town built a huge monument at Reid's grave, and with a simple inscription summed up what he meant to the honest citizens: "He gave his life for the honor of Skagway." The original gravestone of Soapy Smith was whittled away by souvenir hunters, and now only a simple plank marks his burial place.

However, his "hangout" still exists. Soapy Smith's Parlor and Museum, on First Avenue, near the site of the gun battle, is privately owned. Sometimes it's open so visitors can see inside the quaint little building. The Trail of '98 Museum, Seventh Avenue and Spring Street, is open every day in summer so that visitors have every opportunity to see a fascinating collection owned and operated by the citizens of Skagway. The museum is on the second floor of the first granite building in Alaska. It was scheduled to be a college in 1900, but became a federal courthouse instead. The city of Skagway bought it in 1956. City offices are on the first floor. Above you can browse as long as you wish over old court records preserved under glass, including Frank Reid's will and the papers disposing of Soapy's estate. Besides Native artifacts, memorabilia of pioneers, stampeders, and the Arctic Brotherhood, there are unusual miscellaneous items. How about a blanket made from the skin of duck necks and fortified by pepper bags sewn behind the skins for moth protection? The gambling paraphernalia from the old

Board of Trade Saloon is on display, and on the grounds is a vintage White Pass & Yukon Route steam locomotive.

Local residents are full of enthusiasm. In summer they stage "The Soapy Smith Show" and "Skaguay in the Days of '98," with cancan girls, and preceded by play money gambling, in the Eagles Hall, 6th and Broadway.

You can drive—or take a taxi—to Dyea, where a tent city of 10,000 sprang up overnight. Here the Klondike-bound began the long, agonizing trek to a lake, where they built boats to continue onward. The fearsome Chilkoot Trail, starting from near sea level, climbed a perilous slope to 3,739-foot Chilkoot Pass. They say that if a climber had to step out of line, he could freeze to death before someone would stop long enough to let him get back in. The last half mile was so steep that some enterprising souls built a "stairway" to the top, cutting 1,500 steps—and charged those who used the stairway a heavy toll. In 1898 an avalanche at Sheep Creek swept more than 60 men to their death. Many lie in Slide Cemetery, near the Dyea townsite.

For more than 60 years the Chilkoot Trail lay silent and in time became overgrown. Then the state began to clear and restore the trail, starting from the beach at Dyea to the Canadian border. The hike today is still not an easy one, but from the heights there are impressive panoramas. Many mementos of the early Chilkoot Trail are around, so the hike is a walk through history. Each year hikers make the trip to Lake Lindeman or Lake Bennett. The National Park Service requests that they "leave nothing but footprints and take nothing but photographs." Bear sightings and current trail condition information is available from U.S. rangers at Skagway, Dyea, and Sheep Camp, and from Parks Canada wardens at Lake Lindeman. The Klondike Gold Rush Park Visitor Center has maps and brochures. Or write to the Superintendent, Klondike Gold Rush National Historical Park, Box 517, Skagway, AK 99840.

PRACTICAL INFORMATION FOR SOUTHEAST
ALASKA

HOW TO GET THERE. By air: From Seattle, *Alaska Airlines* serves Southeastern points: "First City" Ketchikan, Wrangell, Petersburg, Juneau, Sitka, and Yakutat. *Western* flies to Ketchikan and Juneau via Seattle, Portland, or Salt Lake City. There are no major jet carriers that fly directly to Haines or Skagway, but *L.A.B. Flying Service* and *Wings of Alaska* fly to both from

Juneau. Because of deregulation, route shifting, and rumors of airline mergers, air travelers should see their travel agents or contact airlines directly for current information on schedules and fares—and Southeast gateways.

By water. *Ferry:* The ferries of the Southeast System of the *Alaska Marine Highway* broke the isolation of the Inside Passage towns in 1963. They connect Seattle and/or Prince Rupert with southeast Alaska ports. The main ports are Haines, Juneau, Ketchikan, Petersburg, Skagway, Sitka and Wrangell.

Largest of the ferry fleet is the *MV Columbia,* which carries 1,000 passengers, 184 vehicles, and has 96 staterooms. The *Malaspina, Matanuska,* and *Taku,* also named for big Alaskan glaciers, are not much smaller. More like liners than ferryboats, most have cocktail lounges, cafeterias, and solariums. Reserve staterooms. Otherwise it is acceptable to sleep in a reclining deck chair between ferry ports, or roll out on deck in a sleeping bag. Public washrooms with showers are available.

Whether you travel on foot, or by car or camper, motor bike or bicycle, the Inside Passage is a popular and scenic alternate route to driving the whole distance on the Alaska Highway. Passenger and vehicle fares are rated on a through basis, with no charge for stopovers. Foot passengers simply get a stopover from the purser. Vehicle space has to be reserved ahead, when you buy your ticket. Cabin fare is port-to-port for one continuous trip. Meals are not included. The fare structure is complex, depending on numerous variables including the size of the vehicle you're traveling with. The schedule is also involved, and departures sometimes depend on the right time and tide. Distances are figured in hours of running time, rather than miles. Seattle to Skagway is about a thousand miles, or about 60 hours, if all goes well. It's about 6 hours Ketchikan to Wrangell, the next port, and 3 to Petersburg, beyond. It takes only an hour from Haines to Skagway. Three smaller ferries connect with smaller ports with intriguing names: Metlakatla, Hollis, Hoonah, Angoon, and Pelican. The *LeConte, Chilkat,* and *Aurora* ferries have no staterooms, but do have cafeterias and snack and liquor bars. Write to *Alaska Marine Highway,* Division of Marine Transportation, Pouch R, Juneau, AK 99881; phone (907) 465–3941 or 465–3940. In Seattle: Pier 48, Seattle, WA 98104; (206) 623–1970. Toll free in South 48 (800) 544–2251; in Alaska, (800) 551–7185. **Be sure to reserve well in advance.**

Contact the *B.C. Ferry Corp.,* 818 Broughton St., Victoria, B.C., Canada V8W 1E4; phone (604) 386–3431. In Vancouver, B.C., phone (604) 669–1211; in Seattle, WA (206) 682–6865. Canadian ferries operate between Vancouver Island, and Prince Rupert, B.C., Canada and connect with the Alaska ferry system.

Cruise ship: The strong competition along the Alaska cruise route continues. Watch for promotional schemes, including fly-frees, or with discounts, from home to embarkation point, intended to woo cruisers. Contact your travel agent or send for information and brochures from the following companies and compare before choosing among many fine ships being dispatched to Alaska this summer.

These are some main contenders along the Inside Passage and some sample prices, based on 1985 rates per person, double occupancy. *Costa Cruises,* One Biscayne Tower, Miami, FL 33131; phone (800) 462–6782. 7-day round trip from Vancouver on the *Daphne,* from $1,190. *Cunard/Norwegian American Cruises,* 555 Fifth Ave., New York, NY 10017; (800) 223–0764. 7-day cruises from Vancouver to Whittier (near Anchorage) on the *Cunard Princess,* and the reverse, from $1,225. 11-day cruises on the *Sagafjord* from $2,160. *Exploration Cruise Lines,* 1500 Metropolitan Park Bldg., Seattle, WA 98101; (206) 624–8551; toll free (800) 426–0600. 8-day/7-night round-trip cruises from Ketchikan along the length of Alaska's Inside Passage on the *Majestic Alaska Explorer* and the *Great Rivers Explorer* are priced from $1,499. They also offer 3-night segments from $675, and 4-night segments from $899. *Holland America Westours Cruises,* 300 Elliott Ave. W., Seattle, WA 98119, (206) 281–3535, from $1,895 for 10-day cruises out of Vancouver on the *Nieuw Amsterdam, Noordam* and the *SS Rotterdam.*

Pacquet French Cruises, 1007 North American Way, Miami, FL 33132; (800) 327–5620; seven nights Vancouver to Anchorage, from $1,325. *Princess Cruises,* 2029 Century Park East, Los Angeles, CA 90067; (213) 553–7000; (800) 421–1600. 10-night, round-trip cruises on the *Royal Princess* out of San Francisco, from $2,410. 7-night cruises out of Vancouver on the *Sun Princess,* from $1,337; on the *Island Princess,* from $1,505. (See also *Princess Tours* in "Tours," *Facts at Your Fingertips.*) *Royal Viking Line,* 1 Embarcadero Center, San Francisco, CA 94111; (800) 634–8000; 11-day, round-trip cruises from San Francisco on the *Royal Viking Star,* from $2,107. *Sitmar Cruises,* 10100 Santa Monica Blvd., Los Angeles, CA 90067; (213) 553–1666; (800) 421–0880. 12 days on the *Fairsky,* from $2,175. *Sundance Cruises,* Suite 2200, 520 Pike St., Seattle, WA 98101; (206) 467–8200; (800) 222–5505. *Stardancer* takes vehicles and passengers to Vancouver, Skagway, and Haines, allowing luxury cruising combined with on-your-own touring. 7-day, round-trip passenger fare from $775; vehicles from $450. *World Explorer Cruises,* 550 Kearny St., San Francisco, CA 94108; (800) 222–2255 in California, (800) 854–3835 rest of U.S. Optional shore excursions along with 14-day program cruises on the *SS Universe* from Vancouver, from $1,595.

The *Cruise Lines International Association* (CLIA) keeps track of some 87 ships which practically cover the world. The rundown, including ships cruising seasonally to Alaska, is given in their *CLIA News about Cruises,* sent out from 17 Battery Pl., Suite 631, New York, NY 10004; (212) 425–7400.

By car. You can drive to the Southeast, but the only access highways taking off from the Alaska Highway are the 110-mile Klondike Hwy. 2 and the 159-mile Haines Hwy. leading to the two northernmost ports in the Panhandle: Skagway and Haines.

By bus. Bus service between Whitehorse (Canada), Skagway, Haines via *Alaska Yukon Motorcoaches,* 349 Wrangell Ave., Anchorage, AK 99501; (907) 276–1305 or 555 Fourth and Battery Bldg., Seattle, WA 98121; (206) 682–4104. Also contact *White Pass & Yukon Motorcoaches,* P.O. Box 100479, Anchorage 99510; (907) 277–5581; toll-free (800) 544–2206.

CLIMATE AND WHAT TO WEAR. The climate is comparable to the rest of the Pacific Northwest, but wetter. Don't complain about the rain to a native; they brag about it. It's been measured on a guage that says at the top, "Busted in 1949—202.55 inches!" in Ketchikan. They even drink to it there in a waterfront bar, *The Rainbird*. Summer highs are in the mid-60s; winter lows, low 20s. Full raingear that is light and easy to pack is a must. Include something to keep your feet dry on city streets or while exploring and hiking farther afield. Lightweight sneakers, pants suits, and slacks are comfortable for spring and summer. In autumn, the days may still be mild, but warmer slack outfits and perhaps a convertible-type topcoat will feel good for cooler evenings. In winter, add some wool, an overcoat or parka, heavier shoes or boots, head and hand covering, and you'll be up to anything going on out-of-doors.

Although clothing is casual aboard the cruise ships, as a rule there are also opportunities to dress up. Women may want to take an evening dress and men a jacket and tie. Just ask ahead about how formal or informal it may be aboard the particular ship you choose. Then you'll also be prepared for any special nights out in town.

GETTING INTO TOWN. Ketchikan: Flights land at Ketchikan International Airport on Gravina Island across Tongass Narrows from Revillagigedo Island. Ferries make the 10-minute trip every half-hour from the airport to the Airport Ferry Terminal (near the State Ferry Terminal) on Revillagigedo for $1.75.

Wrangell: Ferries and cruise ships dock close to downtown. If you arrive at the airport, taxis are available, but may be expensive—even if shared. Inquire from your hotel about courtesy service from the airport.

Petersburg: The airport is a mile from town; ferries dock nearly a mile south of Petersburg. Taxis meet both planes and ferries.

Juneau: Docks are downtown. Air passengers can take a bus to town from the airport—about 9 miles for around $5. A Haida Cab will cost about the same per person, if you can find others to share it. Cars are for rent at the airport and in town. Reserve ahead for one if the state legislature is in town; sometimes they run into the tourist season in June and space may be tight.

Sitka: Ferries dock about 7 miles from town. Buses run to downtown hotels from the dock and airport. There are also taxis and cars for rent.

Haines: The airport and the ferry terminal are about 3.5 miles from town, served by local bus and courtesy car from some motels.

Skagway: There is taxi service year-round, and by Skagway Hack (horse & buggy) in summer. Avis car rentals at Klondike Hotel.

Wooden Creek Street is a reminder of Ketchikan's more notorious past. Dolly's House for instance, once a "house of ill repute," is now a museum. *(Photos: Bob Spring for Exploration Holidays and Cruises.)*

The beauty of Sitka's setting was one of the reasons the site was coveted by both the Tlingit Indians and the Russians.

The capital of Alaska, Juneau, is accessible only by sea or air. Just beyond the mountains that tower over the city is the 4,000-square-mile icefield, the Mendenhall Glacier. *(Photos: Bob Spring for Exploration Holidays and Cruises.)*

Glacier Bay National Park attracts nature lovers, wildlife watchers, and fishermen. Retreating glaciers have left miles of waterways for birds, seals, whales, porpoises, and visitors.

The Anchorage-Seward Highway and the Alaska Railroad parallel Turnagain Arm from Anchorage to Portage.

The sun may still be high at midnight in Kotzebue, thirty miles above the Arctic Circle.

The Richardson Highway near Thompson Pass. *(Photo: Bob Spring for Exploration Holidays and Cruises.)*

HOTELS AND MOTELS. Lodging prices tend to be lower in the Southeast than in the big cosmopolitan areas. Mostly they fall into the *Moderate* to *Expensive* range (plus tax). *Deluxe* here will mean "Alaska Deluxe"—the best available, probably the most expensive, and considered tops by the local residents. Based on double occupancy, a *deluxe* room will probably cost over $100 per night. *Expensive* will probably be $80–100; *moderate,* $60–80; and *inexpensive,* under $60. (Be aware that the number of available rooms in hotels in small towns is not overwhelming. Reserve ahead, unless you are prepared to camp out.)

KETCHIKAN
(Zip Code 99901)

Hilltop Motel. *Moderate.* 3434 N. Tongass Hwy.; (907) 225–5166. 46 units across from air and ferry terminals. Two levels, large rooms. Family-type. Restaurant and cocktail lounge.

Ingersoll Hotel. *Moderate.* 303 Mission St.; (907) 225–2124. Historic downtown 54-room, three-story hotel, with front rooms overlooking the waterfront. Restaurant; lounge; and deli-sandwich shop.

Super 8 Motel. *Moderate.* 2151 Sea Level Dr. (near Airport Ferry terminal); toll-free (800) 843–1991; (907) 225–9088 in Ketchikan. "First City" was the first Alaskan city to have a member of this chain. 83 rooms, among them 6 suites with view of Tongass Narrows. Many "extras" included; some rooms with water beds; some special rooms for handicapped persons; and a freezer to hold the catch of visiting fishermen.

Gilmore Hotel. *Inexpensive.* 326 Front St.; (907) 225–9423. 42 rooms at downtown waterfront near restaurants and shopping; airporter bus service. Newly renovated with color TV; phones; cocktail lounge.

WRANGELL
(Zip Code 99929)

Harding's Old Sourdough Lodge. *Moderate.* Box 1062, (907) 874–3455 or 3613. Majors in fishing and hunting and memorable Alaska-style menus.

Roadhouse Lodge. *Moderate.* Box 1199; (907) 874–2335. Four miles out the Zimovia Highway, but they'll send courtesy car. Lounge and restaurant; dancing. They also have bikes and cars for rent and offer hiking, charter fishing, tours, and outdoor fish bakes.

Stikine Inn. *Moderate.* Box 990; (907) 874–3388 or 874–3389. 34 rooms, with television; coffee shop; dining room; bar. Free phone. Liquor store. A block from ferry; overlooks city dock.

Thunderbird Hotel. *Moderate to Inexpensive.* 223 Front St., Box 110; (907) 874–3322. 36 rooms, all with bath, TV, phone. Free coffee in lobby; laundromat adjoining. Downtown.

PETERSBURG
(Zip Code 99833)

Tides Inn. *Expensive.* 1 mi. W. of ferry terminal, N. 1st & D Sts.; (907) 772–4288. Modest-size motel, with 23 units. Free continental breakfast. Hunting and fishing information, charters.

Beachcomber Inn. *Moderate.* 4 miles south of town, Box 416, (907) 772–3888. Homey, once a cannery. Boats and float planes tie up at dock. Rooms with baths; restaurant and bar. A picturesque setting and a local favorite.

King Salmon Motel. *Moderate.* Box 869; (907) 772–3291. Handy to ferry dock. Restaurant and bar.

Mitkof Hotel. *Inexpensive.* Box 689; (907) 772–4281. Over 70 years established downtown. Color TV and phones. Has clean, comfortable rooms with and without bath.

JUNEAU
(Zip Code 99801)

Sheffield House Juneau. *Deluxe.* 51 W. Egan Dr; 586–6900; toll-free (800) 544–0970; in Alaska call collect (907) 274–6631. 104 rooms with first-run color movies. Banquet and meeting facilities. Downtown. Restaurant; lounge.

Baranof Hotel. *Expensive.* 127 Franklin St.; 586–2660; toll-free (800) 544–0970; in Alaska call collect (907) 274–6631. 225 rooms, in the center of town. Telephone; TV; restaurant; bar; banquet and meeting rooms; 7-day-a-week coffee shop.

Prospector Hotel. *Expensive.* 375 Whittier Ave., in Sub-port area; (907) 586–3737. Modest-size hotel with full facilities. Restaurant, bar. Sightseeing tours available.

Bergmann Hotel. *Moderate* (for rooms with baths) to *Inexpensive* (without baths). 434 Third St.; (907) 586–1690. A vintage hotel reflecting "old Juneau."

Breakwater Inn. *Moderate.* 1711 Glacier Ave.; (907) 586–6303. Motel overlooking boat basin. Dining room; bar; laundromat.

Driftwood Lodge. *Moderate.* 435 Willoughby Ave.; (907) 586–2280. Motel with 47 units, some with kitchens. Several two-bedroom apartments. Laundromat; restaurant.

Super-8. *Moderate.* 2295 Trout St.; (907) 789–4858. 75 rooms near airport; courtesy car.

The Tides Motel. *Moderate.* 5000 Glacier Hwy.; (907) 780–4622. 22 rooms, 30 camper spaces; all facilities; nearby shopping.

Alaskan Hotel. *Inexpensive.* 167 S. Franklin St.; (907) 586–1000. In downtown historic area. Rustic bar; health spa.

SITKA
(Zip Code 99835)

Shee Atika Lodge. *Moderate.* Box 78; toll-free (800) 426–0670 (inc. AK and HI); in Washington State call (800) 552–7122; (907) 747–6241. Now a Vance

Corporation hotel. 97 rooms. Native Corporation-built hotel across from convention center. Features large public areas and Alaska Indian Art Shop.

Sheffield House. *Moderate.* Box 318; toll-free (800) 544–0970; in Alaska call collect (907) 274–6631. On the waterfront overlooking marina. 80 rooms, banquet facilities, dining room, lounge, disco, and boat dock.

Potlatch House. *Inexpensive.* 709 Katlian St., Box 58; (907) 747–8611 or 8606. Several blocks from downtown, but there is a courtesy car. Mt. Edgecumbe and harbor view. Restaurant and cocktail lounge.

Sitka Hotel. *Inexpensive.* 118 Lincoln St., Box 679; (907) 747–3288. Downtown hotel with elevator and 24-hour phone service. 60 rooms, some with choice harbor and island views. Easy walking to historic sites from Tlingit Indian/Russian American/Alaska Territorial past.

HAINES-PORT CHILKOOT
(Zip Code 99827)

Captain's Choice. *Deluxe* motel units overlooking Lynn Canal, at 2nd and Dalton. Box 392; (907) 766–2461. Captain's Suite has wet bar.

Fort Seward Condos. *Expensive to Moderate.* Overlooking Lynn Canal. Box 75; (907) 766–2425 or 766–2801. If you want to stay awhile, inquire about these completely furnished apartments available by week or month (3-day minimum).

Eagle's Nest Motel. *Moderate.* On Highway 7 near town center and airport; Box 267; (907) 766–2352. Open year-round; camper park, full hookup; also National Car Rentals available.

Mountain View Motel. *Moderate.* Box 62; (907) 766–2900. Adjacent to Fort Seward, within walking distance of downtown Haines. Kitchenettes, TV, laundromat, restaurants, art shops nearby. Handy to the action at beaches, harbor, parks, and performing arts center.

Thunderbird Motel. *Moderate.* 2nd & Dalton Sts., Box 159; (907) 766–2131. Modern motel units in this small downtown facility, all with private baths. TV. Also rent-a-cars.

Halsingland Hotel. *Inexpensive.* Located in Port Chilkoot, Box 158; (907) 766–2000. Affording a view of Lynn Canal and surrounding glacial-sided mountains, this moderate-size, family-style hotel is in vintage army quarters of old Fort William Seward, facing parade ground. Cocktail lounge; family style dining room featuring Swedish cuisine and fresh local seafood. Alaska-Yukon Motorcoach depot. Nearby wooded Port Chilkoot Camper Park (766–2755) with electric hookups, water, dump station, showers, laundromat.

SKAGWAY
(Zip Code 99840)

Golden North Hotel. *Expensive.* 3rd and Broadway, Box 431; (907) 983–2294. A gold rush remainder. All 35 rooms different; furnished with charming antique touches. You can't miss it; its golden dome is a landmark. Restaurant.

The Klondike. *Expensive.* Box 515; toll-free (800) 544–0970; in Alaska call collect (907) 274–6631. Next to the Historic District. 171 rooms, lounge, restaurant, banquet facilities, outdoor barbecue. Houses tour groups. Original section recreates theme of gold rush through colorful decorations.

Skagway Inn. *Moderate.* Box 129; (907) 983–2289. Aura of gold rush preserved in this vintage building, once a saloon, on unpaved boardwalk-lined main street. Rooms (with and without private bath) have women's names instead of numbers.

Wind Valley Lodge. *Moderate.* Box 3543; (907) 983–2236. 22nd & State St. on the Klondike Highway. 12 well-appointed rooms near historic district and restaurants.

Fifth Avenue Bunkhouse. *Inexpensive.* At 5th and Broadway; Box 48. For the thrifty. Bring your own sleeping bag and they'll furnish the bunk. $10 a night; showers $1; laundromat nearby. Towels and blankets for rent if needed. No reservations.

 BED-AND-BREAKFASTS. In Ketchikan: *Ketchikan Bed-and-Breakfast,* Box 7735, 99901; (907) 225–3860 or 9277. **In Wrangell:** *Clarke's,* 732 Case Ave. 99929; (907) 874–3863. **In Sitka:** *Les's,* 210 Crabapple Dr. 99835; (907) 747–3633. **In Haines:** *Ft. Seward,* in Chief Surgeons Quarters, House #1, Box 5, 99827; (907) 766–2856.

In Juneau: Contact: *Alaska Bed-and-Breakfast Association,* 526 Seward St., 99801; (907) 586–2959. Also: *Alaska Guest Homes,* 1941 Glacier Hwy.; (907) 586–1840.

 YOUTH HOSTELS. No reservations at these; don't count on kitchen facilities. **In Ketchikan:** Sponsored by the First United Methodist Church, Grant and Main Sts.: Box 8515, 99901; (907) 225–3780. Operates Memorial Day to Labor Day.

In Sitka: *Sitka Youth Hostel.* Box 2645, 99835; (907) 747–6332. Summer only.

In Juneau: *Juneau Youth Hostel.* Northern Light Church, 11th & A St., Box 1543, 99802; (907) 586–9559 or 586–6457 or 789–9229. Summer only.

In Haines: *Bear Creek Camp and Youth Hostel.* Small Tract Rd., Box 334, 99827; (907) 766–2259. Inexpensive, primitive, rustic cabins—"a step above a tent." Cook on a wood stove, haul water, bring own bedding. No electricity. Parking for self-contained campers; tenters welcome. Operates year-round.

 CAMPING AND CABINS. There are plenty of places to camp throughout the Panhandle—public and private. See "Camping" in *Facts at Your Fingertips* for the addresses of the federal and state agencies offering camping facilities. These charge a small fee, may limit your stay, and do not take reservations. The local visitor information center will direct you to campgrounds in the area—campgrounds within sight of mountains and glaciers, bordering saltwater beaches and freshwater lakes and streams.

The Forest Service is in charge of cabins in national parklands, including the 155 cabins in southeast Alaska's *Tongass National Forest.* More than 50 are in the Ketchikan area. Some are accessible by hiking; some by boat; most are fly-ins. The Ketchikan Area Supervisor is in the Federal Bldg., Ketchikan, AK 99901; (907) 747–6671. The Chatham Area Supervisor: Box 504, Sitka, AK 99835; (907) 747–6671. The Stikine Area Supervisor: Box 1329, Petersburg, AK 99833; (907) 772–3841. In Juneau, consult the Information Center at Centennial Hall, 101 Egan Drive; phone (907) 586–7151. Reservations are necessary for the cabins; only $10 per night per party.

See also the sections on "State Parks" and "National Forests, Parks and Preserves" later in this *Practical Information.*

 WILDERNESS LODGES. Around Ketchikan: *Clover Pass Resort,* 15 paved miles north of the city, is headquarters for the salmon derby. Hopeful fisherman strike out from here to hook fighting king salmon. Six cabins for rent, and the RV park has complete hookups for up to 30 campers. Amenities include showers, restaurant, and laundromat, tackle and rental shop. Better check space in fishing season—especially during Derby Days. Write Box 7322A, Ketchikan, AK 99901; (907) 247–2234. You can also drive to *George Inlet Lodge,* Mile 12, So. Tongass Hwy., which offers personalized fishing packages. P.O. Box 5077, Ketchikan 99901–0077; phone (907) 225–6077.Go by boat or fly to *Yes Bay Lodge,* 45 miles northwest of Ketchikan. Write The Hack Family, Yes Bay, AK 99950 for rates and reservations for packages that include all: family-style meals, room, equipment, guide, and many activities. They feature hunting, fishing, hiking, beachcombing, birdwatching and photography. Near an Indian village, Klawock, on **Prince of Wales Island** is reached by ferry, small plane, and boat. The Fabry Family Guides take over at their tenter's lodge, *Log Cabin Sports Rental,* Box 54, Klawock, AK 99925, (907) 775–2205, helping guests to learn about Tlingit Indian traditions and steering people toward wholesome outdoor pursuits in this backcountry paradise. Nearby, more elaborate accommodations—restaurants and rooms with baths—offer sport fishing and recreational packages. Contact the *Prince of Wales Lodge,* Box 72, Klawock, AK 99925, (907) 755–2227. Besides fine fishing, this area features crabbing (cook it on the beach), and "Craiging." Craig, about 6 miles away, is where to find the stores—including three liquor stores—bars, and the island's newest *Haida Way Lodge,* P.O. Box 90, Craig, AK 99921; (907) 826–3268. *Waterfall Resort* is recycled from a historic cannery 62 miles west of Ketchikan, about 40 minutes by air. There are amenities in the restored cabins and buildings that workers of the 1910 cannery wouldn't believe. Bar, restaurant, and cabin decor are in vintage style, but with modern comforts. "Where sportfishing is for kings" is the resort motto, and they welcome visiting boats and planes. Reservations and queries go to Waterfall Resort, Box 6440, Ketchikan, AK 99901, (907) 225–9461 or (800) 544–5125. *Thayer Lake Lodge,* Box 5416, Ketchikan, AK

99901, (907) 945–3343 (October–May), is within Admiralty Island National Monument. It's American Plan, and also has 2 cabins for up to 4 people, with cooking facilities for do-it-yourselvers.

Around Juneau: To the north is *Taku Glacier Lodge.* Contact Manager #2 Marine Way, Suite 228, Juneau, AK 99801, (907) 586–1362. It is 30 air miles from Juneau in mountain and glacier wilderness. The vintage log lodge opts mostly for day visitors, who come for the delicious salmon bake, and for the flightseeers en route over the Juneau Ice Field. Reserve ahead for overnight stays, guided trips to glaciers, and for sportfishing.

Around Glacier Bay: *Glacier Bay Lodge,* at Bartlett Cove, is the only over-night hotel within the National Park. For information on the abundant sightsee-ing, flightseeing, naturalist programs, and sportfishing from late May through late September, the year-round contact is the Reservations Manager, Glacier Bay Lodge, 1500 Metropolitan Park Bldg., Seattle, WA 98101; (206) 624–8551. Outside the park, near the jet airport serving Glacier Bay daily in summer, is small, homey *Gustavus Inn,* Box 31, Gustavus, AK 99826, (907) 697–2255 (winter 586–2006), now being operated by children of the original 1928 home-steaders. *Salmon River Rentals,* Box 121, Gustavus, AK 99826, (907) 697–2245, rents economy housekeeping cabins, bicycles, and sleeping bags May through September. Grocery, showers, and washing facilities are nearby. King and silver salmon abound in the surrounding waters of Icy Strait and Glacier Bay. Cut-throat and Dolly Varden trout haunt the Salmon River. From Gustavus, bus transportation is available to Glacier Bay National Park and Preserve, 10 miles.

Lodges with some of the best all-inclusive fishing packages and live-aboard yacht charters, especially out of Ketchikan and Juneau, are rounded up in *Fish Our Alaska!* the brochure of *Alaska Sportfishing Packages,* Suite 1320, 4th & Blanchard Bldg., Seattle, WA 98121; (206) 382–1051; toll-free (800) 426–0603. Also consult the state-compiled Travel Index of the Division of Tourism's official vacation planning guide. (See "Tourist Information Sources," *Facts at Your Fingertips.*) The Information Office of the *Alaska Sportfishing Lodge Asso-ciation* is at 500 Wall Street, Suite 401, Seattle WA 98121; (206) 622–3932. Hunters should write the Executive Director, Alaska Professional Hunters Association, Box 4–1932, Anchorage, AK 99509, phone (907) 276–3236, for sporthunting and big game guide leads.

On islands more remote: At Baranof Island's Warm Springs Bay, Indians were the first to appreciate the warm water, then commercial fishermen, and now guests of the *Baranof Wilderness Lodge,* Box 210022, Auke Bay, AK 99821. Whenever possible, the *Explorer* ship captains delight in dropping by to grant cruisers shore leave for sampling the relaxing, therapeutic experience of a good, hot soak. If you like the idea of staying on your own island in a lighthouse, only a few minutes (by skiff) from Sitka, write Burges Bauder, Box 277, Sitka, AK 99835; (907) 747–3056.

HOW TO GET AROUND. By air: Following are some of the local carriers that operate scheduled air service through southeast and/or charters and flightseeing. From Ketchikan, *Tyee Airlines,* 1515 Tongass, Ave., 225–9810, and *Westflight Aviation,* 1719 Tongass Ave., 225–9693, serve logging camps, fishing areas, and many small communities. From Haines, *L.A.B. Flying Service,* Box 272, 766–2222, flies to Juneau, Skagway, Hoonah, Gustavus, and Excursion Inlet. From Juneau: *Wings of Alaska,* 1873 Shell Simmons Dr. #119, 789–0790, also flies to Western Canada. *Alaska Airlines,* 789–0600, flies to Gustavus, where there are buses to take visitors to Glacier Bay National Park. For many years *Channel Flying,* 2601 Channel Dr., Juneau, AK 99801, has been the charter and scheduled flying link to small Southeastern towns, always with an eye for the scenic routes that delight the passengers. Amphibious aircraft, too. *Around Glacier Bay: Glacier Bay Airways,* Box 1, Gustavus, AK 99826, has an office in the Glacier Bay Lodge lobby, as well as at Gustavus Airport, to expedite glacier flightseeing, camper drop-offs, and group transfers in the area.

By water: The *Alaska Marine Highway* ferries will help you travel up (or down) the Panhandle. Reservations are required for vehicles and cabins. Walk-ons may travel without reservations (except from Seattle); this means you'll be sleeping on lounge chairs or on the deck, itself. Southeast ports include Ketchikan, Wrangell, Petersburg, Sitka, Juneau, Haines, and Skagway. For reservations and information contact: Alaska Marine Highway, Division of Marine Transportation, Pouch R, Juneau, AK 99811; (907) 465–3941 or 465–3940. See also "How to Get There" earlier in *Practical Information for Southeast Alaska.*

By car: Only two Southeastern towns are connected to the *Alaska Highway:* Haines, via the Haines Hwy. and Skagway, via Klondike Hwy. 2. See "Hints to Motorists" in *Facts at Your Fingertips* for information about driving in Alaska.

By rail: The *White Pass & Yukon Route* railroad between Skagway and Whitehorse, Y.T., remains mothballed; but motorcoaches cover these routes and connect with interior Canadian and Alaskan points (see "How to Get There: By Bus," above).

TOURIST INFORMATION. Fish and game information is freely dispensed in sporting goods and fishing gear stores, as well as at the fish and game department offices listed here. **Ketchikan:** *Visiotrs Bureau* office is on the downtown dock; open daily 8:00 A.M.–5:00 P.M. (noon–6:00 P.M. Sundays) in summer; business hours the rest of the year. 131 Front St., Box 7055, Ketchikan, AK 99901; 225–6166. Call 225–5571 for 24-hour visitor information. *Dept. of Fish and Game* is located at 415 Main St., room 208, Ketchikan, AK 99901; 225–2859. Open Mon.–Fri. 8:00 A.M.–4:30 P.M.

Wrangell: *Visitor Information Center* is in an A-frame on the corner of Brueger St. and Outer Dr., Box 49, Wrangell, AK 99929; 874–3901; open when cruise ships and ferries are in port and at other, flexible hours. *Dept. of Fish and*

Game, 215 Front St., Wrangell, AK 99929; 875–3822. Weekdays 8:00 A.M.–4:30 P.M.

Petersburg: *Chamber of Commerce and Information Center:* on Harbor Way in the Harbormaster Bldg., Box 649, Petersburg, AK 99833; 772–3646; open Mon.–Fri. 10:00 A.M.–4:00 P.M. *Dept. of Fish and Game:* Main St., Petersburg, AK 99833; 772–3801; open weekdays 8:00 A.M.–4:30 P.M.

Sitka: *Visitor Bureau,* open summer Mon.–Sat. 9:00 A.M.–9:00 P.M. Sun. noon–4:00 P.M. Weekdays 9:00 A.M.–5:00 P.M. the rest of the year. It's in the Centennial Bldg. on Harbor Dr., Box 1226, Sitka, AK 99835. *Dept. of Fish and Game:* 304 Lake St., Sitka, AK 99835; 747–5355; weekdays 8:00 A.M.–4:30 P.M.

Juneau: *Visitor Information Center* is in the Davis Log Cabin, 134 Third St., Juneau, AK 99802; 586–2201 or 2284. Open year-round 8:30 A.M.–5:00 P.M. Mon.–Fri.; summer 2:00–5:00 P.M. Sat., Sun., holidays. There's also an *Information Center* at Centennial Hall, 101 Egan Dr.; 586–7151. *Department of Fish and Game,* 230 S. Franklin St., Box 3–2000, Juneau, AK 99802; 465–4270 or 4180. 8:00 A.M.–4:30 P.M.

Haines: *Visitor Information* at 2nd and Willard St., Haines, AK 99827. Open daily 8:00 A.M.–5:00 P.M. June through August; 766–2202. *Dept. of Fish and Game,* Haines Hwy., Box 431, Haines, AK 99827, can be reached at 766–2830, 8:00 A.M.–4:30 P.M.

Skagway: *Convention and Visitor Bureau,* booth, Box 415, Skagway, AK 99840; 983–2297, and the National Park Service Visitor Center, are in the former railroad depot, 2nd and Broadway. Hours vary. Also see *Alaska Sightseeing* at the Golden North Hotel 983–2241 or the travel desk at the *Klondike Hotel,* 983–2291; their desks are manned most of the time May–Sept.

TOURS. Names like *Misty Fiords* and *Glacier Bay* suggest a kaleidoscope of mountains, deep inlets, forests, wildlife, and glaciers—nature's spectaculars. The companies listed here have tours that visit America's newest national monument, Misty Fiords, and veteran Glacier Bay, formerly a monument, but now a national park and preserve. There are many more than these examples; the following firms can direct or take you to other worthy tour destinations also, in the Southeast-and farther north. (Note the spelling of "fiords." It was offically decided to spell it that way when the monument was established.)

Alaska Discovery, Box 26, Gustavus AK 99826, (907) 697–2257 majors in seven great wilderness areas including Glacier Bay. Their strong points are kayaking and backpacking adventures. For about $100 a day, or perhaps a little more than that, calculated from where the tour departs, they cover guide service, all charters involved, insurance, three meals a day, tents, cooking and camping gear, and all expedition equipment. They offer discounts if you sign up for connecting trips for their *Alaska Discovery Wilderness Series.*

Alaska Exploration Holidays and Cruises, 1500 Metropolitan Park Bldg., Boren and Olive Sts., Seattle, WA 98101; (206) 624–8551; toll free (800) 426–0600. Their *Majestic Alaska Explorer* and *Great Rivers Explorer* cruise from Ketchikan to Misty Fiords and penetrate deep into the heart of the monument. Dinner the first night is served among the beauty of sheer granite walls laced with waterfalls, before the ship goes north along the Inside Passage on its 8-day/7-night round-trip cruise. The 158-passenger *North Star* sails from Prince Rupert and spends a morning in Misty Fiords northbound during her 8-day round trip. Besides a whole day in Glacier Bay, they also explore winding *Tracy Arm,* a lovely, narrow fjord, long cherished by boaters.

Leisure Tours, 3436 Tongass, Ketchikan, AK 99901, (800) 544–4187, handles combination cruise and air tours, a stay in Ketchikan, and a visit to Misty Fiords. Give them an idea of your special interests and they may be able to come up with a customized package—as they did for the touring Texans (mentioned in the "Touring Alaska" essay in the introductory section of this book).

Outdoor Alaska, Box 7814, Ketchikan AK 99901, 247–8444, offers assorted cruise/fly tours, some overnighting in the monument, with drop-off and pick-up service for canoers and kayakers. Dave Pihlman, a second-generation Alaskan, scheduled the first tours into solitary, little-known Misty Fiords. He also offers a *Historical Waterfront* cruise.

Alaska Travel Adventures, 200 N. Franklin, Juneau, AK 99801 (586–6245), handles some unusual water excursions. Ask about the Ketchikan *Indian-Style Canoe Trip,* the Juneau *Mendenhall Glacier Float Trip* (for all ages), and *Marine Wildlife Exploration* around Sitka's islands, by yacht and motorized raft. With *Chilkoot Trail Float Tours,* 5th and Broadway, Skagway, AK 99840 (983–2370), take in the history and sites of Dyea and a scenic, slow float down the Taiya River. Eagles are the main attraction during float trips through the Chilkat Bald Eagle Preserve, offered by *Alaska Cross Country Guiding & Rafting,* Box 124, Haines, AK 99827 (766–2040).

Whether a novice or an experienced rider, you'll see wildlife and spectacular scenery during guided *Mount Juneau Equestrian Tours;* write 3–6500, No. 180, Juneau, AK 99802, or call 586–4782.

AIR TOURS OF NOTE IN THE SOUTHEAST. Weather permitting, at some time during your stay try to take an air tour of the vicinity. Some are short enough to fit in between ship sailings or during ferry stopovers. Some favorites are flightseeing tours that include a lift off and splash down right in front of busy harbor at **Ketchikan** or **Juneau.** *Tyee Airlines,* 1515 Tongass Ave., Ketchikan, AK 99901, based on Ketchikan's waterfront, offers a 40-minute flight that covers the waterfront, during which the experienced Alaska bush pilot pinpoints totem parks, rain forests, and anything else interesting below before he heads through open spaces between the mountains for a look at the lakes behind Ketchikan called Mirror, Punchbowl, Goat, Swan, and Grace, and cliffs of granite rising two thousand feet above the fjords. If you have up to 3 hours, ask about the *Bonus Bush Flight Tour* (on space-available basis only), a working trip supplying outlying communities. Fellow travelers may be loggers, Natives, and fishermen.

Alaska Island Air out of **Petersburg,** Box 508, Petersburg, AK 99833 operates a 9-passenger amphibious aircraft to many Southeast destinations.

In **Sitka,** *Bellair,* Box 371, Sitka, AK 99835, 747–3220 or 747–8636, and *Mountain Aviation,* Box 875, Sitka, AK 99835, 747–6000, offer area flightseeing tours. They specialize in "personalized" photo and flightseeing. Depending on your time and budget, you may see a bird reserve where hundreds of eagles nest, look into the once-active volcano crater of Mt. Edgecumbe, a Sitka landmark, hover around the heights where mountain goats gather—and it's likely that whales or seals will surface in the water around the many islands.

Juneau sits under the vast expanse of the Juneau Ice Field. Take a helicopter tour that includes landing on or near a glacier. *Temsco Helicopters,* 1873 Shell Simmons Drive, # 111, Juneau AK 99801; 789–9501, offers a 45-minute Mendenhall Glacier Tour ($99 in 1985), and a 1½-hour Glacier Explorer ($179). Price includes round-trip transfer between town and heliport and boots for stepping out to examine this frozen world close up.

You'll appreciate the planes and *Colossal Aeronautical Tours* of *Skagway Air Service,* Box 357, **Skagway, AK** 99840. They stick with the local theme in cleverly and brightly painted Cherokee Sixes, and the slogan "We Can-Can-Can!" Climbing gold rush passes and tracing the Trail of '98 by air is about a 45-minute tour, a real thriller for the money. Stop in at their office at 4th and Broadway and ask about prices of that and other air-taxi and charter flights.

 STATE PARKS. See *Facts at Your Fingertips* for general information about the system. An ideal state park in southeast Alaska is *Chilkat State Park,* south of **Haines** on the Chilkat Peninsula. Here you can see bald eagles, fish for salmon, go beachcombing, and, of course, enjoy the breathtaking scenery. Hike and boat in the summer; cross-country ski in the winter. For further information contact Haines Chamber of Commerce, 2nd & Willard, Haines, AK 99827; (907) 766–2202.

 NATIONAL FORESTS, PARKS AND PRESERVES. *Admiralty Island National Park* includes Admiralty Island, one of the largest islands in southeast Alaska. Parts of the island are less than 12 miles from Juneau, but this is still wilderness: brown bears outnumber people and there is the largest concentration of bald eagles known in North America. The principal settlement is Angoon, accessible from Juneau by scheduled flights and ferries. There are public-use cabins here (about 15). Contact the U.S. Forest Service, Admiralty National Monument, Forest Service Info. Center, 101 Egan Dr., Juneau, AK 99801, (907) 789–3111. *Misty Fiords National Monument* displays some of

Alaska's most spectacular scenery. Sheer granite cliffs rise from the ocean; crystal-clear waters and mirror lakes abound. The U.S. Forest Service maintains cabins here. Access to the monument is only by plane, boat, or occasional ferry. Information can be obtained from the Tongass Visitor Center in the Federal Building, **Ketchikan,** or from Monument Ranger, Misty Fiords National Monument, Tongass National Forest, Federal Bldg., Box 6137, Ketchikan, AK 99901; (907) 225–2148. For specific information on *Glacier Bay National Park and Preserve* contact the Superintendent, Box 1089, Juneau, AK 99802; (907) 586–7137. *Tongass National Forest,* America's largest, includes most of southeast Alaska and is ideal for backpackers. There are U.S. Forest Service campgrounds near **Ketchikan, Juneau, Petersburg,** and **Wrangell,** and about 150 public-use cabins in outlying areas, accessible by boat, trail, or chartered aircraft. Most of the communities in the forest are ports for the Alaska state ferry. Contact Regional Forester, U.S. Forest Service, Box 1628, Juneau, AK 99802; (907) 586–7282.

SKIING. Juneau: *Eaglecrest Ski Area* on Douglas Island offers 1,400-foot vertical drop, lessons, a lodge and a snack bar. Call (907) 586–5330.

THE INDIAN HERITAGE. Ketchikan: About 2 miles south of Ketchikan, behind Saxman Indian Village, on South Tongass Hwy., is *Saxman Totem Park.* There are over 20 poles here, among them a reproduction of the Lincoln totem. Open year-round, no admission charge.

Totem Bight State Historical Site, about Mile 10 on the N. Tongass Hwy., is about 25 minutes north of Ketchikan. There are excellent reproductions of poles here and a tribal house. Open year-round, no admission charge.

Tongass Historical Society, 629 Dock St., exhibits Indian artifacts. Hours vary depending on whether or not cruise ships are in port. Generally open afternoons year-round. Small admission fee. 225–5600.

The *Totem Heritage Cultural Center,* 601 Deermount St., provides the background for the totemic culture, with 33 poles and fragments from old Tlingit and Haida Indian Villages. Native tour guides during summer months and a small admission fee. 8:30 A.M.–5:00 P.M. Phone 225–5900.

Wrangell: Cross the footbridge in the inner harbor at the bottom of Front St. to Chief Shakes Island where totems—some of the finest examples of this art—surround the restored *Bear Tribal House.* Inside, some of the chief's wealth is displayed along with other treasures. Phone 874–3505 for hours and admission fee. Look around town for some exemplary totems tucked away in unusual places. The weathered mortuary pole with a kind-faced man hugging his knees may be back in its usual place—thanks to the restoration program—standing guard over by the oil docks. Walk the beach near the ferry dock at low tide to see Indian rock carvings. Experts say these petroglyphs may have been chipped into the rocks as long as 8,000 years ago. (Totem carvers may be seen at work on Shakes Island or Front St., creating replicas.)

The *Wrangell Museum* is at the corner of Second and Bevier sts., a few blocks from the ferry terminal. Totems and local historic artifacts are inside. Open Monday–Thursday, Sat. 1:00–4:00 P.M.; Fri. 1:00–3:00, May–Sept. In winter: Wed. 1:00–4:00; also open for cruise ships and ferries and by appointment year-round. Small admission fee. 874–3770.

Sitka: The *Sheldon Jackson Museum* on the Sheldon Jackson College Campus houses some of the finest Indian arts and crafts, and Russian relics to be found in Alaska. Open 9:00 A.M.–5:00 P.M. daily in summer; 1:00–4:00 P.M. in winter, closed Sat. and Mon. Small admission fee. 747–5228.

At the Fort Site of *Sitka National Historical Park,* at the end of Metlakatla St., the emphasis is Tlingit Indian. Totem poles outside and inside the visitors center, excellent audio-visual programs, and people—including some natives who may be at work in the craft shops—help to interpret this side of Sitka's rich cultural heritage. The park's visitors center is open Mon.–Sat. 8:00 A.M.–5:00 P.M., mid-Sept.–mid-May; daily 8:00 A.M.–6:00 P.M., mid-May–mid-Sept. Park grounds are open daily, 7:00 A.M.–10:00 P.M., year-round. No admission fee. 747–6281.

Juneau: The *Alaska State Museum,* Whittier St. off Egan Dr., displays a large collection of Indian artifacts, including the Lincoln totem. Also exhibits from Alaska's gold rush period, Russian-American historical displays, natural history exhibits. Open weekdays in summer 9:00 A.M.–9:00 P.M.; weekends 1:00–9:00 P.M.; in winter, weekdays 9:00 A.M.–5:30 P.M., weekends 1:00–5:30 P.M. No admission charge. 465–2901.

If Chief Walter Williams happens to be on guide duty in town, you'll get a rundown on all he knows (considerable!) about his Indian heritage, plus his interpretation of some of his favorite dances.

Haines-Port Chilkoot: Indian lore, arts, crafts, and dance are perpetuated on the historic grounds of turn-of-the-century *Fort William Seward.* Artists and craftspeople work in the Alaska Indian Arts Skill Center in one of the vintage buildings; they're usually there in summer 9:00 A.M.–5:00 P.M. weekdays and when cruise ships and ferries are in town. Some may be working outside if the project is large enough—a house pole, or perhaps a dugout canoe. June through September the Chilkat Dancers perform frequently, wearing authentic costumes crafted in the Alaska Indian Arts program. Ask at the visitor's center for a schedule for the dancers. Phone 766–2202. Small admission charge. On the post parade ground is *Totem Village,* including a replica of a tribal ceremonial house, a pioneer's cabin, pelt-drying racks, and some large totems. For information on Ft. William Seward contact the Halsingland Hotel, which will also provide walking tour maps for the fort.

The *Sheldon Museum and Cultural Center,* 25 Main St., houses a collection of pioneer and Tlingit artifacts. Open 1:00 P.M.–4:00 P.M., daily in summer, by appointment the rest of the year. Small admission fee. 766–2366.

Skagway: Here was the namesake ancestral home of the Tlingit Indian tribe that once guarded these mountain passes. Stop in at *Native Carvings* on the main street and you may find Richard Dick, an Alaska Tlingit Indian, working in wood and stone and willing to pass on some Native lore.

Scattered around the islands, in smaller Indian villages, are many signs of Native Alaskans. *Klawock* (Kl-wahk'), an Indian community a short flight or a ferry ride from Ketchikan, has a notable collection of totems on a hill in town. Kake, Hydaburg, Angoon, and Hoonah, are also reached by air or sea. On the way, bush pilots are inclined to circle and try to point out some remains of deserted village sites—perhaps a totem or part of a tribal house—if they think you are interested.

 OTHER HISTORIC SITES. Ketchikan: The *Creek Street Historic District,* a wooden street set on pilings along the Ketchikan Creek, was Ketchikan's "red-light district." Here, Dolly, Black Mary, and Frenchie plied their trade for over 50 years—until 1954. *Dolly's House,* 24 Creek St., is a brothel turned museum. Open during the summer for tour groups, or check at the visitors bureau (225–6166); a small admission fee. Phone 225–6329.

Sitka: *Castle Hill* was the site of Governor Baranof's castle. Here the first U.S. flag was raised when Alaska changed from Russian to American hands. Walkway to the site is next to the post office on Lincoln St. Open to the public free of charge, year-round.

The focal point of the town's Russian history is *Saint Michael's Cathedral,* on downtown Lincoln Street. Built in 1844–48, this building was one of the finest examples of rural Russian church architecture, until a fire in 1966 destroyed it. The rebuilt cathedral is an exact replica and contains many art treasures—including the Sitka Madonna icon—from the days of the Czarist rule. Open daily June–Sept., 11:00 A.M.–3:00 P.M., other times by appointment. Visitors are reminded that this is an active parish conducting weekly services. 747–8120.

Haines: *Fort William Seward* reflects the Indian heritage of this community (see "Indian Heritage" earlier in this section), as well as a military history. At the fort you can see barracks, the commanding officer's quarters, the guardhouse, the mule stables, and more. Details and a map for a walking tour are available at the Halsingland Hotel, 766–2000, or call the visitor's center June–Sept. 766–2202. Free.

Skagway: The Skagway unit of the *Klondike Gold Rush National Historical Park* encompasses a 6-block area of the community's business district and includes many wooden buildings dating from the gold rush days, among them the Arctic Brotherhood Hall and vintage railroad depot, now housing the Park Visitor Center, open 9:00 A.M.–8:00 P.M., mid-May–mid-Sept. Phone 983–2400.

Soapy Smith's Parlor and Museum, on First Ave. is near the site of the duel between infamous outlaw "Soapy" Smith and Frank Reid—representing the side of law and order. The museum is privately owned. Contact the Convention and Visitor Bureau for information, 983–2297.

The Trail of '98 Museum, Seventh and Spring Sts., is on the second floor of the first granite building constructed in Alaska (1899–1900). The purpose of the museum is to preserve Alaskan historical material and to display reminders of Alaskan pioneer life. Some of Soapy Smith's personal items are here. Open daily in summer, 10:00 A.M.–8:00 P.M. Oct.–May for groups by appointment only. Small admission fee. 983–2420.

 FISH. **To learn about them** visit **Ketchikan's** *Deer Mountain Hatchery* adjacent to the Totem Heritage Center. It's self-guiding, and there'll be someone on hand to interpret, too. It's free, open year-round. Call 225–6760.

Besides totems, Indian community **Klawock** also majors in fish. Alaska's first salmon cannery was built in Klawock in 1878 by the Northern Pacific Trading and Packing Company.

At **Petersburg,** study the fish sculpture considered to be one of the Pacific Northwest's finest pieces of bronze art. It's outside the *Clausen Museum,* Second and F sts., and it honors all fish, including the halibut, Petersburg's mainstay. The museum is open daily during the summer 1:00–4:00 P.M. 772–3598. Free.

Also in Petersburg, the *Crystal Lake Fish Hatchery* on Mitkof Hwy.—a hatchery for coho, king, and chum salmon and steelhead trout is open to visitors. No tours but personnel will explain what goes on here. Best time to visit: 8:00 A.M.–4:00 P.M., Mon.–Fri.

In **Juneau** you can watch migrating and spawning salmon, late July–Sept. Try Fish Creek, N. Douglas Hwy.; Sheep Creek, Thane Rd.; Montana Creek, Montana Creek Rd.; Steep Creek, near Mendenhall Glacier Parking Area; Peterson Creek, Glacier Hwy.

To catch them. All Southeast communities, regardless of their other interests, go in for sport and/or commercial fishing. And they all hold fishing derbies in the summer (usually May and June) in which visitors are invited to participate. Winning fish are usually well over 50 pounds, and the prizes add up to thousands of dollars. Local fish and game department offices, marine charters, and sporting goods stores, usually next to or on the waterfront, have current contest rules, licenses for sale, and lots of advice (free). *Alaska Sportfishing Lodge Assn.,* 500 Wall St., Suite 401, Seattle, WA 98121 (phone 206–622–3932, toll-free 800–352–2003), and *Alaska Sportfishing Packages,* Suite 1320, Fourth & Blanchard Bldg., Seattle, WA 98121 (206–382–1051, toll-free 800–426–0603), keep tabs on peak seasons for various species of fish and best places to catch them during lodge season, May through September.

To eat them. Throughout the Southeast, visitors will meet fish on the menu, and in some places be exposed to a favorite institution, the salmon bake, a summer event, usually all you can eat for $16 and up. **Wrangell** offers one that usually coincides with a cruise ship being in port. It's part of the sightseeing tour that ends up at the *Roadhouse Salmon Bake,* a few miles out of town.

At **Juneau,** the *Gold Creek Outdoor Salmon Bake* at Last Chance Basin, where millions in gold has been mined, has long been popular with visitors and residents. It's held rain or shine every night, 5:30–9:00 P.M. Only groups of over 20 need make reservations; 586–1424. Be at the Baranof Hotel at 6:00 P.M. for free transportation. While in Juneau it's also possible to combine flightseeing with that old Indian custom the salmon bake in a setting among glaciers and wilderness at Taku Glacier Lodge. Three-hour tours by float plane fly via the Juneau Ice Field, massive source of many mighty glaciers, including the Taku. They land at the dock of Taku Lodge, situated in a mossy rain forest. The dining room overlooks the aptly named Hole in the Wall Glacier. Coming and going, the skillful and obliging pilots identify landmarks and glaciers and watch for wildlife on the move. In the long, light summer evenings, sharp eyes may spot black bears bent on berrying, and sheep and goats on mountain ledges. Phone 586–1362 for information. The Taku Glacier Lodge office is at #2 Marine Way, Suite 228, Juneau, AK 99801.

Sitka is inclined to put a masterly salmon bake in the all-purpose Centennial Building, when requested by cruise ships or on other special occasions. Just ask at visitors information if one is scheduled.

Another favorite is the *Port Chilkoot Potlatch,* where fresh local salmon is prepared over an open alderwood fire, then served on the Parade Ground of Fort William Seward, adjacent to **Haines.** The potlatch is held daily 5:30–7:30 P.M. Inquire at the Halsingland Hotel nearby, facing the quadrangle; 766–2641.

MUSEUMS. Ketchikan: *Dolly's House,* 24 Creek St., is a brothel turned museum. Open during the summer, small admission fee. Phone 225–6329 or the visitor bureau for information, 225–6166.

Tongass Historical Society Museum is in the Centennial Bldg., 629 Dock St. Collection features Indian artifacts, pioneer history, photos. Hours vary depending on whether or not a cruise ship is in port. Usually open in the afternoon throughout the year. Small admission charge. 225–5600.

Wrangell: The *Wrangell Museum,* Second and Bevier Sts., houses displays of local and Tlingit history, and petroglyphs. Open May–Sept., Mon.–Thurs., Sat., 1:00–4:00 P.M.; Fri. 1:00–3:00 P.M. In winter: Wed. 1:00–4:00 P.M.; also open for cruise ships and ferries and by appointment year-round. Small admission fee. 874–3770.

Bigelow Museum, Stikine Ave. "Our Collections" is a private collection of artifacts and 19th-and 20th-century memorabilia. Open when ferries are in port and by appointment. Phone 874–3646 and they'll send a courtesy car.

Petersburg: *Clausen Museum,* Second and F Sts., features the world-record king salmon caught commercially (126½ lbs.), as well as local, historical displays. Open daily in summer 1:00–4:00 P.M. 772–3598. Free.

Sitka: The *Sheldon Jackson Museum* was the first museum in Alaska and houses an outstanding collection of Indian and Russian art and objects. Open in summer 9:00 A.M.–5:00 P.M. daily; 1:00–4:00 P.M. in winter, closed Sat. and Mon. 747–5228.

Juneau: *Alaska State Museum,* on Whittier St. off Egan Dr., houses a variety of displays ranging from Indian cultural displays, exhibits on mining, wildlife, and the trans-Alaska pipeline to Russian-American exhibits and the Lincoln totem. Summer hours: 9:00 A.M.–9:00 P.M. weekdays; 1:00–9:00 P.M. weekends. Winter hours: daily, 11:00 A.M.–5:30 P.M. No admission charge. 465–2901.

House of Wickersham, 213 Seventh Ave., houses historic collections of early 20th-century Alaska. The State targets 1986 for its reopening after a half-million-dollar restoration.

Haines: *Sheldon Museum and Cultural Center,* 25 Main St., exhibits Russian and Indian items. Open 1:00–4:00 P.M., daily, in summer; by appointment the rest of year. Small admission fee. 766–2366.

Skagway: Join a short walking tour of historic Skagway leaving from the Visitor Center at 10:00 A.M., noon, and 2:00 P.M., led by a National Park Ranger. The buildings, restored or in the process, are outdoor museum pieces!

Trail of '98 Museum, Seventh and Spring Sts., displays one of the best collections of gold rush memorabilia in the state. You can see some of Soapy's own belongings here. Open summers 10:00 A.M.–8:00 P.M.; in winter, for groups by appointment only. Admission charge, $2. 983–2420.

THEATER AND ENTERTAINMENT. In **Ketchikan,** the farcical melodrama *Fish Pirate's Daughter* is staged June–Sept. at the Frontier Saloon, 127 Main St. Tickets available on cruise ships and from the visitors bureau, and—if available—at the door. Write Box 6653, Ketchikan, AK 99901; 225–9950.

In **Sitka,** everyone applauds the traditional Russian folk dances performed in summer by the *New Archangel Dancers* on the stage of the Centennial Bldg. Performances are timed according to cruise ship arrivals or by special arrangement. Small admission charge. Write Box 1687, Sitka, AK 99835.

In **Haines,** see *Lust for Dust,* a melodrama created by the Lynn Canal Community Players during their 3-year-long centennial celebration. Performed at the Chilkat Center for the Arts, Ft. William Seward; call 766–2160. June–Sept. the *Chilkat Dancers* also perform here about twice a week. Ask at the visitor's center for schedule information; 766–2202. Small admission charge.

In gold rush gateway **Skagway** there's no lack of 1898 atmosphere. You can see *In the Days of '98* shows throughout the summer. These historical comedy-dramas are performed nightly (also some matinees and mornings) mid-May–mid-Sept. Eagles Hall, 6th and Broadway. Tickets sold at door, or write for reservations to Soapy Smith, Box 1897, Skagway, AK 99840; 983–2545.

SHOPPING. Everywhere you sightsee and explore you'll be tempted by the myriad shops and art galleries. They'll be selling traditional and modern creations made from Alaskan materials. The source of supply may be a small "cottage industry" or a cooperative venture of several local artists and craftsmen. Some items and materials may be unique to an area.

Ketchikan's mix of artists and craftsmen—silversmiths, potters, sculptors, photographers, etc.—supplies the *Puffin* on Creek Street. *Scanlon's* near the welcome sign downtown deals in traditional, contemporary, and Native Alaskan fine art works. *Nancy's Jewelers',* 209 Main St., great variety of gold nugget jewelry includes a 14-karat-gold Rainbird charm. Look for Native crafts at the

Alaska Treasure Cache, 224 Front St. and *Trading Post,* 201 Main St. *Authentic Alaska Craft,* 318-A Dock St. specializes in locally made totem poles, skin masks, and other collectible items of Alaska clay, soapstone, and fossil whalebone. *The Foxy Lady,* 435 Dock St., not only has the latest fashions but also up-to-date information on Ketchikan's current attractions.

In **Wrangell** you can buy a garnet from a Boy Scout. An unusual garnet ledge about five miles from town near the Stikine River flats was deeded to them. You are bound to find an Alaskan souvenir at *Sylvia's General Store* in a house renovated in 1906 style, 109 McKinnon.

Sitka, as in its Russian past, has a reputation for having well-stocked stores. On Cathedral Circle you'll find everything from Alaska Wild Berry Products to T-shirts: *Tops & Things* has T-shirts with Alaskan motifs and phrases, created by Stella Conway, a charter member of the New Archangel Russian Dancers; The *Russian Bell* and the *Russian-American Co.* have both Russian and Alaskan curios. *Old Harbor Books* has a wide selection of books, maps, and nautical charts; *Ceramitique* makes things of native Sitka clay. *Alexanders* on Harbor Drive has Alaskan paintings. Walk along Katlian Street behind the waterfront Sheffield House for picturesque shops in the "old town." They buy and sell old books and charts in *The Observatory* and *Books Books Books. Taranoff's Sitkakwan Shop,* also on Katlian St., like its name, reflects a Tlingit/Russian background with Alaskatique. Mrs. Taranoff designed the "Little Drook" (*friend* in Russian) button that city guests get when they sign in at the greeting desk in the Centennial Building. Wear it. Everyone is *extra* helpful when they know you are a visitor.

In **Juneau,** on Franklin St., two historic buildings are developing shopping malls. You'll find intriguing handmade items such as Russian action toys of wood at *Olde Towne Classics* in the *Senate Mall.* In the turreted *Emporium,* the *Heritage Coffee Co.* sells "fresh roasted" by the bag or cupful in their *Espresso Bar.* The *Latitude 58,* on Franklin St. across from the Red Dog Saloon, displays the hand insignia, which stands for authentic native handicrafts. *Nina's Originals* on Seward Street creates distinctive fur apparel, and the *Baranof Gift Shop* off the lobby of the hotel has collector's items, including rare Russian icons, on display. The proprietress, Martha Edwards, has served as president of the Alaska Visitors Association, the first woman to be elected to that position. If you're a bookworm, don't miss browsing in the *Baranof Book Shop* a few doors seaward. The *Merchant's Wharf,* on the waterfront, of course, was recycled from the dock and an old seaplane hangar. It's now an intriguing shopping mall with restaurants.

As you have gathered from the exploring section, **Haines** and **Port Chilkoot** are oriented toward Indian crafts. *Helen's Shop,* on Main St., has been an outlet for fine craft work and a source of local information cheerfully dispensed for over 30 years. At Port Chilkoot, for almost as long, they have been turning out authentically designed totem poles, masks, silver etchings, soapstone carvings, and other handicrafts. What they don't use in the Chilkat Dance programs they'll sell through the *Alaska Indian Arts Skill Center.* Look for notable newcomers on the arts-and-crafts scene. They display and sell their work at the *Art*

Shop, in a 1904 building, originally the telegraph office for Fort William H. Seward at Port Chilkoot. *The Sea Wolf* sculpture studio on the parade grounds and the *Whale Rider Gallery* in downtown Haines have the work of Tresham Gregg, who grew up in a nearby officer's quarters made into a family residence. The magnificence of upper Lynn Canal scenery has inspired many artists, including long-time resident Gil Smith, whose paintings hang in the State Museum and Governor's Mansion, the Anchorage Fine Arts Museum, and at the University of Alaska.

Skagway has a most interesting assortment of stores lining boardwalk-bordered Broadway. There are snack shops, restaurants and well-stocked grocery stores and bars. You can buy music, books, scrimshaw, Indian art, handicrafts, and sightseeing tours and charter flights. The *Red Onion* now sells curios, jewelry, objets d'art, and drinks, but go around back and upstairs. This 1898 building with beckoning mannikin in the window was once a bawdy house. Visitors can see and take pictures of the interior of this gold rush brothel, including the two restored "cribs." Long-established shops such as *Kirmse's Curio Store* dealt with the Yukon stampeders. *Dedman's Photo* has Alaska books and color slides, including a gold rush collection. And stop in at *Native Carvings, Richter's Jewelry, Keller's Curios,* the *Door Knob* and the *Trail Bench,* dealing in skins and furs. *Princess Charlotte Gallery* is a cooperative outlet for one-of-a-kind items created by several local artists. Along with a storeful of quality merchandise, *Corrington's,* Fifth and Broadway, has an Eskimo museum and a large collection of ivory pieces for sale. In two shops on Broadway you may find "scrimshanders" at work. Both David Present and William Joseph Sidmore etch on ivory, using the same skills that were used by sailors during long periods at sea, and that are still used by Eskimos, the master ivory carvers in the Arctic. You could spend hours in Skagway browsing, buying, and talking with the friendly shopkeepers.

PANNING FOR GOLD. In **Juneau,** *Alaska Travel Adventures* will help arrange gold panning and gold mine tours, 200 N. Franklin, Juneau, AK 99801; 586–6245.

Thane Ore House, Juneau, combines gold panning with a feast in their Miner's Cookhouse—all you can eat of salmon, halibut, BBQ ribs, etc., for around $15; call 586–6245. They guarantee that after lessons there will be gold in every pan. Included is a mining museum tour and transportation from hotels and cruise ships. May 15–Sept. 30.

 DINING OUT. Meals, especially if you take advantage of local specialties, are fairly reasonable in the homey restaurants of smaller southeast towns. They may run *less* in cost than this overall budget estimate: $4 to $8 for breakfast or lunch, and $8 to $30 for dinner. Major credit cards are widely accepted, but it's probably wise to call ahead to double check. The categories and ranges for a complete dinner are: *Deluxe,* $30 and up; *Expensive,* $20–$30; *Moderate,* $15–$20; and *Inexpensive,* under $15.

KETCHIKAN

Clover Pass Resort and Restaurant. *Expensive.* Mile 15 N. Tongass Hwy.; 247–2234. Seafood specialties, probably fresh caught in their "front yard," the ocean, served with view. Salad bar and cocktail bar. Open Apr. 1–Oct. 1.

Gateway Club. *Expensive.* Mile 7, N. Tongass; 247–2470. Salad bar has 17 (at least) ingredients to go with beef and seafood specialties. Open 9:30 A.M. to wee hours. Free shuttle from downtown Fridays and Saturdays.

Charley's. *Moderate.* 303 Mission St.; 255–5090. Off Ingersoll Hotel lobby; honors Charles Ingersoll, builder of this mainstay of "The Block," in the heart of historic downtown Ketchikan.

The Fireside. *Moderate.* 335 Main St.; 225–2006. Popular supper club located in downtown Ketchikan. Fresh seafood a specialty. Lounge, music, and dancing.

Gilmore Gardens Restaurant & Lounge. *Moderate.* 326 Front St.; 225–9423. Newly beautified, with small hotel charm.

Hilltop Restaurant. *Moderate.* 3434 Tongass Ave.; 225–5166. Features daily specials, sandwiches, fountain. Across from ferry terminal.

June's Cafe. *Moderate.* Corner of Creek & Stedman Sts.; 225–4305. Open 7 days for all meals; take-out phone orders.

Kay's Kitchen. *Moderate.* 2813 Tongass Ave.; 225–5860. Home cooking, especially soup and pies; crab and shrimp Louis. Lunches only. Clever decor and great location overlooking busy Bar Harbor boat traffic. Closed Sundays and Mondays.

Angela's Delicatessen. *Inexpensive.* Mission St. Custom-made sandwiches produced cafeteria style, next to Ingersoll Hotel.

Diaz Cafe. *Inexpensive.* On Stedman St., across from the Salvation Army; 225–2257. Small, popular, good family food. No booze.

The Galley. *Inexpensive.* 2334 Tongass; 225–5400. Variety of fast food; beer and wine.

Harbor Inn. *Inexpensive.* Under the Welcome Arch on Mission St., 225–2850. Open 24 hours.

Jackie's Restaurant. *Inexpensive.* At the Midtown Mall; 225–4545. A pleasant, casual spot for tasty food.

Stephanies. *Inexpensive.* 1287 Tongass St.; 225–2966. Another good bet for a reasonably priced meal.

You can pick up delicious fast snacks, especially seafood, from vendors set up at the City Dock.

WRANGELL

The Diamond C Restaurant. *Moderate.* 116 1st St. (behind the Totem Bar, Front St.); 874–3677. Specialties are tasty homemade soups and tiny Wrangell shrimp, the best you'll ever eat.

The Dockside. *Moderate.* In the Stikine Inn; 874–3388. You can count on the convivial atmosphere in the Stikine Bar, and fresh local seafood in season in the dining room.

The Hungry Beaver. *Moderate.* At Wrangell's oldest site (formerly Fort Dionysius, now the Marine Bar); 874–3005.

The Roadhouse. *Moderate.* Mile 4, Zimovia Hwy.; 874–2335. Lounge, evening dining and dancing. Outdoor fish bakes on request for 10 or more.

The Wharf. *Moderate.* Also on Front St.; 874–3681. Come as you are. Home cooking and Alaska hospitality.

PETERSBURG

Viking Room *Expensive.* At Beachcomber Inn, Mile 4, Mitkof Hwy.; 772–3888. View of Wrangell Narrows comes with fresh local seafood and steak dinners. Shipwreck Room for cocktails. Reservations needed.

Harbor Lights Restaurant. *Moderate.* Pizza in historic Sing Lee Alley; 772–3424.

Irene's. *Moderate.* Downtown, near Fisherman's Wharf, G and Main Sts.; 772–3702. Seafood and salad bar.

The Homestead. *Moderate.* Indian St.; 772–3900. Healthful home cooking.

SITKA

The Shee Atika Lodge. *Deluxe.* Uptown, across from convention center; 747–6241. Newest, large hotel built by the Native Corporation. Fine dining and entertainment.

Sheffield House. *Deluxe.* Built on a former dock, overlooking the beautiful, historic waterfront and islands. 747–6616. Excellent food, entertainment, bars.

Staton's Steak House. *Deluxe.* Downtown overlooking Sitka Sound; 747–3396. Popular with residents. Also bar.

Channel Club. *Expensive.* 3½ miles out the Halibut Point Rd.; 747–9916. A local favorite for view, steaks and salad bar.

Paul and Judy's Canoe Club. *Expensive to Moderate.* In the Potlatch House, end of Katlian St.; 747–8606. Alaskan specialties served 7 nights a week 5–11 P.M. with piano bar and view of Mt. Edgecumbe and harbor.

Lory's Sitka Cafe. *Moderate.* 116 Lincoln St.; 747–6488.

Nugget Saloon. *Moderate.* Airport. Seafood and do-it-yourself steaks.

Revard's. *Moderate.* On Lincoln St. near Cathedral Circle.

Fish Factory. *Inexpensive.* 407 Lincoln. Menu varies with the catch.

Marina Pizzeria. *Inexpensive.* On Lincoln near Circle; 747–8840.

JUNEAU

The Diggings. *Deluxe.* 340 Whittier Ave.; 586–3737. At the Prospector Hotel there is live entertainment nightly, dancing and cocktails.

The Gold Room. *Deluxe.* 2nd and Franklin; 586–2660. Alaskan decor including paintings by Sydney Laurence help decorate this handsome restaurant in the

Baranof Hotel. Entertainment often reflects early Juneau life. Ice Worm Cocktails are the bar specialty.

Breakwater Inn Restaurant. *Expensive.* 1711 Glacier Ave.; 586–6306 or 6303. All remodeled, except the view of the channel. Serves seafood specialties plus regular fare.

Summit Restaurant. *Expensive.* 455 S. Franklin; 586–2050. Intimate, serves only 18 for dinner in Gold Rush Era atmosphere. Try the tempura prawns.

Woodcarver Restaurant and Lounge. *Expensive.* 51 W. Egan Dr.; 586–6900. In the Sheffield House; elegant and excellent.

Bellezza Ristorante. *Moderate.* In the Court Plaza Bldg. 3rd & Main; 586–1844 for reservations. Italian cuisine; homemade pastas, bread, and pastries.

Chinese Palace: No. 2. *Moderate.* 434 3rd, in Bergmann Hotel, a registered historical landmark; 586–6414. Walk from the ship to "best of the Orient" cuisine.

Fiddlehead Restaurant & Bakery. *Moderate.* 429 W. Willoughby. 586–3150. Healthful things, homemade; blueberry/buttermilk pancakes to salmon quiche; true sourdough, breads, and memorable pastries.

Glacier Lounge and Restaurant. *Moderate.* Located at airport. 1873 Shell Simmons Dr.; 789–9538. Usually has seafood on the menu. Overlooks Mendenhall Glacier.

Second Street Restaurant. *Moderate.* 1102 Second St., Douglas (across the bridge); 364–3271. Formerly Mike's, a Juneau institution; seafood, steak and salad bar specials are served with an Italian accent now.

Silverbow Dining Room. *Moderate.* 120 2nd St.; 586–4146. Smoke-free atmosphere while enjoying classic country French and regional American dishes, in renovated historic building.

Viking Restaurant. *Moderate.* 218 Front St.; 586–2159. Welcomes families; features stuffed baked potatoes—10 different specialties!

Brown Bear Cafe. *Inexpensive.* 220 Front St.; 586–2202. Open 24 hours.

Bullwinkle's Pizza. *Inexpensive.* 318 Willoughby Ave.; 586–2400. When you're in the mood for pizza, this is the place to go.

City Café. *Inexpensive.* 439 S. Franklin; 586–1363. Variety of food and quick service in this clean, convenient café across from downtown ferry terminal.

Fisherman's Wharf Restaurant. *Inexpensive.* 22 Egan Dr., on Merchants Wharf; 586–3369. Try a halibutburger.

Pattie's Etc. *Inexpensive.* 230 Seward St.; 586–9555. A local favorite.

HAINES-PORT CHILKOOT

The Lighthouse. *Expensive.* Overlooks the Haines small boat harbor and bordering snow-clad mountains; 766–2442.

Hotel Halsingland. *Moderate.* At Parade Ground in Port Chilkoot; 766–2000. Super Swedish and American meals. Fresh-caught salmon and other Alaskan seafood are menu favorites, along with wildberry deserts. Magnificent scenery from hotel area. Family-style meals have scheduled hours.

The Post Exchange. *Moderate.* On the Parade Ground; 766–2009. New restaurant in vintage Fort Seward building, once a PX and bowling alley. Live entertainment twice a week, including the "Ft. Seward Follies."

33-Mile Roadhouse. *Moderate.* 766–2172. 7 A.M. to 10 P.M. daily. Also fill your gas tank; 92 miles until more.

Dan and Barb's. *Moderate to Inexpensive.* At the Main St. Y, downtown Haines; 766–2588. Good value.

The Pizza Cutter in the Fog Cutter Bar. *Moderate to Inexpensive.* Main St.; 766–9109. A good spot for a drink, too.

Porcupine Pete's Sourdough Restaurant. *Inexpensive.* 2nd Ave. and Main St. Family restaurant offers free sourdough starter.

SKAGWAY

Golden North Restaurant. *Expensive.* Broadway and Third; 983–2451. Gourmet gold rush cuisine.

Irene's Inn. *Expensive.* Broadway and Sixth; 983–2520. Spacious dining room (and a few modern rooms) in a once-illicit 1899 gaming parlor next door to "Days of '98" show. Family operation. Alaskan food. Good salad bar.

Chilkoot Dining Room. *Moderate.* In Klondike Hotel, 3rd and Spring; 983–2291. Bar.

Northern Lights Café. *Moderate.* Long-time Broadway favorite; 983–2225. Fresh salmon and halibut with sourdough rolls and, with dinner, their special Old Fashioned Klondike Dessert is only 25¢.

Prospector's Sourdough Restaurant. *Moderate.* 4th & Broadway. Features sourdough hotcakes and waffles, king crab omelettes, and reindeer sausage.

Sweet Tooth Saloon. *Moderate.* Broadway, between 3rd and 4th; 983–2405. Featuring home-baked goods, homemade soups, sandwiches, in attractive old-fashioned ice-cream parlor decor.

 BARS AND NIGHT LIFE. The favorite watering holes in towns usually are well patronized by the residents, who are quick to point them out to visitors. Some "in" places that you might want to sample include the *Fireside Supper Club,* 335 Main St., in **Ketchikan;** *Kito's Kave,* a den of many decibels, in **Petersburg;** on G St., past Main, near the new boat harbor.

In **Sitka,** the locals head for the excellent lounge and entertainment at the uptown *Shee Atika Lodge,* across from the convention center, the *Channel Club* out Halibut Point Rd., and the disco in the waterfront *Sheffield House.* In **Skagway** gold rush atmosphere can be found in *Moe's Frontier Bar,* on Broadway between 4th and 5th, and the *Red Onion Saloon,* 2nd and Broadway, with sawdust floor, antique backbar, and potbelly stove.

Juneau's *Red Dog Saloon,* 159 S. Franklin St., with sawdust on the floor and a bear-trap-and-snowshoe decor, may be the best known in Alaska, but don't overlook the genteel and charming atmosphere in the *Alaskan Hotel* bar at 167 S. Franklin St. It's renovated in its original Alaska-Victorian style and listed in the National Register of Historic Places. **Wrangell's** *Marine Bar* is on the site of Ft. Dionysus; follow Front St. to Shakes St.—it's by the bridge to Shakes Island.

ANCHORAGE

Alaska's Big Apple

If you have been intrigued by the variety in Alaska's skylines so far, wait until you see Alaska's "Big Apple." They've been busy adding towers to already tall buildings—the Anchorage Westward Hilton, the Captain Cook—and building new ones, such as the Sheraton. Facing mountains on three sides and with marine views as well, they are surrounded by scenery that is probably unsurpassable in quantity and quality. In addition, situated at the upper end of Cook Inlet, the city is in a hub position in relation to the rest of Alaska, as well as the world. The roads converge in Anchorage. The busy International Airport is a world air crossroads.

Starting as a tent camp in 1913, this old city has gone further in less time than almost any world city you might name. Modern, cosmopolitan Anchorage is the financial and business metropolis of the state, as

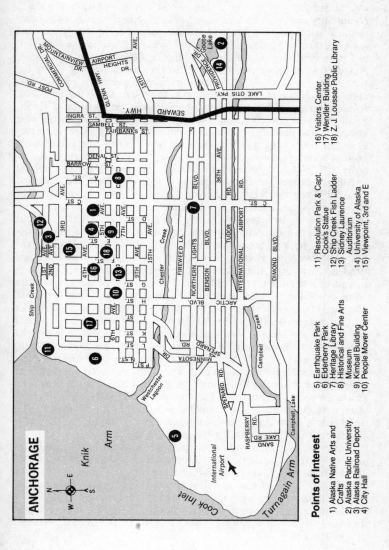

Points of Interest

1) Alaska Native Arts and Crafts
2) Alaska Pacific University
3) Alaska Railroad Depot
4) City Hall

5) Earthquake Park
6) Elderberry Park
7) Heritage Library
8) Historical and Fine Arts Museum
9) Kimball Building
10) People Mover Center

11) Resolution Park & Capt. Cook's Statue
12) Ship Creek Fish Ladder
13) Sidney Laurence Auditorium
14) University of Alaska
15) Viewpoint, 3rd and E

16) Visitors Center
17) Wendler Building
18) Z. J. Loussac Public Library

well as the focal point for the creative arts and education. Besides a community college and a branch of the big University of Alaska, there is a new institution in town—a four-year private school being recycled from the former Alaska Methodist University, closed because of financial problems. Its goals are far-reaching, as defined by its new name, Alaska Pacific University. Its aim is to prepare pioneering spirits for the twenty-first century. Here, in developing, stategically located Anchorage, they hope to spur a meeting of the minds involving all Pacific Rim countries, affiliating with the colleges and universities of Japan, South Korea, Samoa, Hawaii, and especially China. It's an ambitious endeavor, and funding no small problem. If it works, a valuable cultural and economic link will be established between these nations and the United States.

By 1917, Anchorage was established as the busy construction base and headquarters for the nation's first federally built and operated railroad. Then the Alaska Railroad extended from seaport terminal Seward to Nenana and on to Fairbanks, with branch lines to some mining areas with intriguing names like Chickaloon, Chatanika, and Moose. Still in use are the Fairbanks-to-Seward track and a spur across the narrow neck of the Kenai Peninsula south of Anchorage. It was built in 1942 from Portage, where Turnagain Arm (off Cook Inlet) deadends, through the mountains to Whittier on Prince William Sound. It was needed in World War II for moving military necessities from tidewater to Anchorage and Fairbanks. This Whittier cut-off shortened by about fifty miles the distance between inland Fairbanks and access to an ocean port. It gave the railroad two important terminal ports, at Seward and at Whittier, connecting with oceangoing vessels.

In 1940, Anchorage was still only a small town of 3,500, but World War II triggered the action, and the keynote has been growth. New industries and energy-resource discoveries, particularly oil-related ones, have managed to keep the city and its environs booming. Studies made ten years ago predicted there would by 225,000 people living in Anchorage by 1980. Those statistics are pretty much on target. The 1978 census showed a population of more than 202,000, and they now forecast continued growth for the last half of the '80s.

Annually, over three million people pass through Anchorage International Airport, on domestic and foreign flights and cargo operations to and from major world cities. Over the pole, London is only nine hours away. The national capital, New York, and the rest of the eastern United States are 7½-hour flights. Seattle is 3 hours away; Los Angeles 5; Honolulu, on the same time as Anchorage, is 5½ hours south. Japanese visitors, of which there are many, fly from Tokyo to Anchorage in 7½ hours.

Because it's big, there is more to see in Anchorage than within any other city in the state. Moreover, the active Alaska Visitors Association is headquartered there and the enthusiastic Anchorage Convention and Visitors Bureau are determined to make the city a destination for all seasons and all people. Some brochures now are printed in Japanese and German to accommodate some of their best customers. They are developing a language bank, and they claim that when needed they can call on people to help out in Arabic, Afghanistan, Native Alaskan, Finnish, Chinese, Dutch, French, Hebrew, Hungarian, Italian, Korean, Malayan, Norwegian, Polish, Portuguese, Spanish, Russian, Swedish, Turkish, Vietnamese—in addition to Japanese and German. There are also special aids for the deaf and blind, as well as other handicapped persons.

Anchorage is young among world cities, and perhaps some of its folks are a little self-conscious about not having an image they can really pinpoint and call their own. It's not a gold rush gateway, ex-Russian capital, salmon capital, oil capital, etc.—titles that other, smaller Alaskan towns can claim. But they can't compete with Anchorage's lively, cosmopolitan bustle, only minutes away from vast frontier wilderness. This helps make it the state's leading convention center, attracting national and international organizations.

Exploring Anchorage

Downtown is neatly laid out with numbered avenues north and south and lettered streets east and west. There is much of interest in a reasonably compact area.

Start at the Visitor Center, 4th and F, to pick up a walking tour map and comprehensive *Anchorage Guide* put out by the Convention & Visitors Bureau. It's more than you can cover during a single session, especially if you try to take in *all* their suggestions. But you will spend some happy hours trying. Following is a downtown tour of some points of interest indicated on the map.

Our tour starts heading west from the information center on the first "main street," Fourth Avenue. You'll note the 4th Avenue Theater, built by an early Alaska character, Cap Lothrop, who started his empire by supplying Cook Inlet gold miners by steamer, and expanded it to include radio stations and movie houses. He spent some of his millions to bring culture to Anchorage. This unusual and handsome theater, built only 25 years after the founding of the frontier railroad town helped set its course toward becoming the cosmopolitan city of today. The elegance inside includes murals of bronze and silver and the state flag symbols—Big Dipper and North Star—outlined in twinkling lights in the ceiling.

In the next block, art lovers will want to step into the lobby of the Alaska Bank of Commerce, graced with five historical paintings by three top Alaskan artists: Sydney Laurence, Josephine Crumrine Liddell, and Fred Machetanz. The quaint Wendler Building, its corner turret once dwarfed by the modern towers of the Captain Cook Hotel, has been moved from its 1915 building site at 4th & I to the southwest corner of 4th & D. It's listed on the National Register of Historic Places.

Take a small detour to Elderberry Park, a place to watch whales, birds, and the Bore Tide—a rushing tide peculiar to the area to be seen when water fills the bays of Cook Inlet. Nearby is the Anderson House, from 1919, open to the public and restored in the early furbishings. Then on L street, head north to Resolution Park on 3rd Avenue, where the statue of Captain Cook looks across at Mt. Susitna's famous "Sleeping Lady" profile. The captain landed on a point to the south that separates Turnagain and Knik Arms of Cook Inlet. This is also a good place to observe the Bore Tide if you are there at the right time. There are other tides farther away, at Earthquake Park, across Westchester Lagoon facing Knik arm, and also along Turnagain Arm, but you'll need transportation.

Walk south on K Street from Resolution Park, and turn east on Sixth. But first stop in at the Gingham House, 615 K, dating from 1917. From 10:00 A.M. to 6:00 P.M. during the week you can watch local craftsmen weave baskets, carve ivory, and sew skins—and buy there, too, if something strikes your fancy. At the Oomingmak Musk Ox Producers, 6th & H, there aren't any of the creatures on hand, just items made of their lovely wool (called qivuit) by members of the co-op; some ladies may be there knitting.

By now you may be ready to try Anchorage's inexpensive alternative to walking (or driving), the local bus system, called the People Mover. Free double-decker buses shuttle the downtown area. The bus network covers residential and business districts with shopping malls where you'll see some major retail stores—Penney's, Lamonts, Montgomery Ward, Nordstrom's, Sears Roebuck & Co.—and many specialty shops. The People Mover is for exploring farther afield, too, like perhaps at the Alaska Zoo, which is about five miles south on the Seward Highway from Anchorage, then left on the O'Malley Road for about two miles.

Alaska Zoo

The zoo is nonprofit, city owned, and leased to the operators who have programs for 8,000 or 9,000 school children and almost one hundred thousand visitors a season, late spring through fall. Some forty species of wildlife inhabit the spacious grounds. Visitors follow the paths to the "stars" of the zoo. Native Alaskans—a polar bear Binky and her cubs—reside in their new grotto and pool. Perhaps a distant relative of the mastodons whose frozen remains are still being found in Arctic tundra, longtime resident Annabelle the elephant lives in a new $150,000 house. Though the zoo charges admission, it also depends on donations. Bring your leftover meat or fish (no bones, please) and cash to put in the containers provided.

Back Downtown

Continuing the downtown stroll, from 6th turn north on F, then take in a couple of blocks of 5th to D St. You'll pass the much-used Sydney Laurence Auditorium, honoring Alaska's best-known artist. The whole block is earmarked for the new performing Arts Complex. Depending on your time, you can linger at the Oriental Gardens, stop in at the new Convention Center, or at the National Park Service Area Information Office, where you will see the displays and perhaps a free movie on the parks (shown daily 12:15 P.M. in winter; 12:15 and 3:15 P.M. in summer). The Kimball Building at 500 W. 5th was bought at the original townsite auction, and it has preserved its early storefront look while selling dry goods and also antiques, coffee and assorted teas.

Ask the sales clerk at Alaska Native Arts and Crafts Cooperative, 425 D Street, about watching Native craftsmen at work there making items of wood, horn, ivory, woven reeds, and leather. Here they also make and sell Laura Wright parkas, the colorful warm Eskimo-style parkas visitors get to borrow while they are on Arctic tours.

Back to 4th Ave., turn west to E, then north to a viewpoint at the corner of 3rd and E St. You can ponder and photograph much of historical and scenic interest. It overlooks Ship Creek, where the tent city developed in 1915 when the government decided to build the Alaska Railroad. The large parking lots on 3rd Ave. from E to A streets, are part of the buttress system worked out to support and stabilize this area, most heavily damaged during the 1964 earthquake. The Port of Anchorage is Alaska's largest, handling tankers and container ships. It begins near the mouth of Ship Creek, where there is a marina and small boat harbor, and includes several miles beyond the bluff along Ocean Dock Road up Knik Arm. In the distance beyond the Creek, you'll sometimes see planes taking off and landing at Elmendorf Air Force Base, or helicopters at Fort Richardson Army Base, to the east.

If you are still in a walking mood, you might want to walk down the steps through the parking lot to the Railroad Station. Outside are totem poles and a locomotive built in 1907 for the Panama Canal Railroad. Inside is a photo display and gift shop. Nature lovers will want to go farther north along Ship Creek to the pond in front of the green power plant. Waterfowl gather there, even in winter, appreciative of the warmer water due to the plant. Salmon swim up Ship Creek to jump a spillway in the dam. It's easy to watch them from a viewing platform. Kings are most likely from early June until mid-July; other salmon species, from mid-August until September.

This chapter focuses primarily on the city of Anchorage, proper. For information on the surrounding areas, see the following chapter, "Southcentral and Interior Alaska."

PRACTICAL INFORMATION FOR ANCHORAGE

HOW TO GET THERE. By air: Scheduled airlines fly direct to Anchorage from gateway cities in the Lower 48 states and Canada. The deregulation of air travel may cause carrier changes. In spite of higher fuel costs and other inflationary causes, more competition encourages air-fare bargains. Watch the ads and ask your travel agent about discounts, coupons, and other "super-savers." For up-to-date flight information, how to get to gateway cities, and fares, contact travel agents or the nearest main or local airline office of: *Alaska Airlines,* Box 68900, Sea-Tac International Airport, Seattle, WA 98168 (currently direct flights from L.A.; San Francisco; Portland, OR; Seattle); *Northwest Orient Airlines,* Alaska Sales Office, 4300 West International Airport Road, Anchorage, AK 99502, and *United Airlines,* (800) 841–8005, fly direct from Seattle and Chicago; *Western Airlines,* Regional Sales Office, 3830 International Airport Road, Anchorage, AK 99502 (from Salt Lake City, Seattle, Portland, OR). (Though not flying at this writing *Wien Airlines,* Inc., 4100 International Airport Road, Anchorage, AK 99502 is expected to resume service.) On their international flights, *Air France, British Airways, Japan Air Lines, K.L.M. Royal Dutch Airlines, Korean Airlines, Lufthansa German Airlines, Sabena World Airways,* and *SAS Scandinavian Airlines System,* touch down in Anchorage, with stopover privileges.

Smaller carriers and local air-taxi operators commute between Anchorage and other, even remote, spots in Alaska. *Alaska Aeronautical Industries,* Box 6067, Anchorage, AK 99502 flies to Homer, Kenai, and Kodiak. *MarkAir,* Box 6769, Anchorage 99502 flies to far north, far west, and southwest towns. *Reeve Aleutian Airways,* 4700 W. International Airport Rd., Anchorage, AK 99502 flies "the chain." *SEAIR,* Box 6003, Anchorage, AK 99502 schedules connections to over 60 bush communities. *Valdez Airlines,* Box 6714, Anchorage, AK 99502 flies to Cordova, Homer, Iliamna, Kenai, Kodiak, and Valdez.

By bus: *Alaska Yukon Motorcoaches,* 249 Wrangell St., Anchorage, AK 99501, or 555 Fourth and Battery Bldg., Seattle, WA 99501. Connects with the State Ferry System at Haines and Skagway. *Valdez/Anchorage Bus Lines,* 743

W. 5th Ave., Anchorage AK 99501, (907) 272–1935; Valdez phone, 835–5299. For the many ticketing and boarding points for *White Pass & Yukon Motorcoaches:* P.O. Box 100479, Anchorage; (907) 277–5581; toll free (800) 544–2206.

By rail: The *Alaska Railroad* runs between Anchorage and Fairbanks via Denali National Park and Preserve daily, May to September. Express trains stop to board or detrain passengers at Denali Park Station. Along with more than 50 regular stops, local trains halt to let off or pick up fishermen, hikers, or homesteaders. Informative brochures provide a running account of what is to be seen, and the upper doors of the vestibules are open for the benefit of photographers. This helpfulness on the part of the railroad is reflected in the camaraderie of the passengers; by the time destinations are reached strangers are "old friends." Reservations should be made no less than 2 weeks prior to travel. Contact the Alaska Railroad, Passenger Sales Representative, Pouch 7–2111, Anchorage, AK 99501. Phone (907) 265–2494.

By water: The *Alaska Marine Highway System* will bring you to Skagway and Haines where you can connect with *Alaskan Yukon Motorcoaches* to Anchorage. (See "How to Get There" in *Practical Information for Southeast Alaska* and "By Bus," above.) Cunard's *Princess,* Exploration's *North Star,* Paquet's *Rhapsody,* and Sitmar's *Fairsky* extend their Inside Passage cruises to include the Gulf of Alaska to Whittier, with a train connection to Anchorage.

By car: Anchorage is a hub of the road system in southcentral and a gateway to interior Alaska. Getting there by car, camper, trailer, or motorcoach via the *Alaska Highway,* the *Glenn Hwy.,* and other historic highways is a real wilderness-road adventure. (See "Hints to Motorists" in *Facts at Your Fingertips.*)

GETTING INTO TOWN. If you are on tour, you'll be met by a representative, who will see that you get what's coming to you with your tour price. Otherwise it's about $6 one way for *limousine* service from the airport to major downtown hotels (about 7 miles). *Taxi* service is also available, as is the *People Mover* bus service. Follow the signs from the baggage claim area to the bus stop. Or, you can rent a car. (See "How to Get Around," below.)

HOTELS AND MOTELS. You'll find the widest choices here in Alaska's "Big Apple" and vicinity. Also contact the usual visitor information sources for addresses, rates, and the assorted amenities of other available transient housing. Rates are based on double occupancy. Expect to pay $100 and up for *Deluxe* accommodations; $80–100 for *Expensive;* $60–80 for *Moderate;* under $60 for *Inexpensive.*

Anchorage Sheraton. *Deluxe.* 401 E. 6th Ave., 99501; toll-free outside Alaska (800) 325–3535; in Alaska call collect (907) 276–8700. Near downtown. Elegant décor, including jade stairway in foyer. Rooftop restaurant/lounge, ballroom, and healthclub with whirlpool and saunas.

Anchorage Westward Hilton Hotel. *Deluxe* (Bristol Bay Native Corp.). 3rd and E St. 99510; 272–7411. 500 rooms in downtown double tower. Coffee shop, dining rooms, bars.

Captain Cook Hotel. *Deluxe.* 5th & K St., 99510; toll free continental U.S. (800) 323–7500; in Alaska and Hawaii (800) 323–1707; in Canada (800) 661–1262. Large, well-decorated rooms in huge hotel. Three towers of view rooms. Some suites. Parking lot. Coffee shop, dining room, cocktail lounges with entertainment.

Sheffield House. *Deluxe.* 720 W. 5th, Anchorage, AK 99501; 276–7676; toll free continental U.S. (800) 544–0970; in Alaska call collect 274–6631; Zenith 06003 from Canada. Three blocks from Convention Center; two restaurants and 3-level Penthouse Lounge, highest in Anchorage, with view.

Anchorage International Airport Inn. *Expensive.* 3333 International Airport Rd., 99502; (907) 243–2233. Big, down to its king and queen size beds. Restaurant, bar, convention facilities, courtesy car service.

Sheffield TraveLodge. *Expensive.* 3rd and Barrow, 99501; 272–7651; toll free continental U.S. (800) 544–0970; in Alaska call collect 274–6631; Zenith 06003 from Canada. Pleasant, three-story motor inn with coffee shop, dining room, bar.

Anchorage Eagle Nest Motel. *Moderate.* 4110 Spenard Rd., 99503; (907) 243–3433. Motel only, but two restaurants on same block. 5 minutes from airport, with free pickup and delivery. Rooms include kitchen.

Best Western Barratt Inn. *Moderate.* 4616 Spenard Rd., 99503; (907) 243–3131; toll free Continental U.S. (800) 528–1234. 150 rooms, a few with kitchenettes. Restaurant, bar, and courtesy car to and from airport, 3 minutes away.

Hillside Motel & Camper Park. *Moderate.* 2150 Gambell St., 99503; (907) 338–6006. 26 rooms, some with kitchenettes. All hookups, even phone, hot showers, laundry.

Holiday Motor Inn. *Moderate.* 239 W. 4th Ave., 99501; (907) 279–8671. (Call collect in Alaska, or make reservations by calling any Holiday Inn, anywhere.) Large motor inn, three levels. Attractive rooms. Indoor pool. Dining room, cocktail lounge with entertainment nightly, except Sun.

Inlet Towers. *Moderate.* Near downtown at 1200 L St., 99501; (907) 276–0110. 140 hotel-apartments, kitchenettes; beauty shop, sauna rooms, laundromat.

Mush Inn Motel. *Moderate.* 333 Concrete, 99501; (907) 277–4554. Large motel near Merrill Field. Free transportation to and from airport. Restaurant and bar nearby. Covered parking; security guards. Family rooms, kitchenettes. Heated water beds.

Northern Lights Inn. *Moderate.* 598 W. Northern Lights Blvd., 99503; (907) 561–5200. 144 rooms. Restaurant, lounges (live music), beauty and barber shops. Free parking.

Red Ram Motor Lodge. *Moderate/Inexpensive.* 5th & Gambell; 279–1591. 19 rooms with phone and color TV. Restaurant, lounge, beauty salon.

Voyager Hotel. *Moderate.* 501 K St., 99501; (907) 277–9501. Rooms with kitchenettes, bath, color TV. Separate, but on the lower level of the building is the Corsair restaurant and bar. Highly recommended for location and comfort.

The Inlet Inn-Downtown. *Inexpensive.* 539 H St., 99501; (907) 277–5541. An older hotel; rooms with baths and some kitchenettes. Seasonal rates. Limo service. 119-rooms. Convenient to all downtown activities, including restaurants.

John's Motel 'n Camper Park. *Inexpensive.* 3543 Mt. View Dr., 99504; (907) 277–4332. Small motel with hookups, showers, near Mt. View Shopping Center. Many conveniences within walking distance.

BED-AND-BREAKFASTS. You can **"Stay with a Friend"** by contacting 3605 Arctic Blvd., #173, Anchorage, AK 99503; (907) 274–6445. Or try **Alaska Private Lodgings,** Box 110135, Anchorage, AK 99511; (907) 345–2222. More than 70 B & B units are available in Anchorage. Rates start at about $30, double.

YOUTH HOSTELS. The **Anchorage Youth Hostel** at Minnesota St. and 32nd Ave., Box 4–1226, Anchorage, AK 99509, is open year-round and has kitchen facilities. There are laundromats nearby. $6.25 per night in summer; $7.25, in winter. Nonmembers allowed for 1 night at $8.25. Curfew at 11:00 P.M. For reservations phone (907) 276–3635; after 7:00 P.M. call (907) 276–9522. Hostel membership cards are available at Allways Travel, 302 G St., 274–3641, or at the hostel.

WILDERNESS LODGES. Anchorage is a big city, but the Alaskan wilderness experience can be had closeby. Airwise, a little north of Anchorage: Float planes serve *Judd Lake Silvertip Lodge* and *Silvertip on the Tal.* Besides spectacular fly fishing on the Talachulitna River and headwaters, there are float trips on the Tal and on the Chelatna River. Contact Manager, Silvertip Lodges, Box 6389, Anchorage, AK 99502; (907) 243–1416. Also consult Ketchikan Air Service, 2708 Aspen Dr., Pouch B, Anchorage, AK 99503 (243–5525) and Rust's Flying Service, P.O. Box 6325, Anchorage, AK 99502 (243–1595). They've been exploring the area by fly-ins for many years. You can drive north of Anchorage on the Parks Highway to rustic *Chulitna River Lodge,* Box 374, Star Route B, Willow, AK 99688, (907) 733–2521.

HOW TO GET AROUND. By bus. The *People Mover* bus service will take you around town for 50¢; children, 25¢, senior citizens with passes and handicapped free. Exact change required. The central station is downtown at Sixth and G. Pick up a schedule there or call 264–6543. There are also free, double-decker shuttle buses downtown.

By car. *Avis, Budget, Dollar, Hertz,* and *National* car rentals are handy at the airport, and there are others—even *Rent-A-Wreck*—which you can arrange for there, or ahead of time through the local office in your area. It's a good idea to reserve in advance during peak travel months July and August. Gas and oil are extra; license regulations are the same as everywhere else. It's possible to rent one place and drop off another by arranging ahead. Other motoring possibilities include: *Alaska R.V. Tours/Rentals,* 3002 Spenard Road, Anchorage, AK 99503, (907) 274–2573, and *No. 1 Motorhome Rentals of Alaska,* 322 Concrete, Anchorage, AK 99501, (907) 277–7575, collaborate with airlines on fly/drive packages.

 TOURIST INFORMATION is dispensed at the *Anchorage Convention & Visitor Bureau* (ACVB) centers at the airport. They vary their hours with flight schedules. The *Domestic Information Center,* phone 266–1437, is in the Baggage Claim area; *International Information Center* (same phone) is in the customs intransit area. The ACVB *Downtown Information Center,* phone 274–3531, is in the attractive log cabin at Fourth and F Streets. Mailing address is 201 E. Third Ave., Anchorage, AK 99501. It is open daily 8:30 A.M. to 6:00 P.M. in summer, and from 9:00 A.M. to 4:00 P.M. in winter. Ask for the current *ACVB Anchorage Visitors Guide* that tells all about Anchorage, including tours. Also ask to see their menu collection. Looking through them and comparing prices helps a traveler to stay within a budget. The hot line *"All about Anchorage"* at 276–3200 is a recording that gives the events of the day, the time, and the place, and the number to call for more information, or for reservations if needed. There may be a rock-climbing demonstration or a film on mountain rescue, a musical at the Fine Arts Museum, a trip through the Candy Kitchen, an ethnic exhibit where you can sample the food, and perhaps something special in the way of nightlife. Alaska Dept. of Fish and Game, 333 Raspberry Rd., Anchorage, AK 99502; 344–0541, or 349–4687 for a recorded message. *National Park Service Area Information Office* is a treasure of information for backpacking throughout Alaska. Reservations for Forest Service cabins can be made here: 2525 Gambell, Anchorage, AK 99503; 271–4243. Open weekdays 8:00 A.M.–5:00 P.M.

 TOURS. Sightseeing comes from many angles, including aloft in an air taxi, helicopter, even hot air balloon. Consult the tourist information centers listed above, hotel travel desks, or the following firms. *Alaska Sightseeing* (349 Wrangell, 99501; 276–1305), *Atlas Tours* in the Holiday Inn, 239 West 4th Ave., phone 276–1909, *Grayline* 547 W. 4th, 99501, 277–5581, and *Royal,* in the Captain Cook Hotel, 5th & K, 99510; 277–5566, have sightseeing and activities to all major motorcoach destinations and beyond, including *Exploration Holiday's* off-the-beaten-path tours to the Arctic, the Remote Pribilof Islands, etc.

STATE PARKS. Located in the mountains just east of Anchorage *Chugach State Park* affords travelers the opportunity to get out of the city into real wilderness. Hike, view the wildlife, pick berries, ski, snowmobile, camp. *Ranger hikes* of varying degrees of strenuousness are offered on summer Saturdays, Sundays. The park office is at 2601 Commercial Dr., 99501; 279–3413. Phone 274–6713 for recorded information on current rules and conditions.

OTHER NATURAL ATTRACTIONS. Many Anchorage areas within easy reach are definitely for the *birds.* They gather at *Ship Creek* ponds, *Lake Hood, Lake Spenard,* and *Potter's Marsh,* a state game refuge, on the Seward Highway, where you might also see a coyote. The *Anchorage Audubon Society* keeps track of the best local bird-watching spots. Check their hot line (274–9152) for prerecorded word on current sightings and field trips.

Unique to Anchorage is the *Bore Tide,* along the Seward-Anchorage Hwy. For determining the best time to view, first check the low-tide schedule in the newspaper. To see it at Mile 32.6 from Anchorage, add 2 hours and 20 minutes. Another good spot is about 4 miles farther; add 22 hours and 45 minutes to the low-tide time. Besides the tide, which is impressive in its 30-foot—and more— rise and fall in 6 hours, watch for beluga, the smaller white whales, breaching and surfacing as they follow the fish. Look, but don't try to walk on the exposed tide flats. It's muddy, and some places act like quicksand.

Probably the most unusual site and tourist attraction is one created by nature in 1964. The 135-acre *Earthquake Park* at the west end of Northern Lights Blvd. is a testimonial to the devastating shake-up, left as it was, to be healed by nature, with time. From here there are grand views of 20,320-ft. Mt. McKinley, 17,400- ft. Mt. Moraker, the Talkeetna Mountains to the northeast, and the Chugach Mountains to the east.

ZOOS. The *Alaska Zoo* houses polar bears, brown and black bears, reindeer, moose, wolves, foxes, musk ox— over 40 species of wildlife in all. Located on O'Malley Rd., south of downtown off the Seward Hwy. Open daily, year-round, 10:00 A.M.–5:00 P.M. Small admission charge. Phone 344–8012 for details.

PARTICIPANT SPORTS. Cycling. Thanks to a cycling legislator, Alaska has many fine bike trails. Anchorage has 78 miles of paved ones that crisscross the city between Cook Inlet and the Chugach Mountain foothills. In winter these serve as **ski** trails. You can bike free through the municipal "Earth Cycle" program Monday through Saturday 9:00 A.M. to 5:00 P.M. Just leave a picture ID card and a $5 deposit when you pick up your bike at the corner of 4th and F. This is catty-corner from the Log Cabin Visitor

Center, where they will have trail maps, and also information on other bicycle rentals.

Dog Sledding. In winter, international teams and mushers compete on Saturdays and Sundays, 11:00 A.M. at the Tudor Road Race Track. Inquire at *Alaska Sled Dog Racing Assn.,* 272–9225, about other winter—and summer—activities. Also contact the *Chugach Express Dog Sled Tours* at Box 261, Girdwood, AK 99587; 783–2266; and *Goose Lake Dog Sled Rides,* Box 757, Girdwood, 272–3883 or 783–2266.

Golf is played in summer at *Elmendorf Golf Course,* 18 holes on the Air Force Base, phone 752–2773, open summers. Green fees are $9–12. You can also play at the *Moose Run Golf Course,* 18 holes at Fort Richardson, phone 864–1181. The name may be a clue to what else you might see. Green fee is $10. Inquire locally about some 9–holers in the vicinity.

Hiking is year-round and the trails are prolific, with many scheduled hikes—some on snowshoes when necessary. Ask at the visitor center if you are interested in joining a sponsored hike and want maps showing access and trails. The *Alaska Handicapped Sports & Recreation Assn.,* P.O. Box 714, Girdwood, 563–4060 has information on trails, campgrounds, and activity geared to those with handicaps.

Skiing. The closest ski area is in *Arctic Valley,* and it operates weekends and holidays only from Dec. 1 to the end of April. A day lodge serves soup and sandwiches. Phone 276–7669 for ski conditions. Cross-country skiing is available, but trails are not maintained. Shuttle bus service available from downtown. *Mt. Alyeska Resort,* 40 miles from Anchorage is fully developed. It has double chairlifts, poma lift, rope tows, ski school, rental equipment, overnight accommodations, dining room, cocktail lounge, day lodge with sundeck and snackbar, and the Skyride Restaurant at top of Chairlifts #1 and #4. The ski season is November thru April including heli-skiing, dog sled rides and horse-drawn sleigh rides, plus lively "apres-ski" entertainment.

When the snow leaves, this year-round resort shifts years. Summer visitors sightsee by chairlift, and by hiking to viewpoints above the lodge. Other activities include hang gliding, parachuting, balloon rides (in winter, too), and gold panning at the nearby *Erickson Crow Creek Gold Mine.* For super seasonal ski packages and reservations, and information on visiting other times of the year, write General Manager, Alyeska Resort, Box 249, Girdwood, AK 99857; 783–2222.

Swimming. You can swim at several health clubs, and in hotel pools. Four high schools have pools where visitors may swim for a couple of dollars: *West High,* 1700 Hillcrest Dr.; 274–5161; *East High,* 4025 E. 24th Ave., 274–6430; *Dimond High,* 2909 W. 88th Ave., 243–2317; *Chugiak High,* Birchwood Loop Rd., off Glenn Hwy. north of the city, 688–2010. Phone the *Cultural & Recreational Service,* 264–4475, for more on the aquatic possibilities. Outdoor public areas are maintained from 10:00 A.M. to 6:00 P.M. in summer at *Goose Lake,* 3 miles from downtown Anchorage at Northern Lights Blvd. & Providence Dr.; at *Jewel Lake,* 6½ miles from downtown at Jewel Lake Rd. and Dimond Blvd.; and at *Spenard Lake,* 3 miles from downtown at Spenard Rd. and Lakeshore

Drive. These areas also have picnic areas, restrooms, and playground. (Note: swimming in Cook Inlet is extremely dangerous.)

HISTORIC SITES. The *Anderson House,* one of the city's first homes, has been beautifully restored. It's in Elderberry Park, at the foot of Fifth Ave. Open 1:00–4:00 P.M., Tues.–Sun. Phone 274–2336. Small admission charge. *Delaney Park,* on 9th Ave., still looks like a landing field, which it was—Anchorage's first air strip used by the bush pilots. The *Pioneer School House,* 3rd Ave. & Eagle St., first in Anchorage, is surrounded by *Crawford Park,* location of log cabins built in the early days of Anchorage. For Alaska's Russian heritage, call before coming, and someone will show you *St. Innocents Russian Orthodox Church,* 6724 E. 4th; 333–9723. Another is *St. Nicholas of Myra Rectory Byzantine Rite,* 2200 Arctic Blvd.; 277–6731.

LIBRARIES. The *Heritage Library,* in the National Bank of Alaska Building, Northern Lights Blvd. and C St., displays a most important collection of historical costumes, artifacts, tools, maps and publications. It's open Mon.–Fri., 1:00–4:00 P.M., 276–1132. The *Z.J. Loussac Public Library,* 524 W. 6th Ave., 264–4481, has a comprehensive section on the North. Open 9:00 A.M.–9:00 P.M., Mon.–Fri.; Sat. 9:00 A.M.–6:00 P.M.

MUSEUMS. All sorts of things go on among the collections and exhibitions of the *Anchorage Historical & Fine Arts Museum,* 121 W. 7th Ave. It has both permanent and changing displays of Indian and Eskimo art and artifacts, and there is often a cultural event—lecture, film, even a mini-concert—scheduled in the auditorium. They sell publications and craft items in the gift shop. In summer it's open daily Mon., Wed., Fri., Sat. 9:00 A.M.–6:00 P.M., Tues., Thurs. 9:00 A.M.–9:00 P.M., Sun. 1:00 P.M.–5:00 P.M.; in winter, Tues. through Sat. 9:00 A.M.–6:00 P.M., Sun. 1:00–5:00 P.M. Phone 264–4326. No admission charge.

Both *Elmendorf Air Force Base* and *Fort Richardson* have free **Wildlife Museums** with large displays of mounts of Alaska birds, mammals, and sportfish. Elmendorf is at the Boniface and Glenn Hwy. intersection; ask at the gate directions to Bldg. 4803. Phone 552–2282. Mon.–Fri. 7:45 A.M.,–4:45 P.M.; Sat. 10:00 A.M.–3:00 P.M. Free. Fort Richardson Wildlife Museum is 5 miles northeast of Anchorage on the Glenn Hwy., Bldg. 600; call 863–8113. Mon.–Fri. 9:00 A.M.–5:00 P.M. Free.

THEATER AND ENTERTAINMENT. No matter when you visit Alaska's "metropolis" you'll find plenty to keep you busy, looking, or doing. Alaskans come up with hard-to-resist activities not only in summer but the year-round. In fact, many a visitor has declared Anchorage (and other Alaska destinations) even *more* intriguing with a dash of "off-seasoning." They are surprised to find a lively social season in fall, winter, and spring, and that there are many organizations bent on enriching community life.

Tickets, Inc. in the lobby of Alaska Pacific Bank Bldg., 524 W. 4th, 279–9695, is open 10:00 A.M. to 5:00 P.M. Mon–Fri. during the busiest cultural season—winter; they shorten their hours in summer. They sell tickets and have information on the productions mentioned here and on other groups that perform in season, such at the *Theater Guild, University of Alaska Anchorage Theatre,* and the *Community Theatre.* For recorded information on cultural events of the week, call 276–ARTS (276–2787).

The *Alaska Repertory Theatre,* 705 W. 6th, 276–2327, or 5500 (box office), produces plays in both Anchorage and Fairbanks, and also tours through Alaska every year. Its Anchorage season is from November into April. The Alaska spirit and grandeur of the land is portrayed in unique ways; the *Alaska Experience Theatre* shows a 40-minute film at Cinema 180, 705 W. 6th St.; call 276–3730 for show times. June into Sept: Larry Beck recites the most famous poems of Robert W. Service and presents other nostalgic reminders of pioneer and gold rush days during the *Alaska Show* daily at 8:00 P.M. (adults $12; children 6–12, $10) at the Egan Convention Center, 555 West 5th Ave; phone 278–3831 for reservations or ask at travel and tour information desks in hotels.

MUSIC. During its September to March season, the *Anchorage Civic Opera* puts on not only whole operas, but also entertainment for dinners. They perform in the Sydney Laurence Auditorium, 6th and F; 276–8688. The *Anchorage Concert Association* signs up top names for its season series October to April, plus some specials: Champagne Pops (ouch!) Concert, and a Viennese Waltz Night. They can be reached at 360 K St., Suite 230, 99501; 272–1471.

For free: *Concerts in the Park,* mid-June to mid-August on Thursdays at 7:00 P.M. in Delaney Park Strip, 9th & P sts. The Alaska Air Command Band sounds off there with Dixie to Pop, and also performs *Tunes at Noon* at the Old City Hall, 4th & F, June–August, on Wednesdays. Another free outdoor concert downtown features guest artists: *"Meet Me at the Plaza"* takes place at the Alaska Mutual Bank, 601 W. 5th., Fri. noon, June–Aug.

SHOPPING. The best buys in Alaska are products of native materials made by Natives and other artists and craftsmen living in the state. Look for carvings out of ivory, soapstone, jade, and wood, and items made from fur. You'll find a wide choice of jewelry, mukluks, masks, totem poles, paintings, baskets, and even food items that *look* Alaskan. But how does one know that an item was produced in Alaska and is an authentic souvenir?

The state has adopted two symbols that guarantee authenticity of crafts made in Alaska by its people, and it supplies them with tags and stickers to put on their work. If the piece you covet has a hand symbol, it was made by one of the Native peoples. A dipper-shaped flag symbolizes that it was made in Alaska, by a resident, of materials which can be found in the state (though they may have been imported, as well, to be crafted here). If some items with these emblems seem more expensive than you expected, examine them and you'll probably see that they are one of a kind and have been made by hand. There are many more shops than those listed here; part of the fun is discovering for yourself!

In a city that has a whole festival dedicated to it—the Fur Rendezvous—there are bound to be places where visitors can see it, feel it, and buy it. These companies also have free tours, but call ahead: The *Anchorage Fur Factory,* at 105 and at 539 W. 4th Avenue, 277–8414, owned and operated by a large Mexican family; *David Green Furriers,* 130 W. 4th Avenue, 277–9595; and *Martin Victor,* 428 W. 4th, 277–7683, who urges you to "Soften Up. Bring Home A Fur."

An Ulu may be just the thing for chief cooks in the family. Pronounced "ooloo" and used by northern Natives for centuries for all sorts of cutting tasks, including filleting, it's bound to be a conversation piece. You'll find them in most shops, or buy direct from *The Ulu Factory,* 198 Warehouse Ave. They demonstrate the Ulu's uses at the *Alaskan Food Cache* in a historic building at 819 W. 4th, where they garner delectable provisions from America's Last Frontier, and pack them cleverly. Free sampling! Salmon—canned and smoked—reindeer sausage, and Homestead Kitchens jams and jellies are among their best sellers. Pick up a catalog for "at home" shopping when you hunger for those Alaskan goodies.

You may be able to watch Native craftsmen at work at *Alaska Native Arts and Crafts Cooperative,* 425 D St. You'll certainly be able to buy goods of wood, horn, ivory, reed, and leather, there. Browsers are welcome at the *Rusty Harpoon,* 411 W. 4th in the Yellow Sunshine Mall. Their long suit is carving wood and soapstone and doing scrimshaw—etching on ivory—an art that came from the whalers and was readily picked up by the artistic Eskimos. You'll see an artistic Eskimo doing unusual pen and ink Native scenes on animal skins at the *Alaska Treasure Shop,* 436 W. 4th Ave. *Bering Sea Originals* feature Alaskan Native clay ceramics in their gift shops in the University Center Mall, Dimond Center, and Northway Mall. *The Gilded Cage,* 715 W. 4th, has special Alaskan items like wildflower seeds, sourdough starter, and jellies, along with many other unusual and handcrafted things. It is operated by volunteers for the Alaska Treatment Center for Crippled Children and Adults. *At Alaska Heritage Arts,* 211 E. 5th, you'll see ivory and soapstone carvings, paintings and prints created by fine artists.

For the wool from the musk ox visit *Oomingmak Musk Ox Producers,* 6th Ave. and H St.

Jewelry made from gold nuggets, ivory and jade is hard to resist. Shop around; here are some places for starters where you can see it being created. At both *McGrane Jewelers,* 427 D St., and the *Nuggetree,* 809 W. 4th Ave., they fashion jewelry from natural gold nuggets, and you're welcome to watch. *Stella Designs,* 700 W. 58th, manufactures clever cloisonné jewelry and T-shirts—with original Alaskan motifs, for sale in many shops. At the *Kobuk Valley Jade Shop,* in the parking lot just below Alyeska Resort, you can watch the fine art of jade cutting.

They have caches for more than food. (An Alaskan cache is a mounted, covered miniature cabin in which supplies and furs are stored. It is elevated to prevent bears and animals from getting at the contents.) The *Arctic Cache,* 429 W. 5th, 274–7110, has jade, ivory, and soapstone jewelry and carvings, and Eskimo yo-yos, which they'll demonstrate. There are thousands of books at the *Book Cache* which has a store downtown, 333 W. 4th, and at 436 W. 5th Ave., at the International Airport, and at 8 shopping centers in Anchorage.

The shopping possibilities are extensive both downtown and in the major shopping centers and malls throughout the city. And don't overlook the handy gift shops in the hotels with a wide range of items, including clothing.

PANNING FOR GOLD. *Action Alaska's Hospitality Plaza,* 440 L St., 279–1406, will know all about the best panning in the area, prices, and how to get there. Near Girdwood, south of Anchorage on Highway #1 about 40 miles, the Ericksons' 1898 *Crow Creek Gold Mine* and historic buildings are open to visitors (fee charged). Drive 3 miles up the Crow Creek Road, part of the Old Iditarod Trail, to pan for gold or camp overnight. Box 113, Girdwood, AK 99587, or contact by phone through Mt. Alyeska Resort, 783–2222.

 DINING OUT. Dining can be as elegant or as informal as you wish to make it. Many restaurant chains go all out to protect your pocketbook. Look for specialty restaurants that lean toward healthful foods, and also those serving assorted ethnic dishes. Generally, budget about $35 per day per person for restaurants other than the fast food kind. These categories will give a clue to the tab.

Breakfast or lunch may run $4 to $8; dinners, $10–$20. Restaurants are listed according to their price category. Categories and ranges for a complete dinner are: *Deluxe:* $30 and up; *Expensive:* $20–$30; *Moderate:* $15–$20; and *Inexpensive:* under $15. A la carte meals would cost a bit more. Many establishments accept major credit cards. Call ahead for reservations; some close Sun. or Mon.

Crow's Nest. *Deluxe.* 5th & K St.; 276–6000. Sweeping view of historic Cook Inlet from this fine restaurant atop 9-story Captain Cook Hotel. Seafood and steak. Also the **Quarter Deck** *(Expensive)* in Tower 1 and **Whale's Tail** room, on ground floor, a bar that serves lunch Mon.–Fri. and hors d'oeuvres Mon.–Sat.

House of Lords. *Deluxe.* 720 W. 5th. 276–5404. Ground-floor restaurant in Sheffield House. Elegant food and service. Try the just right Filet of Halibut Olympia with a special fluffy sauce. Fitting climax to a spectacular meal is Café Diablo, prepared with style at your table.

Josephine's. *Deluxe.* 201 E. 6th Ave.; 276–8700. The Sheraton's elegant roof-top restaurant.

Nikko Gardens. *Deluxe.* 2550 Denali St.; 272–4522. Like a "Phoenix," the Japanese-style favorite, once destroyed by fire, rises again, but in a new location, the Denali Towers.

Top of the World Restaurant. *Deluxe.* 3rd and E Sts.; 272–7411. Award-winning restaurant. Located in the Westward Hilton Hotel, this is a most popular spot for fine dining. Wide selection on menu. Cocktail lounge. Reasonable coffee shop also available. Restaurant and lounge open afternoons and evenings.

Stuckagain Heights. *Deluxe.* 9871 Basher Rd.; 333–8314. In the Chugach Mountains, overlooking the city, once so exclusive they didn't tell you how to get there until you made reservations. Their Moose Gooser bus system schedules pick-ups and returns to hotels.

Clinkerdagger, Biggerstaff and Petts. *Expensive.* In the Calais Building on C St., 3301 C St.; 274–5628. Very popular; reserve! Old English-Tudor atmosphere, and a wide selection of anything you want.

Club Paris. *Expensive.* 417 W. 5th Ave.; 277–6332. Locals like the basic dinners and conviviality.

Elevation 92. *Expensive.* 3rd & K Bldg.; 279–1578. 92 feet above sea level; superb inlet view.

Garden of Eatin'. *Expensive.* 2502 McRae Rd.; 248–3663. Theater served with dinner in this Quonset hut that was first a homestead. Open 6–10 except Sun. and Mon. (and all winter, when it is closed). Reservations required.

Simon & Seaforts. *Expensive.* 520 L St.; 274–3502. A saloon and grill dedicated to capturing the spirit (and spirits) of the turn-of-the-century grand saloon. Congeniality with good food.

Tiki Cove. *Expensive.* 5th & I, across from the Captain Cook Hotel; 276–8454. Polynesian food and drink.

The Upper 1. *Expensive.* Located at Anchorage's International Airport; 243–4331. Local favorite is "Sunday Smorgasbord Supreme" from noon daily. Varied menu. Cloudhoppers Lounge.

The Cauldron. *Moderate.* 328 G St.; 276–0301, and 700 E. Benson Blvd; 276–5957. Good-for-you things leaning toward, but not entirely, meatless. Homey, with live folk or classical music nightly. Also takeout lunch menu.

The Cellar Food & Spirits. *Moderate.* At the Red Ram, 5th & Gambell; 279–1591. Make reservations for dinner shows in intimate dining atmosphere.

Downtown Deli. *Moderate.* 525 W. 4th; 274–0027. Local food landmark between the Captain Cook and the Anchorage Westward Hilton. Many notables have endorsed their tasty specialties and unique made-to-order dinners.

Great Alaska Beef and Sea. *Moderate.* 3230 Seward Hwy. (near Sears); 274–4664. Cocktails, lunch and dinner.

Gwennie's Old Alaska Restaurant. *Moderate.* 4333 Spenard Rd.; 243–2090. Colorful, can't-miss-it, out Spenard way. Try it for an all-Alaskan breakfast, lunch, or dinner.

Marx Bros. Café. *Moderate.* Operated by 3 "brothers" in refurbished 1916-building at 627 W. 3rd; 278–2133. Specialties are fresh local seafood and exotic wild game.

One Guy from Italy. *Moderate.* In the "Z" Plaza at 3024 Minnesota Dr.; 277–6823 or 9231. *The* place for Italian food (closed Tuesdays). At least 43 different specialties, 25 kinds of pizza. They're open to suggestions . . . those written in Italian are given priority.

Oriental Gardens. *Moderate.* In relaxing surroundings 7 miles out of town on Old Seward Highway; 349–8633. Japanese and Asian specialties are lobster, tempura, seafood.

Peggy's Airport Café. *Moderate.* At 1675 E. 5th St. Opp. Merrill Field; 338–7602. One of Anchorage's long-time popular dining spots. Visitors are urged to try sourdough hotcakes and Peggy's homemade pies.

Rabbit Creek Inn. *Moderate.* Mile 10 Old Seward Hwy.; 345–1313. Attractive dining room with fireplace. Charcoal-broiled steaks and seafood served in Hearth Room. Roast prime rib specialty. Soft lounge entertainment on weekends.

Rice Bowl. *Moderate.* 232 W. 5th St.; 272–7931. Good Chinese-American cuisine. Also charcoal-broiled steaks. Orders to go.

Tea Leaf. *Moderate.* Lower Level of the Sunshine Plaza, 411 W. 4th; 279–0134. 12-page menu of Oriental treats; open kitchen preparation.

Harry's. *Inexpensive.* 101 West Benson Blvd.; 561–5317. (Formerly Donovan's, renamed for Harry Truman who refused to leave his home when the eruption of Mt. St. Helens threatened.) Besides its fabulous step-down bar, it's noted for hamburgers and giant salads. A fun place. **Note:** Among Anchorage's circa 250 restaurants there are familiar fast-food chains, e.g. **Arby's, Burger King, McDonald's, Wendy's**—even **Wienerschnitzl.**

 BARS AND NIGHTLIFE. Try the *Signature Room* at the Anchorage-Westward Hilton Hotel, 3rd and E St.; the *Elbow Room,* 417 C St.; and *Darwin's Theory,* 426 G. The *Paimuit Lounge* at the Sheraton, 401 E. 6th Ave., is a favorite meeting place of the cosmopolitans. Entertainment nightly at *Lucy's in the Sky,* Holiday Inn, 239 W. Fourth Ave. Captain Cook Hotel, 5th and K St. has *Whale's Tail* on the ground floor and *Crow's Nest* on top. *Upper 1,* at Anchorage International Airport, has a clear view of planes flying in from and taking off for distant lands. *Penthouse Lounge* in Sheffield House 720 W. Fifth, is as high as you can get. Great floor-to-ceiling window on Mt. McKinley and Cook Inlet. *Simon & Seafort's Saloon,* 420 L, has old-time decor. *Harry's,* 101 Benson Blvd., is a well-stocked, convivial Irish pub. *Chilkoot Charlies,* 2435 Spenard Road, is a rustic saloon where they claim the longest bar in the state, and that they make cheechakos feel like sourdoughs. "Catch the light" (laser) and sound shows at 3103 Spenard Road at—would you believe—*Spenardo da Vinci's! The Bird House* at Bird Creek, Mile 26, Seward Hway., is a leftover from Alaska R.R. construction days. It's jerry-built so crooked that when things start to look straight it's time to call it quits.

SOUTHCENTRAL AND
INTERIOR ALASKA

Where the Roads Go

The bulk of Alaska, with plural personalities and multiple faces, is contained in the huge, pan-shaped peninsula that extends several hundred miles to the north and to the west of the Southeast Panhandle. This diversity is reflected in the character of the people, in the characteristics of the land, and in the economy. Thus, within the Interior, visitors may encounter Native Athabascan Indians, and in the Gulf of Alaska–Cook Inlet southcentral areas there'll be descendants of Eskimo offshoots and of Russian settlers. City populations blend people from all over the United States and the world. The mix is concentrated in the two largest cities, Anchorage, at the gateway to the Interior, and Fairbanks, within it.

133

There is great variety in a terrain that has been shaped by major rivers and geologic upheavals. It's a land still being formed, sometimes violently, by earthquake and by volcanic eruption. Mountains contrast with flat valleys, sculptured by now retreated glaciers. The climate, mild to severe, influences the activities of the residents (and visitors). The economy depends on the use of a wealth of natural resources including such notorious ones as oil and gold, as well as other minerals. Coal may be on the verge of redevelopment as a source of energy in some areas. Agriculture has a good start in the rich valleys of the Tanana and Matanuska rivers.

Many routes lead to Southcentral and Interior destinations, where the highway network lends itself to circuit travel. This is the best way for visitors to see the most without duplication, whether they are on their own or with a tour. Anchorage and Fairbanks are pivot points. International airports link them with the world. Highways connect them, through Canada, with the rest of the continental states, and with each other.

On to the Yukon

The summer-only Klondike Highway 2, connecting seaport Skagway with the Alaska Highway south of Whitehorse, though improved each year since its opening in 1978, is still an adventure road. Steep, winding, and narrow, more than a third of it dirt and gravel, it's open and maintained from about the first of May to mid-October, though some hope it will eventually be open year-round. Sometimes paralleling the now-abandoned, narrow-gauge tracks of the White Pass & Yukon Route railroad, the road traverses spectacular mountain scenery and historic goldrush sites on its way to the summit of 3,290-feet-high White Pass.

This summit, 14 miles from Skagway, marks the U.S.–Canadian border and a time change, from Pacific Time to Yukon Time (one hour earlier). Everyone entering the United States must stop at the U.S. Customs station, about 6 miles from Skagway. The same rule applies to entering Canada, at the Canadian Customs station at Fraser, about 22 miles from Skagway. Be aware that both are open only in summer from 8 A.M. until midnight (7 A.M. to 11 P.M. Yukon time). There are no facilities for travelers at the stations.

At the summit there are turnouts in the road for views of the tracks and trestles of the vintage railroad across the gorge. Massive glacier-carved valleys and waterfalls, especially aptly-named Pitchfork Falls, which drops dramatically from Goat Lake, tempt photographers. A clue to the steepness of the highway grade are the "runout ramps" strategically placed to aid descending southbound traffic, particularly trucks, which might lose their air brakes.

Beyond the summit the road widens, continuing northbound through the rocky valley of Summit Lake, highlighted by a view of the Tormented Valley's unusual stunted trees and many lakes. The road crosses the rail tracks at now-deserted Log Cabin, the Northwest Mounted Police customs checkpoint during the gold rush. Chilkoot Pass hikers once caught the White Pass & Yukon train here before it ceased to operate in 1982, after 87 years of service. Now they follow the tracks to the intersection with the highway, to hitch a ride to Skagway or Whitehorse, after their Chilkoot Trail hike from Dyea.

Continuing on beyond the site of Log Cabin, the road heads past Tutshi Lake, then follows Windy Arm. Track and road meet again at the town of Carcross. First a caribou crossing (whence its name), Carcross has continued in its crossroads role, serving the railroad, sternwheelers, and now drivers.

Among the mementoes proudly displayed in Carcross are the first locomotive in the Yukon, an early stage coach and freighter, and, at the lakeshore, the last of the sternwheelers to ply these waters. In the cemetery are the graves of the three who first discovered gold in the Klondike, a pioneer missionary, and that of a precocious parrot named Polly.

From Carcross, the routes of the train and highway stay together, more or less, through meadows with streams and lakes, including colorful Rainbow Lake and Spirit Lake, and views of oddly-shaped mountains. The highway joins the Alaska Highway 13 miles from Whitehorse, 98 miles from Skagway.

Whitehorse

Yukon Territory is vast, wild, exhilarating. It contains almost 208,-000 square miles and perhaps 20,000 persons, more than half of whom live in and near Whitehorse. Whitehorse, the seat of government of Yukon Territory, has a population of about 14,500. The city incorporated a king-size surrounding area in 1974, making it the largest city in Canada in area—162 square miles—until it was surpassed by Timmins, Ontario, in 1981. No other Yukon town has over 1,000 persons. In all the far-flung territory there are probably 12 communities with a population of more than 100—including Old Crow, an Indian settlement far north on the Porcupine River and remote from any road.

Whitehorse, the territorial capital, is a clean, friendly city, with fine accommodations. They range from hotels to campgrounds and include a youth hostel near the jet airport. Some exceptional restaurants and burgeoning shopping centers are contained in this big bend of the Yukon River.

Meriting visits in and around Whitehorse are: Miles Canyon, through which the dam-tamed Yukon flows; MacBride Museum, on the grounds of which are the Sam McGee Cabin, built in 1899 (Sam McGee being a character in a Robert W. Service poem); the Hydro Dam and Fish Ladder; the spirit houses in the Indian cemeteries; some log "skyscrapers" and the Anglican Old Log Church, built in 1900, and now a church museum; the splendid acrylic mural, depicting the evolution of the Yukon, in the foyer of the Whitehorse City Hall; the special northern art displays in the Yukon Archives; and the sternwheeler S.S. *Klondike,* now a national historic site. Three-hour boat excursions include the M/V *Schwatka* cruise up the Yukon and through Miles Canyon, and downriver to Lake Laberge.

Whitehorse is headquarters for some diverse attractions. One is the Royal Canadian Mounted Police, renowned for keeping law and order in the Yukon since 1894. Others are the Yukon Sourdough Rendezvous at the end of February, featuring dogteam races, and the "Frantic Follies," a local-talent vaudeville show, using the theme of the Gold Rush era, staged nightly from June to mid–September in the Whitehorse Sheffield Hotel. Get tickets early from Atlas Travel, nearby. This family show is hilarious and popular.

The Visitors Information at 3rd and Steele has lists of attractions, and Atlas Travel in the Sheffield Hotel Mall sells all kinds of tours.

Dawson City, Yukon Territory, Canada

Gold rush buffs are bound to want to continue to the end of the Trail of '98 at Dawson, gateway to the Klondike gold fields. Planes and buses go there, but to drive the almost 500-mile Klondike Loop Highway is only about a 100 miles more than taking the direct Alaska Highway route that passes the beautiful Kluane Lake area.

The highway is dirt, but well kept up in summer, and campgrounds, stores for groceries and gas, and accommodations are open for business at well-spaced intervals. Following lakeshores, through forests and over gentle mountains and high scenic plateaus, keeps the scenery interesting, highlighted by old settlements of Indians and miners.

Down to fewer than 900 people, about 30,000 below what it had in 1899, Dawson City clings tenaciously to its fabulous past. Streets remain as they were at the turn of the century, and visitors find glamour in the silent, shuttered, ramshackle stores and houses and the miles of flower-bordered boardwalks. But some pioneer buildings are still open and operative or under restoration by Parks Canada as historic shrines. Stroll past some of these spots: begin at the information center at the corner of 1st Avenue and King street and walk up King Street to the Palace Grand Theatre.

The federally restored theater stages "The Gaslight Follies," nightly at 8:00, during the summer season. Afterward, everyone heads for Diamond Tooth Gertie's in the Arctic Brotherhood Hall on Queen Street. The Klondike Visitors Association runs the operation: floor show with can-can girls and *real* 1900 gaming tables, under special government blessing. It's the only legal gambling hall of its kind in Canada (annual membership $2).

On King Street at 3rd Avenue is the 1901 post office. Head straight down 3rd, make a right onto Queen Street, and you'll be heading toward the Canadian Imperial Bank of Commerce, on First Avenue, where Yukon bard Robert W. Service worked from 1907 to 1909. The "Gold Room," above the Bank of Commerce, has an exhibit of early equipment used for weighing, measuring, and melting gold. The S.S. *Keno,* "the historic sternwheeler that pioneered the Yukon," is now a historic landmark near the bank. But the small paddlewheeler *Yukon Lou* and the new 220-passenger *M.V. Klondike* catamaran pass historic sights as they ply the Yukon out of Dawson. You can drive to dredges on the creeks, to legendary mines, and to "Poverty Bar," where you can pan for gold on Bonanza Creek. An outdoor Mining Museum at Front and Queen streets hoards more mining memorabilia.

The Dawson City Museum is in the old Government Administration Building on Fifth Avenue. It houses a collection of artifacts, including old narrow-gauge locomotives. Next door, the Klondike Mine's railway locomotives rest in Minto Park. Near the museum, on Eighth Avenue, is Robert Service's two-room log cabin where his "ghost" recites poems daily during the summer. Down the street from here is Jack London's cabin; half of the logs are from his original cabin in the bush, where he stayed while on his way to the Klondike.

On or near August 17, all of Dawson and visiting gold buffs take a long holiday to celebrate Discovery Day, when a gold strike was made on Bonanza Creek. Festivities include a raft race on the Klondike River. Reserve ahead to be sure of a place to sleep.

Back of Dawson, from the crest of a mountain called Midnight Dome, men still look down on valleys not much changed since a muskeg settlement was the focus of the world's imagination. On June 21 you can see the midnight sun barely dip down behind the 6,000-foot Ogilvie Mountain range in the north before it rises again.

Crossing big rivers, such as the Pelly and the Stewart, on the Klondike Loop Highway, was more exciting before bridges replaced small ferries. But there is still a ferry across the Yukon River at Dawson that carries people and cars free, when the river is ice free, generally May to October. There are public campgrounds on both sides and a trailer park in Dawson.

From Dawson City, Yukon 9 is locally known as the 60-Mile Road. In the early 1900s it was a wagon road for freighting to the gold mines. The border is 67 miles from Dawson and you can't cross without going through customs. They have their hours: 9:00 A.M. to 9:00 P.M. on the Yukon side, 8:00 to 8:00, Alaska side. Allow enough time to avoid an overnight delay. There are no places to stay on the Canadian side. Moreover, it is 71 miles from Dawson City to the first facilities of any kind, including gas. You'll probably breathe a sigh of relief when you make it to Corbett's Boundary House, 4 miles beyond the border. Camping and trailer spaces, cabins, cafe, gas and oil, tubes and tires, and minor auto repairs. From Corbett's it is little more than 100 miles to Tetlin Junction, on the Alaska Highway at Milepost 1,301.

If you are interested in museum-towns, veer north from the Taylor Highway, also called "Top of the World Highway," at Jack Wade Junction (his deteriorating dredge is still there), to Eagle, a tiny village of almost 200, isolated in winter when the highway is closed by snow.

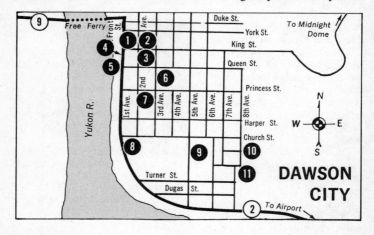

Points of Interest

1) Information Center
2) Palace Grand Theatre
3) 1901 Post Office
4) S.S. *Keno*
5) Canadian Imperial Bank of Commerce
6) Diamond Tooth Gertie's
7) Harrington's Store
8) St. Paul's Church
9) Museum
10) Robert Service's Cabin
11) Jack London's Cabin

There are gold diggings to ponder along the 163 miles, and when you get there you'll find a general store, gas, meals, and lodging, including the pioneer Eagle Roadhouse.

Fur and gold seekers, missionaries, and the Army boosted the population to 1,700 in 1898, gaining a post office. In 1901 Eagle became the first incorporated city in interior Alaska. For many years it was the main port of entry from Canada, via the Yukon River. A telegraph line from Valdez to Eagle was completed in 1903. Eagle was the seat of the first court in the Interior, established by legendary judge James Wickersham. The courthouse is one of Eagle's several museums. The Amundsen Cabin is another. Norwegian explorer Captain Roald Amundsen stayed in this house a few yards from the riverbank. He had trekked overland from his ship, frozen off Canada's Arctic shore to get to Eagle on December 6, 1905. From here he telegraphed the news that his ship, the *Gjoa* had reached Herschel Island, having navigated the Northwest Passage. Some remains of Ft. Egbert, established in 1889 and abandoned in 1901, have been restored, and original buildings preserved. Visitors can walk around the parade ground surrounded by officers' quarters and utility buildings, and see the old Mule Barn with brass nameplates for each mule. The active and eager Eagle Historical Society conducts free tours, through the museum and around town daily in summer.

North via Kluane Lake

The more direct route from the Yukon back to Alaska travels the Alaska Highway. Leaving Whitehorse and the Yukon River, the Alaska Highway moves on to Haines Junction at Mile 1,016. Here, the great pike meets the Haines Highway connecting the Interior and Inside Passage seaport Haines.

Beyond Haines Junction the country is open, with thin woods, except to the west, which is full of the St. Elias Range. Seen on a clear day is a score of pristine, soaring peaks, seemingly impenetrable. Three of the peaks are more than 16,000 feet high with the loftiest, Mt. Logan, 19,850 feet, surpassed only by Mt. McKinley, the highest mountain on the continent.

Canada's Kluane National Park is still in the planning stages, but it's bound to be a an impressive display of wildlife and scenery. Until there is road access to the Park, highway travelers will have to settle for skirting 35-mile-long Kluane Lake, the Yukon's largest. Lodges and motels, some old-timers, some new (but all modernized), and campgrounds and picnic spots are well-spaced along this beautiful lake. Spring through fall the lake trout fishing is big—some over 50 pounds. Boats and guides are for hire at several fish-oriented camps and lodges.

Watch for Dall sheep in the hills at Mile 1,060. Kluane Historical Society, at Mile 1,093, Burwash Landing, has a small but excellent museum of local artifacts. It's open summers 9:00 A.M.–9:00 P.M., and there's a small admission charge. Burwash Lodge, on the shore of Kluane Lake, has been operating since 1904.

Beaver Creek, not too long ago, consisted only of some Indian huts off the road and a lodge. Now there are motels, a trailer park, service stations, cafes, cocktail lounges, some open 24 hours, and some year-round. The post office functions on Tuesdays and Fridays; Canada Customs and Immigration office here is open 24 hours. The Alaska-Yukon Territory border is 21 miles onward. Remember you'll have to set your watch back one hour and to check in at the Port Alcan U.S. Customs and Immigration Station. It is open 24 hours a day, year-round, and everyone entering Alaska must stop.

Sixty miles northward is Northway Junction. The Northway Motel, Garage, and Café, and the well-stocked Stout's Store have most services and supplies travelers may be seeking by then, plus Indian-crafted souvenirs.

The northern end of the Klondike Loop (Taylor Highway) from Dawson joins the Alaska Highway at Tetlin Junction, Alaska, at Mile 1,301.

At Mile 1,314 is Tok (pronounced *Toke*), one of the most important junction settlements in Alaska. Anchorage is 328 miles west; Valdez is 260 miles west, then south on the Richardson Highway. Fairbanks is 206 miles north of Tok. The Alaska Department of Public Safety and hospitable Tok residents maintain the Visitor Information Center and Museum. Along with a public phone, Alaska literature and advice, they offer free coffee. It's open 7:00 A.M. to 10:00 P.M., daily during summer. Tok, as the main overland entry point to Alaska, offers several up-to-date accommodations, cafes, campgrounds, service stations, a clinic, a garage, gift shops, general stores, churches, a four-year high school, and an Alaska State Troopers Post. There are also laundromats, a movie theater, a bank, a post office, guide service, and charter flights. The settlement here is a good place to spend a night, just to get acclimated to Alaska, and to peruse Tok's hospitality helps.

Alaska's Alaska Highway

Beyond Tok, the Alaska Highway slants northeast to skirt the Alaska Range, whose 500-mile arc straddles southcentral Alaska in a tremendous display of raw power and height. The grandest peak is 20,320-foot Mt. McKinley, in Denali National Park and Preserve.

Delta Junction, at Mile 1,422, is technically the end of the Alaska Highway, with an impressive marker saying so. Here the World War

FAIRBANKS 141

II-built Alaska Highway merges with the historic Richardson, originating from gold rush port Valdez, now serving oil tankers. Together they continue to Fairbanks, commonly considered the end for and goal of Alaska Highway travelers.

There's a glowing welcome at the log-cabin information center run by the Delta Chamber of Commerce, open 9:00 A.M. to 6:00 P.M. during the summer. They sell certificates saying you have now reached the official end of the Alaska Highway. From here on to Fairbanks it merges with the Richardson Highway.

Delta Junction is the home of Ft. Greely, a U.S. Army Arctic testing and training center. This, and establishing a permanent pipeline maintenance station here, has bolstered the economy and population. Farming is coming to the fore throughout the rich Tanana River valley. Fishing lakes with pike, trout and whitefish, and many game birds and animals attract visitors, but the biggest novelty is buffalo-watching. (And eating, if you are in Delta the first Sunday in August for the Chamber of Commerce Buffalo Barbecue.) Twenty-three animals were let loose on the Big Delta game reserve in 1928, and now the bison number more than 500. They gather in groups at a saltlick across the Delta River, easily seen from the Richardson Highway about 4 miles from the Junction. They are sometimes seen along the highway and have no qualms about nonchalantly sauntering across the road. There are good tourist accommodations at Delta, and there is a public campground a mile up the highway.

At the End of the Alaska Highway: Fairbanks

Fairbanks has come a long way since 1901, when it got its start on the basis of a rumor and a boat trader's need to make a cache and "hole in" for the winter. The place he picked was here on the bank of the Chena, and the rumor concerned gold possibilities nearby. In 1902, the rumor was verified by Felix Pedro who found gold on his namesake creek. 1903 and 1904 were stampede years. Judge Wickersham moved his District Court from Eagle to the booming gold town. As a favor, boat trader E. T. Barnette named the town for the judge's friend Fairbanks, Indiana Senator, later U.S. Vice President.

Fairbanks today is Alaska's second largest community, with a city population of more than 27,000 and a trading area population (Greater Fairbanks) of more than 60,000. It is a military center, seat of the University of Alaska, a leading airway terminal, an important center of space communication from unmanned satellites, and its international airport also serves Arctic villages and oil fields of the North Slope.

The airport, newly and beautifully refurbished, made the news in 1984 as the meeting place of two famous world figures. Pope John Paul

FAIRBANKS

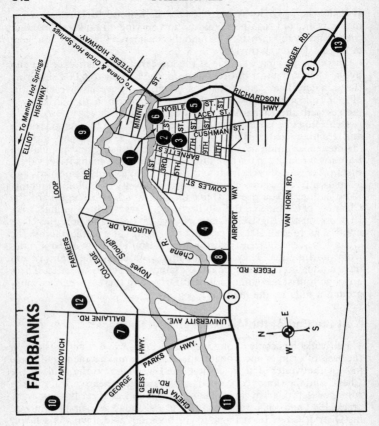

Points of Interest

1) Visitors Information Center
2) Barnette St. and "The Row"
3) City Hall
4) Main School
5) Clay St. Cemetery
6) Griffin Park
7) University of Alaska
8) Alaskaland
9) Creamer's Field Wildlife Refuge
10) Experimental & Musk Ox Farm
11) Riverboat *Discovery*
12) Fairbanks Golf & Country Club
13) Arctic Acres Golf Course

and President Reagan crossed paths there and paused to chat before continuing on their separate missions.

Young (like most Alaska cities) and weathering boom and bust, Fairbanks has been growing and building rapidly. Though generally more costly, there's almost everything here that one might look for in the same sized city in the south 49 states, including tennis, swimming, and golf at the Fairbanks Golf & Country Club, the continent's northernmost.

The signs of the past are everywhere, perpetuated in nostalgic bar decor, entertainment, small cabins overshadowed by tall buildings, and in curio shops and museums. In the environs, large dredges surrounded by piles of leftovers (tailings) are reminders of the glory days of gold mining and smelting. Mixing casually on the downtown streets are Indians, prospectors, big-game guides, homesteaders, famed scientists visiting the university, and hosts of government experts.

Summers are warm and bright. This is emphasized by the annual summer baseball game. Around midnight on the weekend of June 21, a baseball game is started—and played through to the finish without lights. People fish, hike, camp, climb, go boating, and rev up for the big Yukon "800" Riverboat Race.

It can also get cold in Fairbanks. The young people say that winter temperatures of 60 below zero (fahrenheit) are rare; more often the coldest is 40 below. But old-timers recall when for six weeks on end the thermometer never showed above 45 below, and went down to 60 below.

Life does not slow down in winter. Besides many fine cultural events, there are spectator and participant sports, indoor and outdoor: basketball, dog-sled racing, curling, ice hockey, skating, snowmobiling, and skiing (easily-accessible ski slopes are in the Fairbanks area).

Fairbanks is in the heart of the interior. It is the northern terminus of the Alaska Railroad, which extends south to seaport Seward on the Gulf of Alaska. Ft. Wainwright, a cold-weather test field, is next door to town. Eielson Air Force Base is 23 miles away.

The University of Alaska, founded in 1917, spreads out over 2,300 acres. Students from almost every state and many foreign countries attend. It is farther north than any other institution of higher learning in the world. There are more than thirty modern buildings on the main campus in Fairbanks, and branches in Alaska's two time zones. Besides the senior campuses at Juneau and Fairbanks, there are twelve community colleges and ten extension centers throughout the rest of the state. Some 28,000 residents in smaller communities and villages sign up for the assorted courses offered in their area, and almost 7,500 are enrolled at Fairbanks. That's a high percent of learners among the total population.

The university is strong in research, communications and environmental studies, striving toward developing new industries in agriculture and aquaculture, not only for Alaska, but for the world. Besides the traditional curriculum, students can study fine arts such as music and drama, with much community encouragement whenever and wherever they perform, sometimes far afield in a small Native village. More unusual subjects deal with Native heritage and language. The university's location lends itself to geophysical studies of phenomena such as the aurora borealis. And the far north offers unique recreation —dog sledding, ski touring, marathons—when people want a break from their books.

City tours include the attractive University of Alaska campus, with its surprising arrays of bright flowers in summer. The driver points out Constitution Hall where Alaska's constitutional convention was held in 1955, and the museum with its outstanding gold and pipeline exhibits. The beautiful new building has expanded its collection of thousands of items covering arts and crafts, wildlife, botany, anthropology, paleontology, and mineralogy. The aim is to interpret and put into proper perspective Alaska's natural and cultural history.

The University of Alaska's grounds are impressive and its experimental farms are outstanding. In late summer the jumbo products of garden plots can be seen on display at fairs. Many residents, too, are proud to show off their private produce plants. There are more than 400 privately owned greenhouses in Fairbanks. In the area beyond the University on Yankovich Road you'll also see the Musk Ox Farm, where they are trying to domesticate the woolly animals for greater supplies for avid weavers and knitters of the soft, warm wool.

Another nostalgic adventure is to be had out this way. Hoist a couple to the past in the Malemute Saloon at Cripple Creek Resort, once a mining camp. Head out the Parks Highway to Ester, or take the Malemute Saloon Tour offered by Gray Line. (See "Special Interest Tours" in *Practical Information for Fairbanks.*)

You are encouraged to take the free guided walking tours of Fairbank's historical downtown area. It's given twice a day during the summer, depending on the weather, and it takes about an hour and a half. Though it adds to the interest to have a guide, you can park your car in the visitor center lot at First and Cushman and use the walking tour booklet *Ghosts of the Gold Rush* and descriptive brochure to follow the route yourself.

Some highlights: Walking toward the bridge from the center, then left on Turner Street takes you near the spot picked by Captain Barnette in 1901, which was the start of the town of Fairbanks. You'll find Barnette Street a block west of Nordstrom's store, which you'll see on Second Avenue. Walk Barnette to Fourth Avenue; this is where the bawdy houses were from 1910 to 1956, an area called "The Row." At 4th and Cushman is the City Hall, and south at 8th is Main School, on the 1906 site of the first public school. From the school walk east on 8th to Clay Street. Turn left to wander through the old Fairbanks Clay Street Cemetery that has dates from the gold rush period of 1902. Come out at the other side of the cemetery on Fourth Avenue and head west for Noble Street. Follow it north to its deadend at Wendell Avenue for a stroll along the Chena through Griffin Park, before returning to the Visitor Center, via Lacey Street to 1st Avenue.

You'll want to allow plenty of time to explore Alaskaland at Airport Way and Peger Road. It was created in 1967 as the Alaska State Centennial Park, to commemorate a hundred years of American ownership. The city now maintains and operates this large, free outdoor museum of Alaskana. It is open all summer and has an information center at the main entrance. Its 44 acres provide visitors with a "mini tour" of the 49th state. Alaskaland has a gold rush town, constructed primarily from buildings that once stood in Fairbanks's downtown area, with period items in the Hensley House; a charming early church; a Pioneers' Museum; a Robert W. Service Museum; old cabins that house gift shops and artisans; the sternwheeler *Nenana,* in its prime the queen of the Tanana-Yukon fleet; the Crooked Creek and Whiskey Island narrow-gauge railroad, which carries visitors around the 44-acre park; Native Village, with examples of dwellings from all parts of Alaska; and, collected from cabins on creeks around Fairbanks, the Mining Valley section.

If you continue out on Airport Way, you can take advantage of Riverboat Sternwheeler Cruises. To paddle into the past, sign up for the *Discovery*'s 4-hour cruise on the Chena and Tanana rivers, daily during summer. The boat landing is near the airport off the Dale Road exit of Airport Way.

Bird watchers will want to go out College Road beyond Noyes Slough to a former dairy pasture (Creamer's), next to the State Department of Fish and Game Building. Thousands of birds migrate through here and feed on the barley left for them from the yearly plantings. Bring a camera with a telephoto lens and binoculars and watch for all sorts of species, including teal, mallards, Canada geese, and even the less common snow geese and other waterfowl.

PRACTICAL INFORMATION FOR FAIRBANKS

HOW TO GET THERE. By air: Fairbanks is served by several interstate and intra-Alaska carriers, some with direct flights from main cities. Consult travel agents or these for current schedules and best routings: *Alaska Airlines,* Box 68900, Sea-Tac International Airport, Seattle, WA 98168, (206) 433–3100; *Northwest Orient Airlines,* Minneapolis/St. Paul International Airport, St. Paul MN 55111, (612) 726–2362; *United Airlines,* (800) 841–8005; *Western Airlines,* Regional Sales Office, 3830 International Airport Rd., Anchorage, AK 99502, (800) 227–6105; and *Wien Airlines,* 4100 International Airport Rd., Anchorage, AK 99502, (800) 562–5222.

By car: The *Alaska Highway* will take you right to Fairbanks. The *George Parks Hwy.* is the most direct route between Anchorage and Fairbanks. See also "Hints to Motorists" in *Facts at Your Fingertips.*

By bus: Service between Whitehorse and Fairbanks via Beaver Creek and Tok is provided by *Alaskan Coachways,* 3211A Third Ave., Whitehorse, YT, Canada Y1A 1C6 or 206 Wendell St., Fairbanks, AK 99701. *Alaska-Yukon Motorcoaches* travels to Fairbanks from various Alaska cities, including Haines, Anchorage, Valdez: 349 Wrangell, Anchorage, AK 99501; or 555 4th and Battery Bldg., Seattle, WA 98121.

By rail: The *Alaska Railroad* runs between Fairbanks and Anchorage via Denali National Park and Preserve. Reservations should be made at least 2 weeks prior to intended travel date. Contact Passenger Sales Representative, Pouch 7–2111, Anchorage, AK 99510. In Fairbanks contact the depot at 280 N. Cushman. Phone 456–4155.

GETTING INTO TOWN. There are several taxi companies that can take you from the airport to downtown. Some hotels offer free transportation.

HOTELS AND MOTELS. Prices based on double occupancy are: *Deluxe,* $100 and up; *Expensive,* $80–100; *Moderate,* $60–80; *Inexpensive,* under $60.

Captain Bartlett Inn. *Deluxe.* 1411 Airport Way; (907) 452–1888; toll free (800) 544–7528 in continental U.S. 205 rooms. Spruce-log lobby, Alaska decor, and "largest fireplace in Alaska." Near Alaskaland Centennial Park. Restaurant, lounge.

Fairbanks Inn. *Deluxe.* 1521 Cushman St.; toll free Continental U.S. (800) 544–0970; in Alaska call collect 274–6631; toll free in Canada (800) 261–3330. Large, two-story motor inn, with inviting rooms. No pets. Winter plug-ins available. Dining room, cocktail lounge, beauty salon, laundry, valet service. Seasonal rates.

Golden Nugget Motel. *Deluxe.* 900 Noble St.; (907) 452–5141. Two-story motel with comfortable attractive rooms. Sauna and game room. Restaurant, cocktail lounge.

Traveler's Inn. *Deluxe.* 813 Noble St.; (907) 456–7722. Huge, multi-story motor inn, with many different types of units, some studio rooms, some suites. No pets. Coffee shop, cocktail lounge, excellent restaurant.

Golden North Motel. *Expensive.* 4888 Airport Rd.; (907) 479–6201. Near the International Airport. In-room coffee. Restaurant and cocktail lounge nearby. Seasonal rates.

Great Land Hotel. *Expensive.* 723 First Ave.; (907) 452–6661. Spacious rooms, restaurant, and bar.

Polaris Hotel. *Expensive.* 427 First Ave.; (907) 456–4456. Large hotel conveniently located in town, with restaurant and cocktail lounge.

Klondike Inn. *Moderate.* 1316 Bedrock St.; (907) 479–6241. Large rooms with kitchen facilities. Laundry, lounge, and courtesy car.

Maranatha Inn. *Moderate.* 1100 Cushman St.; (907) 452–4421. 100 rooms; full baths. No liquor, but a health bar lounge, and other good things to keep a traveler fit: indoor pool and health spa; sauna; beauty shop.

Tamarac Inn Motel. *Moderate.* 252 Minnie St.; (907) 456–6406. Smaller motel with 20 units.

Towne House Motel. *Moderate.* 1010 Cushman.; (907) 456–6687. Medium-size motel near downtown. Attended pets OK.

Alaska Motel and Apartments. *Inexpensive.* 1546 Cushman.; (907) 456–6393. Wall-to-wall carpets, kitchenettes, and laundry facilities.

Aurora Motel. *Inexpensive.* 2016 College Rd.; (907) 456–7361. Modern cabin units near university campus. Kitchenettes available at extra cost.

Cripple Creek Resort. *Inexpensive.* 10 miles out the Parks Highway at Ester.; (907) 479–2500. Recycled buildings of ghost mining camp. Open summers. Full of atmosphere. Family entertainment and fun in Malemute Saloon. Two dining rooms, one mining-camp style.

BED-AND-BREAKFASTS. For information contact: Box 74573, Fairbanks, AK 99707; (907) 452–4967. Rooms run around $25 single, $35 double, with continental breakfasts. Apartments start at $50, with help-yourself breakfasts.

YOUTH HOSTELS. *Fairbanks Youth Hostel* is a campground at Birch Hill Recreation Area, off the Steese Highway. Box 1738, Fairbanks, AK 99701. Call (907) 456–4979 or 2071 for information. Summer only.

HOW TO GET AROUND. There is daily bus service in town; no service on Sundays or on some legal holidays. Fare is $1 or 1 token for 1 zone; exact change or tokens only. Tokens are available at a variety of businesses for 75¢. Information available through a 24-hour hotline: 452–EASY, or through the Metropolitan Transit Commuter Service offices: 3175 Peger Rd., 452–6623. There are also numerous cab companies in town. Check the phone book.

TOURIST INFORMATION. The log cabin *Visitor Information Center* is at First and Cushman, next to the mileage marker that announces to drivers that they've made it to the end of the Alaska Highway. 550 First Ave., Fairbanks, AK 99701; (907) 456–5774. The information center is open 8:30 A.M.–5:00 P.M., weekdays only in winter, daily in peak season. They'll dispense information on accommodations, restaurants, and various local attractions. The Dept. of Fish & Game offices are on College Rd. and open during business hours. For hunting and fishing information call (907) 452–1525. The new *Public Lands Information Center* in the old Federal Building, 3rd and Turner, will tell you all you'll want to know about Alaska's millions of acres of public lands. Also available are movie and slide programs and even a trip-planning computer.

TOURS. The *Visitor Information Center* sponsors free guided walking tours of downtown historic district. Tours are given twice a day; call 456–5774. Tours by minibus or motorcoach can be arranged through the *Alaska Sightseeing Company,* 452–8518; *Gray Line of Fairbanks,* 456–7741; and *Royal Hyway Tours,* 456–8131. *Gold Rush Tours,* 456–5414, is locally owned and operated. They promise a personalized tour of the golden past, and a free leg garter to set your mood. *Prestige Limousine,* 479–2036, executes its custom tours in style, with chauffeur.

SPECIAL INTEREST TOURS. Narrated **riverboat cruises** take you out for 4 hours on the Chena and Tanana rivers daily during summer. The boat landing is near the airport off the Dale Rd. exit of Airport Way. For information: Riverboat Sternwheeler Cruises, Box 80610, Fairbanks, AK 99708; 479–6673.

Alaska Sightseeing, Gray Line, and Royal Hyway Tours all offer the *Malemute Saloon Tour.* $22 buys transportation, one sourdough concotion or three cheechako drinks—your choice, and keep the souvenir glass—and vaudeville show, including Robert W. Service poetry (no minors).

WILDLIFE REFUGES. *Creamer's Field* is a 2,000-acre migratory waterfowl refuge; 1300 College Rd, 452–1531. In the spring here you may see Canada geese, snow geese, mallards, pintails, shovelers, teal, and other waterfowl. There is a 2-mile nature trail; at the head of which, by the parking lot, you can pick up a descriptive brochure.

SPORTS. The *Visitor Information Center* will have information on local sports. **Baseball** fans can watch the semi-pro *Fairbanks Goldpanners* summers in Growden Stadium. The *Midnight Sun Baseball Game* is played mid-summer without artificial light.

If **curling** interests you, contact the *Fairbanks Curling Club*, 1962 2nd Ave., 452–3011. **Dog sled** demonstrations are held on summer evenings at *R&T Kennels*, on Dalton Trail off Yankovich Rd., 479–3710; and at *Mushers Hall*, 4 Mile Farmers Loop Rd., 452–6874. The *North American Dog Sled Championships* are held in March.

If you'd like to tee off and hit a few balls at the most northern **golf** courses on the North American continent, you are welcome at the *Arctic Acres Golf and Country Club*, 7 Mile Badger Rd., North Pole, 488–6978, and at the *Fairbanks Golf and Country Club* (the northernmost), Yankovich Rd., west of downtown, 479–6555.

You can watch **ice hockey, ice skating,** and other spectator sports under the dome at the *Beluga*, on the U of A campus. Call 474–7205 or 7208.

The *Big Dipper Arena*, Hez Ray Recreation Complex, 19th and Lathrop, 456–6683, offers indoor and outdoor **ice skating.**

Alaska Raft, 529 Front St., 456–1851, rents canoes and rafts for **floating** the Chena, Chatanika, or Tanana River.

There are a number of **ski** areas around Fairbanks. *Cleary Summit* is located 20 miles from town on the Steese Hwy. Overall vertical drop is 1,200 ft. Weekend skiing Nov.–May; Wednesday skiing in spring; no night skiing. Contact: Alpine Haus, 719 Second St., Fairbanks, AK 99701; 456–5520. *Skiland* is near Cleary Summit, about a mile beyond on the Steese Hwy. Overall vertical drop is 700 feet. Main slope is lighted. Open weekends Nov.–May. Write 1015 9th Ave., Fairbanks, AK 99701; 456–4518. *Ski Boot Hill* is about 10 miles from Fairbanks, 4.2 Mile Farmer's Loop Rd. Open Wed nights and weekends Nov.–May. Write 1706 Hilton, Fairbanks, AK 99701; 456–5302.

There are outdoor **tennis** courts at Hez Ray, 19th and Lathrop, 456–6683, and at the *Mary Siah Recreation Center*, 1025 14 Ave., 456–6119. For information on the *University of Alaska Courts*, call 474–7208.

THEME PARKS. *Alaskaland* is a 44-acre historic park. Here you will find authentic old buildings that were once on the streets of Fairbanks, museums, shops, food, entertainment, playgrounds, and a large picnic area. Current and classic movies are shown, and there is old-time entertainment at the

Palace Saloon. A miniature 30-guage train takes visitors for a short ride around. The park is open year-round; summer hours are 11:00 A.M. to 9:00 P.M. daily. The main park entrance is off Airport Way on Avenue of Flags between Moore St. and Peger Rd. A shuttle bus is operated between downtown Fairbanks and the park. Phone 452–4529 for additional information.

 HISTORIC SITES. Historic homes from old Fairbanks can be found in *Alaskaland* Gold Rush Town. Some have been converted into shops, others such as the *Kitty Hensley* and *Judge Wickersham houses* are furnished in turn-of-the-century objects. Also here, the *First Presbyterian Church,* constructed in 1906, and the old sternwheeler *Nenana,* now housing a restaurant. (See "Theme Parks," above.)

 MUSEUMS. The museums in *Alaskaland* (see "Theme Parks," above), are the *Pioneers of Alaska Museum,* dedicated to those who founded Fairbanks, the *Native Village Museum,* featuring Indian artifacts, and *Mininag Valley,* where gold mining equipment is on display.

The *University of Alaska Museum* houses Alaskan ethnographic and archaeological displays, wildlife exhibits, and a historical collection. Located on the west ridge of campus. Open May–Oct., 9:00 A.M.–5:00 P.M., daily, except holidays; winter hours are daily, noon to 5:00 P.M. 479–7505.

 MUSIC AND THEATER. "There is much worthy music being made at the *University of Alaska* in Fairbanks," so said a *New York Times* critic at the Alaska Music Festival where artists from the faculty of the university performed music written by Alaskans. The university sets the pace for Fairbank's theatrical productions as well. Call the theater box office: 474–7751.

Both the *Fairbanks Symphony* (479–3407) and the *Light Opera Theater* (456–1072 or 5774) present excellent productions periodically. In summer the *Alaska Association for the Arts* presents a "Time Out at Noon" concert series on Tuesdays and Thursdays at 12:15 at the Noel Wien Library Auditorium, corner of Airport and Cowles. The Association can be reached at the Alaskaland Civic Center, 456–6485, or 456–2169. The Fairbanks Concert Association has information on local music productions: 456–5952. And for a "Photosymphony" production, phone 479–2130.

SHOPPING. You'll find everything you'll need at the fine, modern shopping centers around town. There are branches of Anchorage fur stores: The *Anchorage Fur Factory* is at 121 Dunkel in Fairbanks, *Martin Victor Furs* is at 212 Lacey.

For Native crafts contact the *Alaska Native Association Arts and Crafts,* 1603 College Road. Also try these for browsing and buying: The *Alaska House and*

Alaska Art Gallery, 1003 Cushman; Eskimo ivory, soapstone, paintings by Alaskan artists. *Eskimo Museum and Gift Shop,* 7 miles from Fairbanks on Richardson Hwy.; Eskimo arts and crafts, ivory, jade, and hematite. The *Last Rush,* a trading post at 4-mile Old Steese Hwy., boasts sod-roofed cabins and mining and trapping artifacts. The *Gold Pan Trading Post,* 16th & Cushman, across from the Fairbanks Inn has a large selection of Native handicrafts and Alaska jewelry. *The Gold Mine,* 402 5th Ave., has it "by the piece or poke." Driving the "Freeway" about 14 miles south of Fairbanks at Mile 1506, it would be hard to miss Con Miller's *Santa Claus House Gift Shop* at North Pole, Alaska. It's noted for a special stamp and the volume of mail handled every Christmas!

PANNING FOR GOLD. You'll easily spot evidence of gold camp remnants in the countryside, and the monstrous dredges that are left behind. If you're interested in trying your hand at panning, *Mining Valley* at Alaskaland, Airport Way and Peger Rd., 452–4244, has the equipment and someone to show you how. Check with *Alaskan Prospectors Supply,* 504 College Rd., 452–7398, for information, especially on how not to jump someone else's claim.

 DINING OUT. A complete dinner is categorized here as follows: *Deluxe,* $30 and up; *Expensive,* $20–30; *Moderate,* $15–20; *Inexpensive,* under $15. Major credit cards are widely accepted although it's wise to call ahead and double check.

Bear and Seal Restaurant. *Deluxe.* In Travelers Inn, 8th & Noble. 456–7722. Fine food, elegant surroundings. Bar.

Sourdough Dining Room. *Deluxe.* Captain Bartlett Inn, 1411 Airport Way, near Alaskaland. 452–1888. Rustic, but elegant: warm wood finish and fireplace, with nearby Dogsled Saloon.

Lord Baranof Castle Inn. *Expensive.* On Airport Rd. at Mile 3. 479–2301. "A bit of the Old World" with specialties from Switzerland, Austria, Germany, France, Belgium, Spain, and Italy. American special is New York steaks for two, served with a bottle of champagne or sparkling burgundy. Bar.

Club 11. *Expensive to Moderate.* At Mile 11, Richardson Hwy. 488–6611. Warm atmosphere with fireside dining. Prime ribs and steaks are the specialties, also chicken and seafood.

Husky Dining Room. *Expensive to Moderate.* In Fairbanks Inn, 1521 Cushman. 456–6602. Alaskana decor features mural in copper of a husky team racing up the wall. Tasty food comes in husky-size portions. Bar adjacent.

Ivory Jack's. *Expensive to Moderate.* Goldstream Road. 455–6665. Restaurant with salad bar 2nd floor, above bar.

Mine Room. *Expensive to Moderate.* Cripple Creek Resort, at Ester, 10 miles on the Parks Highway. 479–2500. "Lodes" of atmosphere in cozy, dim mineshaft decor. Alaskan food featured. Also family bunkhouse dining in larger room, and nightly entertainment at nearby Malemute Saloon.

The Ranch Dinner House. *Expensive to Moderate.* 2223 South Cushman. 452–5660. Fine Mexican food.

Alaska Salmon Bake. *Moderate.* In the Mining Valley at Alaskaland. 452–7274. Fresh salmon, halibut, and ribs are served with salad, sourdough rolls, dessert, and beverage. Alaska fun and history in adjoining Park. A bargain—and delicious. Free transportation from all major hotels.

The Pumphouse. *Moderate.* Don't miss the atmosphere and antiques in this historic Old Chena Pumping Station on the Chena River. Now a restaurant and saloon, it's about 2 miles on the Chena Pump Road. 479–4606. They'll make you welcome whether you come by boat, float plane, car, or bicycle. (You may need a map to find the Pump Road. It takes off where the Geist Road, the Chena Ridge Road, and Highway 3 headed for McKinley come together, a short distance out of town.)

Sandbar Restaurant. *Moderate.* Nostalgic dining aboard the old river queen *Nenana,* drydocked now at Alaskaland. 452–5704. Nearby is the *Palace Saloon* with pioneer flavor and live music.

Tiki Cove. *Moderate.* At 546 3rd Ave. 452–1484. Popular downtown restaurant featuring well-cooked food, good service. Chinese and American dishes. Charming Oriental-Polynesian atmosphere.

Traveler's Inn Coffee Shop. *Moderate.* 8th and Noble. 456–7722. Open 6 A.M. to midnight.

Arctic Pancake and Dinner House. *Inexpensive.* In the Great Land Hotel, 723 1st Ave. 452–6661. Pancakes come in assorted nationalities with Alaskan sourdoughs the specialty.

H. Salt Esquire. *Inexpensive.* 1456 S. Cushman. 452–5944. For fish 'n' chips.

The Omelette Tree. *Inexpensive.* Out College Road, near the end at 1335 Hays, 479–7666. 26 delicious varieties.

Star of the North Bakery and Luncheonette. *Inexpensive.* 543 2nd. 452–4144. Good meals, and where they bake the delicious doughnuts for the sternwheeler *Discovery* cruise refreshments.

 BARS AND NIGHT LIFE. Stop in at *Club 11,* Mile 11, Richardson Hwy.; music and dancing here. Or try the *Dogsled Saloon* at the Captain Bartlett Inn, 1411 Airport Way, near Alaskaland. *Ivory Jack's* is a popular local establishment, with music; on Goldstream Rd., and the entertainment is lively in the *Senator's Saloon* at the *Chena Pump House* (see Pumphouse in "Dining Out," above). The *Malemute Saloon* at Cripple Creek Resort in Ester, 10 miles on the Parks Hwy., features ragtime piano, and readings of Robert W. Service poems by Don Pearson the proprietor. Open summers only.

Highways out of Fairbanks

Although major highways end in Fairbanks, a look at the map shows roads continuing beyond: to the east, to the west, and north to the Arctic Ocean at Prudhoe Bay.

On the brink of the Arctic, some roads lead to hot springs. These were appreciated especially by miners wintering over and waiting for spring thaws in order to begin sluicing again. Watching wildlife, rock hounding, berry-picking in season, and camping are popular along the road, open year-round, that ends 60 miles east of Fairbanks at Chena Hot Springs. Here there are 30 modern units, a restaurant, and pool. The mineral springs were first found by whites in 1907.

Northeast-bound from Fairbanks, the Steese Highway partly follows prospectors' trails. The Felix Pedro Monument stands at the site of his famed Pedro Creek Discovery Claim at Mile 16. Here, in 1902, he found gold that started the stampede to the Alaska interior. The highway passes through once popular mining country, with appropriate mementoes showing up, from remnants of ghost towns and mining sites to residue left by dredging operations—sometimes the dredge itself, rusting and idle. Eagle Summit is the highpoint where, weather permitting between June 20 and 22, there is an unobstructed view of the midnight sun. Many varieties of wildflowers add color to the wilderness vista, and caribou migrate through in fall. Most of the creeks, even the forks, have unusual names, given by miners staking claims. "Tough Luck" and "Lost" creeks could tell a story, perhaps. Mammoth Creek is named for the gigantic fossil remains of animals roaming in Alaska before the glaciers came. The Yukon River stops the Steese at the town of Circle, the northernmost point you can drive to from the continent's interconnecting highway system. Circle's Yukon Trading Post at the end of the Steese Highway is open year-round with supplies and services, including a free campground, hunting and fishing licenses for sale, a base for Sunshine Helicopters and air tours, and a bar with bush Alaska flavor.

An 8-mile branch of the road veers off to Arctic Circle Hot Springs, the "spa" farthest north in the United States—about 35 miles before Circle City. Many people fly to the springs, 136 miles from Fairbanks, to dip in the mineral waters, which are cooled down from their natural 139 degrees. Besides indulging in two warm indoor pools, an Olympic-size outdoor one, and hot mineral baths, guests also explore gold rush sites near the Yukon River, pan for gold, and in mid-June watch the midnight sun. At these springs, first seen by whites in 1893, there are cabins, a trailer and camper park, a cocktail lounge, and fine dining room. A dinner treat is the home-grown produce. Water piped underground from the hot springs encourages the growth of magnificent and tasty vegetables.

Fort Yukon

About 55 miles northwest of Circle City, Fort Yukon lies just above the Arctic Circle, the invisible arc that marks the end of the Frigid Zone at latitude 66° 33 minutes north. Air North flies daily guided tours from Fairbanks in summer, and each passenger receives an "Official Arctic Circle Certificate" as a souvenir of the crossing.

The 2,081-mile Yukon River, cutting an arc to reach the Bering Sea, makes its northernmost bend above the Arctic Circle. Here, where the great stream expands to a width of three miles, stands this log cabin Athabascan Indian village of about 500, or perhaps fewer. Today, even though its population has dwindled in the past two decades, it is the largest Indian village on the Yukon. Although it is above the Arctic Circle—and the post office does a thriving tourist business for that reason—summers are mild, sometimes quite warm. The mercury has climbed close to 100 degrees here—some people say it has actually hit 100—but winter temperatures have gone down to 78 below zero. The 24-hour summer sunshine occasions 10-foot sunflowers and giant strawberries. In winter there are several days when the sun never gets above the horizon.

Athabascan women engage in handicrafts, such as elaborate beadwork. A prized example is an intricately beaded white moosehide altar cover, displayed in a log church, one of many historic buildings dating from 19th-century Hudson's Company trading days when the fort was the farthest westerly outpost. Grave markers in Fort Yukon Cemetery date back to 1868. On display in the Dinjii Zhuu Enjit Museum are collections relating to life and culture of the people of the Yukon Flats. Fur trapping and fishing, in which fish wheels are used to catch salmon, are main occupations. The town has a lot of malamutes, which pull wheel-equipped sleds for summer tourists, and are used in winter, despite snowmobiles, to pull residents' runner sleds.

The Elliott Highway and the "Haul Road"

The Elliott Highway is gravel, well maintained, but tricky when wet and while pulling a trailer. It shares traffic from Fairbanks with the North Slope Haul Road to just beyond the small village of Livengood, a mining town founded about 1915. Then the Elliott heads southwest. At Mile 110, a side road leads 12 miles to the relocated Indian settlement, Minto. Manley Hot Springs, almost 50 miles farther on, was a booming trade town for the mining area in the early 1900s. Now the Manley Roadhouse, old-fashioned hospitality with family-style meals and small museum, and the Trading Post—cabins, store, gas—survive at Mile 157, the end of the highway. The hot springs, with temperatures as high as 136 degrees Fahrenheit, are on a hillside just below the entrance to town. A public campground is near the bridge.

Summer adventurers, willing to share the dust and jarring washboard surface of the poorly maintained "Haul Road" with an increasing number of trucks, may drive as far as Disaster Creek, Mile 210.

They'll see the pipeline as it passes under the highway, and parallels it on high ridges. There are sweeping views as it snakes over hills and disappears into hollows. Approaching the Yukon River, a 5-mile rough gravel road leads to a campground with a boat launching area on the river bank. Beyond the Yukon at Coldfoot, Mile 173, car travelers can share services offered by the "World's Farthest North Truck Stop."

From Disaster Creek Turnaround point, only permit holders may continue on through the spectacular scenery of the Brooks Mountain Range to Prudhoe Bay. Whether to open those last 205 miles to the public and what to do about facilities is one problem the state of Alaska faces. Conservationists argue against opening it, citing cost of maintenance, difficulty of guarding the pipeline, and patrolling such a wilderness road, potential damage to the delicate ecology and to the isolated villages. Meanwhile the road has an official name, the James Dalton Highway, after an Arctic oil exploration pioneer, but a good guess is that its "popular" one will be hard to change.

Day Trips from Fairbanks

Fairbanks residents ride the Alaska Railroad for one-day outings, particularly to Nenana, on the Tanana River, and to Denali National Park. Nenana, a modernized Athabascan village of about 500, offers photographers fish wheels and an ancient cemetery. However, the village is best known for the Nenana Ice Classic. Thousands of Alaskans and Yukoners bet on the exact day, hour, and minute of the ice breakup on the river in the spring, with $100,000 or so in cash going to the lucky winners.

The all-paved George Parks Highway, with many tourist facilities, is the most direct road now connecting Fairbanks and Anchorage. The 370-mile route traverses rugged and beautiful terrain with a bonus. It passes right by the portal of Denali National Park, very convenient for rewarding stopovers. Before this highway was completed in 1971, the only access to the park (except for the railroad) was a long drive via the summer-only, gravel Denali Highway. The Denali veers west from the Richardson Highway at Paxson, south of Delta Junction, and 133 miles later joins the George Parks Highway near the park entrance.

Denali National Park and Preserve

The highlight of Alaska's interior, North America's loftiest peak, has been accustomed to the limelight over the years. It was revered by the Indians, admired by English and Russian explorers, and has been tackled by mountain climbers beginning with three sourdoughs. They missed the true summit in 1910, but another party made it in 1913.

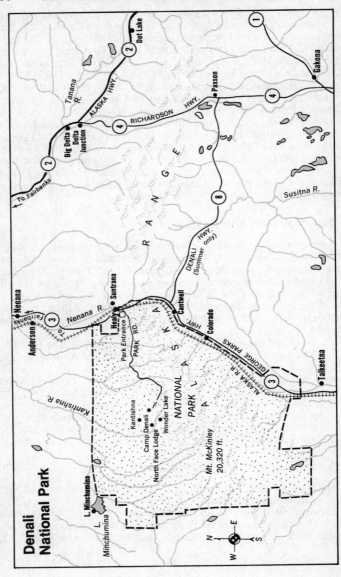

Denali
National Park

Many climbing parties have followed, some making the news because of success, many others because of disaster. In 1979, a successful ascent was made by dog team!

But the most important developments since the large area was reserved and set aside for nature lovers as Mount McKinley National Park in 1917 lie with the expansion and use of wilderness areas here and throughout the state. And there are some who would change the name of the mountain back to its original one. The Indians, who were in awe of the massive snowy peak, called it Denali, meaning "The High One," or "The Great One."

In December 1978, under the 1906 Antiquities Act, President Carter added about 6,094 square miles to Mt. McKinley's 3,030 square miles. Yellowstone was still our oldest, but no longer our largest, national park. Denali National Monument, was expanded to include spectacular scenic areas such as Cathedral Spires, a group of several mile-high geological formations, and also to include all of the Mount McKinley massif which lay outside the former boundary. Another major goal was to preserve ecosystems, leaving undisturbed the calving and migrating territory of the caribou, the domain of the wolf and the grizzly bear, as well as the many lakes that are nesting areas for myriad waterfowl, including the endangered trumpeter swan.

Those able to hike into the back country wilderness from the end of the Park Road or from the George Parks Highway (#3) may use it. To fish, they'll need a license; otherwise the rules are similar to those for the national park. Future developments under discussion are a visitor center and hotel in adjacent Denali State Park.

Everyone agrees that nowhere in Alaska are wild animals better seen in their native habitat than here. More than 130 varieties of birds have been counted in the park; almost 40 species of mammals dwell here, including caribou, moose, bear (grizzly and black), Canada lynx, red fox, Dall sheep, porcupine, and beaver. In late June, caribou assemble on the tundra plains, and early in July the herds, sometimes numbering thousands, begin their annual migration northward to summer ranges.

The forests along the streams in the lower valleys consist of aspen, willow, birch, and black and white spruce. The tundra is a mosaic of alpine shrubs, fireweed, lichens and mosses, monkshood, and lupines. Wildflowers seem to pop up almost everywhere. Waterfowl splash in the ponds, shore birds wing furtively from roost to roost, song birds fill the air.

Some say the best time to see the park, for sheer beauty, is in late August. The trees and tundra flame scarlet and orange, russet and pink, yellow and gold. This incredible tapestry burns with rage for a few days or two weeks at most. Then, quickly, overnight, a frost sets in, and the fire is extinguished. A few weeks later the park hotel boards its windows and closes its doors, the tourists depart, and the long winter sets in. Not everyone leaves then, however. Rangers patrol the park using the sturdy dog teams and sleds that summer visitors saw during demonstrations at Park Headquarters. Winter enthusiasts bent on mountaineering or cross-country skiing can use dog power, too. Denali Dog Tours and Denali Wilderness Treks offer tours and gear-hauling services.

The great attraction of the park is, of course, Mt. McKinley. Its main (south) summit is 20,320 feet high; its north summit, 19,470 feet in elevation. The closest approach to the mountain from the park road is 26 miles, but the space seems to enlarge rather than diminish it. Most summer visitors are not inspired to climb this grand peak and prefer admiring it whenever it reveals itself.

A shuttle bus transports sightseers and recreationers deep into the park. Controlled traffic—in fact very little traffic since private vehicle travel has been replaced by the wilderness shuttle—has increased the possibilities of animal sightings. Some animal counts made a few years ago, and since the shuttle was started, show that visitors have been seeing moose and caribou on over 90% of the shuttle trips into the park. Grizzly bear haunt certain favorite areas, and the sighting of Dall sheep is practically guaranteed. An eight-hour tour, to Eielson Visitor Center, begins through spruce woods. At 2,500-foot elevation the road rises above the timber line. Eight miles from the hotel, one sees the first view of Mt. McKinley. The view from Stony Hill Overlook, 61 miles from the hotel, is dramatic. Though much of the time the mountain may be shrouded by fog or clouds, the chance of seeing all or part of it at any time—even by moonlight—is well worth the gamble.

At Eielson Visitor Center there is a head-on view of Muldrow Glacier, largest northward-flowing glacier in Alaska, which stretches between the twin peaks of the mountain the Indians considered high enough to be the home of the sun. From Eielson, 65 miles into the park, the Denali Park Road continues 20 miles past Wonder Lake, North Face Lodge, and a short distance farther, high on the ridge above, the mountain's namesake, wilderness Camp Denali.

Be advised that in line with their policy of conservation and protection, park authorities warn that anything is subject to change, if they determine it's necessary.

South of Denali Park, the Alaska Railroad and the George Parks Highway (#3) parallel each other much of the distance. They pass through towns of Willow, Wasilla, and Palmer, skirting the Matanuska Valley as they continue to Anchorage.

Another Route from Tok

Instead of traveling north from Tok on the Alaska Highway to Fairbanks, you can travel southwest, along the 125-mile Tok Cutoff, which joins the Richardson Highway at Gakona Junction. There are adequately spaced and well-equipped commercial campgrounds and roadside attractions along this route, such as the Mentasta Athabascan Gift Shop & Store Co-op, Inc., with Native arts and crafts, plus birch-bark items, mukluks, and beaded work. There is also a campground with fireplaces, laundromat, and groceries. The Indians live 6 miles away, but nearby they have built a model of an Indian village to show how it was in the old days.

At Mile 65 a side road leads 46 miles to the old Nabesna Gold Mine, no longer operative, but interesting to see. There are many spectacular views en route, the fishing is good in lakes and streams, but the road may be only fair. Twenty-eight miles up the road to Nabesna is Sports-men's Paradise, a lodge open June to November. Here are sandwiches, gas, fishing, boating.

Onward to Gakona Junction and the meeting of the Gakona and Copper rivers, the scene includes panoramas of the Copper River Valley and the Wrangell Mountains, including 16,237-foot Mt. Sanford and 12,010-foot Mt. Drum. The Richardson and Glenn highways merge here and continue together for the next 14 miles.

Two miles below Gakona Junction is Gulkana, founded in 1903 as a U.S. Army Signal Corps telegraph station. Twelve miles farther, at Mile 139, is the South Junction of the Glenn and Richardson highways. This was the only junction before the Glenn Highway was extended to Tok. Here the highways separate near the town of Glennallen, named for two army officers who were active in mapping the Copper River region. The Richardson continues south to Valdez. The Glenn Highway heads almost due west to Palmer, then follows along the Knik Arm of Cook Inlet to Anchorage.

Beyond the junction the Glenn Highway enters a vast plateau. Back of it are legendary fishing streams that can be reached only by pontoon-equipped planes; from the highway it is possible to see small herds of caribou and an occasional grizzly or black bear. Dall sheep may also come into view. If you tramp into the bush, you may see muskrat and beaver.

The 187-mile road from Glennallen to Anchorage passes streams, forests, wildflower fields and homesteads, lakes, particularly Tolsona, mountain views, such as 17,400-foot Mt. Foraker, and glaciers, includ-ing Tazlina and the Matanuska—one of the oldest and largest in Alas-ka. Its state public campground is at Mile 101 and trails lead along the bluff overlook, a great vantage point for taking photographs. At Glacier Park Resort, Mile 102 (Box 4–2615, Anchorage, AK 99509; [907] 745–2534) you can rent a motel room, or hook up your trailer, and then walk on the mighty Matanuska.

Fifty-four miles from Glacier Park is Palmer, the hub of the Matanuska Valley. It was here that farmers and mechanics from the Middle West arrived in the 1930s, bent on developing agriculture. Very few of the original colonists are still around. But the rich soil of the Matanuska Valley has been productive, and Palmer today is the state's leading farming center, the only one (so far) that is based almost entirely on agriculture. The Matanuska is renowned for its giants—cabbages up to 60 pounds, turnips more than 7 pounds, and Alaska-sized potatoes. They are exhibited at the Alaska State Fair, held annually; 11 days before, and ending on, Labor Day. Matanuska Valley museums at Palmer and Wasilla have early farm tools utilized by first Matanuska Valley colonists as well as arts and crafts of the area. Knik, 14 miles southwest of Wasilla, boasts the Sled Dog Mushers Hall of Fame. Although the Glenn Highway slices through the valley, at the base of the Chugach Mountains, the panorama is best seen by a short drive from Palmer to Wasilla. If the state capital is moved from Juneau, between here and nearby Willow is the chosen site.

Palmer has excellent tourist facilities as well as a city camping park, which can accommodate 40 trailers and 50 campers.

From Glennallen to Palmer there are so many places to camp, obtain automobile services and products, find cafes and lodgings that it seems unnecessary to detail them. From Palmer to Anchorage there is even a greater density of tourist facilities. In the 48 miles between Palmer and Anchorage there is something, it seems, just about every mile. About 15 miles out of Palmer, en route to Anchorage, is the University of Alaska Matanuska Farm, better known in these parts simply as the "Experimental Farm." Corn has been raised here with good results, perhaps indicating a new crop for the valley. A model dairy herd, almost pampered by the agronomists, is for public viewing as well as experimentation. On a summer day the farm is never free of tourists; considering how little publicity it seeks, it gets a lot of visitors. Free tours are given May–Sept., 8:00 A.M.–4:30 P.M. Call 745–3257. Photographers will be interested in the "Family Gardens," where colorful vegetables and flowers form a vivid foreground for the white-clad Chugach Mountains.

On to "Swiss Alaska" via the Richardson Highway

On the Richardson Highway, beyond South Junction, the scenery gets even better. The highway rises to glacier-draped mountain heights

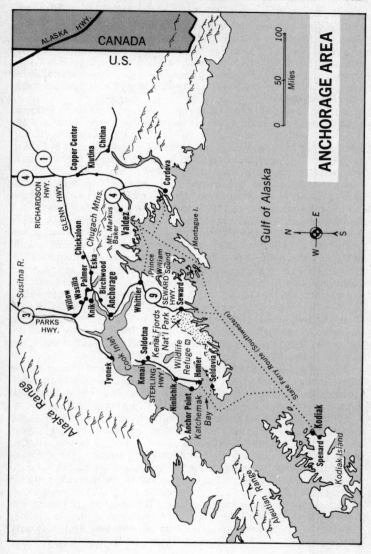

ANCHORAGE AREA

before it drops down to the sea-level delights of Valdez in its alplike setting. Car travelers and motorcoach tours stop to look and photograph impressive views from 2,771-foot Thompson Pass. They drive up to the icy tongue of the Worthington Glacier that almost licks the highway. Some walk the short path to where they can set foot on the mighty river of ice. The route passes through green, waterfall-laced valleys and claustrophobically narrow Keystone Canyon before reaching oilport Valdez.

The road to Valdez parallels an army telegraph line built in 1900 and a trail used by feverish argonauts to reach the Yukon River and the Klondike gold diggings. Now it also parallels the southern portion of the 800-mile pipeline which starts at Prudhoe Bay and ends at Valdez. You'll see the pipeline, from time to time, snaking over the hills, hugging mountains, fording streams and rivers. Accommodations along the way are not only diverse, but interesting. One of the fanciest is The Ahtna, at the Richardson and Glenn Highways Junction, built with local funds from the "People of the Copper River." In contrast is the long-established Copper Center Lodge and Trading Post, still in use, modernized, serving excellent meals, and with cocktail lounge and curio shop. The lodge started as a roadhouse during the Yukon Gold Rush and was the first hostelry in the Copper River Valley, in 1896. Before 1900 there were hundreds of log cabins in and near Copper Valley, built by argonauts who arrived exhausted after crossing the treacherous Valdez Glacier. Many of the men perished from scurvy and frostbite, and a large number returned to Valdez, where they took boat passage back to the States. Only a few indomitable souls remained in the valley, enough to start a post office in 1901. Scarcely one of the log cabins or descendants of the early miner-settlers remains today, but Copper Valley has the "feel" of being rich in tradition.

The informal possibilities for eating, sleeping, and recreating are often spectacular in this vast wilderness area. State waysides and campgrounds are situated to make the best of the rugged, spread-out mountains, the Wrangell Range, and then the Chugach Mountains.

Willow Lake, 5 miles farther, mirrors the lofty peaks of the Wrangell Mountains. Two miles on there is a picnic wayside, affording superb views of the 100-mile-long, 60-mile-wide Wrangell Range. At this point, if you are an imaginative soul, you might think of the Wrangell Range as holding fast in its glacier wildness a mysterious and untamed Shangri-la. Get off the road a dozen miles or so and you may confront grizzly bears, black bears, moose, mountain goats, Dall sheep, beavers, muskrats, ptarmigan, and spruce grouse. If you get lost in season, you can stay alive on fat blueberries and lowbush cranberries; in summer the streams are thick with salmon. There's good fishing, including tasty grayling, at Squirrel Creek Campground.

Near here is a side road leading to Chitina, 33 miles off, on the Edgerton Highway. There is some colorful, rugged scenery along this road, with grand views of the Copper River Valley and of very interesting geologic formations. The first 19 miles are paved and after that the road is gravel. About 24 miles from the junction there is a state public campground at the foot of Liberty Falls. Chitina, a former mining town, is now a supply base for the farms and tiny hamlets of the area. Chitina Cache Store has groceries, hardware, and supplies for anglers; fine salmon fishing in summer and many lakes with grayling. Chitina Saloon has cold drinks and live music on Saturday and Sunday nights. If you want to hear some backcountry music in a real down-to-earth atmosphere, this is the place. Less than a mile from Chitina is a small Indian village, with an old log church. In the three miles to O'Brien Creek there are several spots for do-it-yourself camping. An ancient railroad trestle at the creek will excite photographers.

Along the Richardson Highway there'll be lodges located at fishing rivers: Tonsina Lodge (Mile 79, see "Copper Center Hotels and Motels" in *Practical Information,* below), Tiekel River Lodge (Mile 56; [907] 822–3259), Tsaina Lodge (Mile 34.5; [907] 835–2414)—all generous with information. Besides stores for supplies and gas, there are gift shops with intriguing names: The Grizzly, The Aurora, and Serendipity.

Above-timberline favorites are the campground right at the Worthington Glacier, and Blueberry Lake Wayside, near Thompson Pass. Thompson Pass forms an eastern anchor of the Chugach Range, with Anchorage at the western end. The area is a wonderland of alpine wildflowers—so don't be in a hurry to leave. The structures you see below, as you start to descend the pass, are the remains of an old mining camp and roadhouse. There are, in the next 11 miles, especially in narrow Keystone Canyon, a number of historical markers, waterfalls, and waysides. The highway spans the terminal moraine and milky glacial streams of the Valdez Glacier and a mile later enters the site of Old Valdez, which was so damaged by the Good Friday earthquake of 1964 that the town was relocated several miles to the west of the former townsite. At the entrance to the new town you can park at a turnout and, if you come in August and early September, stroll across the road to see pink and silver salmon spawning.

"Valdez Please"

Valdez, pronounced to rhyme with *please,* has twice—in 1964 and 1981—been named one of the 10 "All American Cities." The honor was given the city's 4,000 community-minded residents by the National Municipal League's Citizen Action Awards program. The city has also been labeled the "Switzerland of Alaska," because of its location near the head of a fjord, surrounded by alplike snowy peaks. Evidence of its gold rush and early seafaring days are in the Valdez Museum. Today the friendly town is a key gateway to camping grounds in the Chugach National Forest. There are enough photographic possibilities in the mountains, fjords, woods, and lakes to fill a book.

Some main attractions are the excellent fishing, cruises to Columbia Glacier, and the tanker ships at the terminal, loading and leaving with oil for refineries to the south. The ice-free year-round port is busy, and especially so in the summer. Make reservations ahead, if not camping, or on a tour.

From Valdez you can take a state ferry to Cordova, Whittier, or Seward.

Cordova, named by Spanish explorer Fidalgo, flourished as the rail port for the Kennecott Copper Mines until they shut down in 1938. Now the town lives off the sea, packing and processing a large percentage of diversified seafood in its modern canneries. Petroleum explorations in the area have raised high hopes for development of oil-related industries. The 1964 Good Friday earthquake lifted the area about seven feet, changing its face and harbor, but not the superb surrounding scenery. Eyak Lake, Cordova, is held fast by mountains never entirely free of snow, and it is a popular winter sports area. Summer recreation includes swimming in the town pool and camping and hiking in the surrounding Chugach National Forest. However, the Chugach National Forest is more than trees; explore the Chugach's watery domain with its sea birds and marine mammals.

Crossing Prince William Sound

State ferries, *Bartlett* and *Tustumena;* cruise ships *Cunard Princess, North Star, Rhapsody,* and *Sagafjord;* and private and charter boats cross between Whittier and Valdez. The *Glacier Queen* round trips in summer with 5½-hour (one way) excursions and longer cruise/tour packages. Contact Columbia Glacier Cruises, 547 W. 4th, in Anchorage. The route is part of the Alaska Marine Highway System which cuts through the Chugach National Forest here, past the land administered by the Forest Service under the U.S. Department of Agriculture. The ferry crossing takes about seven hours and allows a leisurely inspection of sea life and one of the largest of Alaska's tidewater glaciers, the Columbia. Ships approach the face, pause awhile, and are usually rewarded with an ice fall. About half the Columbia's face is visible from the deck of a ship entering the bay. Visitors see 2½ miles of sheer cliff rising 160 to 260 feet above sea level. They say ice may extend down as deep as 2,300 feet in some places.

As glaciers go, this is an active one, flowing seaward about 6 feet a day, faster in summer than in winter, and often calving icebergs from its face. The beautiful deep blue color, most intense on cloudy days where a chunk has just broken off, is caused by reflection and refraction from the highly compressed ice crystals. Like prisms, they break sunlight into all the colors, but reflect back mostly a splendid "glacier blue."

Various forms of food—microscopic animal and plant life and plankton flourishing among the debris carried by the glacier—attract larger feeders to the glacier's face. The naturalist aboard the ferry who interprets the prolific sea life here and throughout the crossing, is often an enthusiastic young college student majoring in forest and wildlife subjects.

Everyone watches for whales, of course. The kind most likely to show in comparatively shallow Prince William Sound are the black-and-white, dorsal-finned killer whales, which are actually the largest of the dolphin family. The small (up to 30 feet) Minke whale is often seen. The humpback whale (up to 50 feet) is seen occasionally, as is the gray whale, especially during late spring.

You can practically count on seeing porpoises. The Dall porpoise is playful, and small schools often follow alongside ships and play in the bow waves. The shy harbor porpoise avoids ships, but watch for them where tidal currents meet or in tide rips. Harbor seals abound, especially around the Columbia Glacier. Ships sneak up on seals sunning on ice cakes so that passengers can try for photos. If you see a small mammal floating on its back, flippers up, possibly carrying a little one on its chest, it is probably a sea otter, once hunted almost to extinction. Protected by the Fur Seal Treaty of 1911, it has recovered and is now about 30,000 in number, mostly in this area.

The Sound is definitely for the birds. Marbled murrelets are the ones you'll see the most of, followed by black-legged kittiwakes, tufted puffins, and glaucous gulls, according to the minimum estimate by the Bureau of Sport Fisheries. Other colorful ones are black oystercatchers, murres, and the spectacular chestnut-colored, blue-and-white-plumed harlequin duck.

The environment is so engrossing that it seems no time at all before the ferry docks at Whittier.

Whittier

With its two almost-skyscrapers, seaport Whittier looks as if it should be a booming community. This was a busy seaport base during World War II, and those gaunt, mostly empty buildings against the mountains once held a self-contained military community of Army men and their families. They housed offices, clinic, people, stores, recreational facilities—a whole city. Now there is a small boat harbor by the docks, and Whittier is the vacation home of some thirty or forty people from Anchorage. They claim it is an excellent base for fishing and other outdoor recreation.

Most visitors in transit spend only enough time here to board the train, which also carries vehicles. The trip from Whittier to Portage takes about half an hour, and you won't see a great deal. The first tunnel is 2½ miles long, and the second is 1 mile. Between them you get an idea of the size of the mountain barrier and glimpses of the Portage Glacier. Those with their own transportation drive onto the railroad flatcars; those on tour hop aboard the waiting motorcoach and ride to where the train stops and lets vehicles off at Portage. Then they are driven north along fjord-like Turnagain Arm to Anchorage.

Exploring South of Anchorage

Car travelers and tours bent on exploring the large wilderness areas to the south reached by road and ferry head out the Anchorage–Seward Highway. The highway and the Alaska Railroad parallel Turnagain Arm as far as Portage, and it's beautiful all the way. Mt. Alyeska Ski Resort and the Portage Glacier, an hour's drive from Anchorage, are probably the most popular tourist attractions in the area. Along the side road to the Portage Glacier Recreation Area, there are easily seen salmon spawning areas. From the parking area, there are clear views across Portage Lake with floating blue-white icebergs to the glacier, 2½ miles distant. The Visitor Center here interprets the area and schedules nature walks. It's open Memorial to Labor Day. For information contact Anchorage Ranger District, Chugach National Forest (Box 10–469, Anchorage 99511, [907] 345–5700). Besides campgrounds and picnic sites, there is a day lodge with dining rooms, bar and gift shop. Scenic raft adventures are also available, leaving from the visitor center, from June to September.

Ten miles beyond the Portage Glacier Recreation Area turnoff is Turnagain Pass, a popular winter recreation area for cross-country skiers and, in recent years, snowmobilers. Twelve miles farther there is a meeting with a road coming in from (or leading out to) Hope, 16½ miles off. A pioneer mining settlement on the Upper Cook Inlet, Hope is still alive, with about 90 year-round residents. It is a summer retreat for some Anchorage people. Porcupine Forest Service Campground is about two miles past Hope.

Nineteen miles past the meeting with the Hope Road, Alaska 1 forks. The left fork, which continues to Seward, becomes Alaska 9. The right fork is designated as Alaska 1. Thirty-eight miles beyond the fork the highway from Anchorage, now Alaska 9, reaches its end at Seward.

Seward

An important port nestled at the foot of the Chugach Mountains, Seward was badly damaged by the big earthquake, but it has been rebuilt. The population of Greater Seward is under 3,000. It is the southernmost terminus of the Alaska Railroad and home port for the state ferry M/V *Tustumena.* On the opposite side of the Kenai Peninsula from the city of Kenai, Seward is a favorite vacation area for sports fishermen from Anchorage, who come to Resurrection Bay to try for salmon and sea bass. Founded in 1903 as a sea (and later railroad) terminal and supply center for the Alaska Railroad, Seward is today considered to be one of the best-equipped and most favorably sited cargo ports and fishing harbors in the North American West. Fishermen may have their catches canned, smoked, or frozen by firms in the city.

Seward is very conscious of the 1964 earthquake. A slide show, "Seward Is Burning," shown at 2:00 P.M. in the Seward Community Library illustrates the damage done by the Good Friday tremor. Other short slide and sound shows are shown on request. Paintings by prominent Alaskan artists, together with Russian icons, are exhibited at the library. Photographs of the big quake are on display at the State and City Office Building at Fifth Avenue and Adams Street, around the corner from the library. A museum in the building's basement holds artifacts of the white pioneers as well as Aleut-made baskets. Continue down Adams Street to Second Avenue and the 1906 St. Peter's Episcopal Church. A painting done in 1925 of the Resurrection, with an Alaska background and motif, hangs here. Travel up Second Avenue, turn right on Jefferson Street, and you'll have reached the Information Cache, in the old railroad car "Seward."

The city has two municipal campgrounds, open May through October 15. Thousands come to Seward on July 4 to see the annual Mt. Marathon Race, to the top of 3,022-foot Mt. Marathon and back. Started in 1909 as a wager between two sourdoughs, the race begins and ends in downtown Seward. The 1981 record is 43 minutes and 21 seconds. Hikers go at a slower pace up a well-marked trail for the view of Resurrection Bay. The Silver Salmon Derby starts the second Saturday in August and runs 8½ days of round-the-clock fishing for more than $100,000 in cash and merchandise prizes. Charter planes fly to Harding Ice Cap, one of the world's largest icefields. Excursion boats explore Resurrection Bay's bird rookeries and come close to a Steller sea lion colony. Hospitable and eager, Seward boasts that it provides "the best and largest camper, trailer, and boat parking facilities in Alaska."

Seward is also a gateway to visiting a portion of the spectacular Kenai Fjords National Park, established in 1980. The Exit Glacier, one of 34-plus glaciers spawned by the amazing Harding Icefield in the Kenai Mountains is now easily accessible. Drive an 8-mile gravel road, park, then cross the Resurrection River on a footbridge and hike an easy mile-and-a-half trail to the visitor center. Here there are exhibits and slide shows. Then it's another half mile to the glacier's edge and the towering pinnacles of ice.

From Memorial Day to Labor Day, the ranger/naturalist interprets the area, and ranger-led hikes and campfires are scheduled on weekends. At Exit Glacier, periodic shuttle bus service is provided especially for senior citizens and the handicapped, running from the bridge toward the glacier, so that everyone may share this glacier experience.

From Seward you can take a state ferry to Kodiak, Port Lions, Seldovia, Homer, Valdez, and Cordova.

Continuing to Explore the Kenai Peninsula

To reach the north side of the Kenai Peninsula, return 38 miles to the forks and turn left, onto Alaska 1, the Sterling Highway. This area has boomed with oil and natural gas exploration and development, and it is popular for recreation and for fishing and hunting. Fishermen line the Russian River during salmon and trout runs. The Kenai-Russian River campground next to the Sportsman's Lodge is starting point for Alaska Campout Adventures floating the Kenai River to Skilak Lake.

The town of Soldotna was established in the 1940s. In its strategic location where the Sterling Highway and the Kenai Spur Road meet, it grew to first-class city status by 1967. It's name, in case you are wondering, was taken from a nearby stream, Soldotna Creek. Some say "soldotna" was from the Russian for "soldier"; others believe it's from the Athabascan Indian word meaning "stream fork."

Though sportfishing is a main attraction in the nearby Kenai River, what they boast of most in the area are the opportunities for recreation in the Kenai National Wildlife Refuge. Among the most popular activities are hiking, canoeing, camping, driving scenic roads within the refuge, and taking pictures. Visit the new visitor center, considered the finest of its kind in Alaska, in the Kenai National Wildlife Headquarters, and they'll fill you in on all the possibilities. To get there, go south through Soldotna, turn left after crossing the Kenai River Bridge, and follow the signs to the headquarters, just off Ski Hill Road (about a mile south of Soldotna).

The Center, open daily, is manned by enthusiastic volunteer hosts and hostesses. They dispense informative free pamphlets, and books and posters are for sale. Specimens of the area's wildlife are mounted in action poses, and you can tune in to wildlife sounds. How about loons calling across a lake or wolves howling in a moonlight display? They show wildlife movies in the theater on weekends; at other times individuals can choose from a list of subjects to view on a small screen. And few can resist the hands-on display.

Drive 11 miles down the Kenai Spur Road to reach Kenai, the largest city on the Kenai Peninsula. Its urban population is some 6,000, and its greater city population (meaning the environs added to the city) is about 17,000.

Kenai

One of the oldest permanent settlements in Alaska, Kenai, on Cook Inlet, was founded by the Russians in 1791. The oldest of the Russian Orthodox churches—Russian Orthodox Church of the Assumption of the Virgin Mary—was built in 1896 and its replica built before 1900 is still in use. But basically Kenai is a very modern community. Discovery of oil and natural gas in the late 1950s turned Kenai from a sleepy village into a swift-paced community. From a scenic outlook in "Old Kenai" you can see, from late spring until autumn, large pods of beluga whales scouring for food fish. They'll be surfacing at the mouth of the Kenai River. The 80-acre Kenai City Park accommodates small pickups and campers.

Everyone in the Greater Kenai Chamber of Commerce is keen on travel to the town of Kenai and the rest of the big peninsula. You'll know it as soon as you step inside their headquarters and information center in "Moosemeat John's" cabin off the Kenai Spur road in mid-Kenai. They'll ply you with maps, literature, and advice, all most useful. They also have rental tour tapes on hand for walking or driving around Old Kenai, and a Black Gold driving tour of the industrial section.

Down Main Street from Moosemeat John's is the Olde Town Gallery, which displays the work of Kenai Peninsula artists.

A visit to Kenai may also include a trip to Fort Kenay Museum at Mission and Overland avenues, across from the Russian church. The displays here include artifacts dating back to the town's origins: primitive tools, mining equipment, Russian icons.

Beyond Kenai the road continues for 27 miles, to Captain Cook State Recreation Area. They are working toward 250 campsites, varying from wooded to beach areas, the delight of rock hounds and beachcombers. Between Kenai and the recreation area, on the shore of Upper

Cook Inlet, there are some thrilling overlooks of Cook Inlet including panoramas of two volcanic peaks, 10,116-foot Mt. Iliamna and 10,197-foot Mt. Redoubt.

The highway passes through moose country, and you'll likely see some in the Kenai National Moose Range. In 1941, this big area was set aside to protect the stamping grounds of moose that grow to giant size on the Kenai. The Kalifonsky Beach Road runs two miles to Kasilof, founded by the Russians in 1786. The Indian fishing village that followed is gone now, and the population scattered, but an old log schoolhouse by the road displays artifacts.

Russian traders founded Ninilchik on fur farming and fish in 1820. Among the area population of 450 are several of their descendants, many Russian-speaking. Antique log homes, fishing shacks and a Russian church high on the hill are reminders of the town's Russian-American beginnings. Ninilchik State Campground may lack water, but the beach has clams and fishing is good.

The Anchor River attracts silver, king salmon, rainbow and steelhead fishermen. The Anchor Point road ends at the beach where a marker informs that this is the most westerly point accessible by continuous road system on the North American continent. During the peak fishing times, the campgrounds will be overflowing, especially at the river mouth. The well-situated Anchor River Inn features the latest fishing information among its many services.

Homer's at the End of the Road

The Sterling Highway gives up at the tip of an almost 5-mile-long finger of land extending into fjordlike Kachemak Bay, the Homer Spit. In summer, much of the town of Homer's activity is based on the salt chuck surrounding Homer Spit, where there is a small boat harbor, ferry and big ship docks, bars, hotel, campground, and beaches. Step into the Waterfront Bar, a fishermen's favorite, with gusty nautical color, or the Salty Dawg Saloon, which has old-fashioned atmosphere plus wonderful views of boats and glaciers. Fishermen cast for trout and salmon from the shore. Campers beachcomb, and "live off the land" by digging clams or catching fresh crab for supper. Delectable seafood is sold in the dock shops and served in the restaurants.

Bird and sea life flourishes among Kachemak Bay's islands, fjords, glaciers, and even volcanoes. St. Augustine on its island 70 miles away across Cook Inlet sometimes entertains with an impromptu "sound and light" show when it erupts. Bay excursions leave from the Homer Spit dock, and the skipper may zero in on seabird nesting islands, lift shrimp and crab pots (traps), pick up and let off campers at Kachemak Bay

State Park, across the Bay, and stop at Halibut Cove, once a thriving fishing town, and now home of several artists.

In the latter 18th century, about the time of the American Revolution, Russian explorers and trappers were paying calls near Homer, even before Captain Cook sailed by. Homer was founded in the spring of 1896, and given the first name of the head man of the first industry there, gold mining. Next came coal mining, followed by the growth of fishing—all kinds—and its satellite industries; farming, including a short-lived fox farming try; and homesteading. Exploratory offshore oil well drilling near Homer in Lower Cook Inlet may turn up an oily future. At present, tourism is a mainstay.

Homer's residents are unusually artistic, probably inspired by the matchless scenic surroundings. Their works are displayed in several galleries and studios, and visitors are welcome. Drop by the Homer Artists Gallery and the 8 × 10 Art Studio, landscaped with native plants and flowers, in town on Pioneer Avenue. The log cabin is full of art and the artist is full of wildflower information. About 12 miles from town is the secluded studio of a long-time respected resident artist, Norman Lowell.

Alaska Wild Berry Products, also on Pioneer Avenue, has a taster's stand in summer, and their kitchens and gift shop, preparing and selling unique berry and sea food packages, are open year-round. The Pratt Museum, off Pioneer Avenue on Bartlett Street, is sponsored by the Homer Society of Natural History. Besides pioneer, Russian and Indian, and sea otter displays, they've added a saltwater aquarium, holding sea life from Kachemak Bay.

Sightseeing excursions follow the Skyline Drive along the rim of the green and flowering bluffs rising behind Homer. They pass original homesteads, many now with modern (and luxurious) log buildings, and pause at views of the Grewingk Glacier, one of many spawned by the Harding Ice Fields just across the bay.

For close-up views, air taxis and helicopters fly out of Homer. Maritime Helicopters hover over volcanic Augustine Island, McNeil River noted for fishing (by people *and* bears), the Barren Islands and Lower Cook Inlet for spotting whales, seals, and porpoises. Homer Air taxi charters fly around the rookeries, islands and fjords of Kachemak Bay. If you are interested in small isolated towns across the bay from Homer, they arrange for sightseeing layovers in English Bay, Port Graham and Seldovia, none of them accessible by road.

Homer, a leisurely day's drive from Anchorage, is a popular weekend destination for Alaskans. Visitors from "outside" fly in from Anchorage for one day, or longer, package tours, and there is bus and ferry service, between some points on the Kenai.

Seldovia

Seldovia seems to retain the charm of an earlier Alaska, perhaps because of its isolation. No roads reach there, only small planes and boats, and state ferries of the Southwest Alaska Marine Highway System. The town's Russian flavoring shows in its onion-domed church and its name, derived from the Russian place name which translated "herring bay." Visiting fishermen use lots of that small fish for bait. With it they catch record salmon and halibut and king and Dungeness crab. They find the fishing good whether dropping lines in the deep water of Kachemak Bay, or casting into the surf for silver salmon while standing on the shore of Outside Beach, near town. But the serious fishing is commercial and large scale, beginning with netting and continuing through the processing in the big Wakefield operation.

Crossing to Kodiak

From Homer, ferries serving the Gulf of Alaska head across a stretch of the Pacific Ocean to the town of Kodiak on Kodiak Island, the largest of a group bordering Shelikof Strait, which leads up to Cook Inlet. Across the Strait are the lofty volcanoes of the Alaska Peninsula.

The waters between the mainland and Kodiak Island are not always calm; indeed, they are at times as turbulent as any waters off the Alaska coast. In giant swells the *Tustumena* pitches, yaws, and rolls, and passengers who rush out on deck to look at the angry sea are stung by salt spray and buffeted by ruthless winds. Still, the scenery is itself worth the voyage. The spooky Barren Islands, the mystic-looking head of Marmot Cape, the broken hills of Afognak Island, and the sunsets, blazing as though the whole world were on fire, give the passage an odd, arresting beauty.

The only other way to get to Kodiak, unless you have your own boat or are signed up with one in the large fishing fleet working out of Kodiak Harbor, is to fly. Alaska Aeronautical, MarkAir, and Wien Airlines fly to Kodiak from Anchorage. Kodiak Western Airlines serves Kodiak on a charter basis and remote areas by scheduled amphibian aircraft. By careful planning and timing you might be able to combine some tours and flights to see the Katmai, Kodiak, and Homer —three choice wilderness areas—before returning to the big city.

Kodiak is a great place for a short course in Russian-American history. It all began here, almost 200 years ago. On tour or on your own, you'll be well exposed to the island's scenic and historic landmarks, with the accent on Russian-American history.

The first Russian settlement, in 1784, was at Three Saints Bay, near present Kodiak, which dates from 1792. The town's heyday was at the turn of the 18th century, when it was headquarters for the rich fur trade, and governed by Alexander Baranof. (He later moved the capital of then Russian America to Sitka.)

The Kodiak colonists hewed and carved Russian-style wooden homes and built ships from plentiful Sitka spruce. They fired bricks and ground grain shipped from Russian settlements in California. Returning ships also carried back ice for bars and restaurants and bells for California missions and Russian Orthodox churches. The iron and brass bells were cast in Kodiak's busy large foundry.

Kodiak's Holy Resurrection Church parish was established in 1794 by Father Herman, one of the original missionary monks. He came from St. Petersburg (now Leningrad) via Siberia by small wooden ship in 1793. In 1970 he was canonized here, Alaska's—and North America's—first saint of the Russian Orthodox Church. Inside the church, thrice rebuilt after disasters, but always in the original style, there are valuable icons and some treasures of St. Herman, also called the "Fisherman's Saint." Among them are the cross and heavy chain he wore to show his love for God.

The one building left from 1793, said to be the oldest wooden structure on the West Coast of the United States, is the Baranof Museum with antique Russian samovars and trays, seal-oil candles, handcrafted silver jewelry, and handwoven Aleut basketry. Some items may be for sale. Portions of the original log walls, chinked with moss, show inside. On the lawn outside is a millstone used by the early Russians.

The Russian American era ended with the Purchase of Alaska by the United States in 1867. For the next 70 years Kodiak plugged along as a fishing town, visited by Baptist missionaries in 1886, and covered by volcanic ash in 1912, when a volcano 100 miles away blew its top. The town boomed when the World War II Naval Base was established at Fort Abercrombie, 8 miles from town. The fort is now a National Historical Site with a campground. There are leftover bunkers here from when Kodiak was "home" for 25,000 troops and was heavily fortified.

Some scenic drives radiate out from town to many attractive, though mostly unimproved, campspots along bays and coves and a fossil beach. A road winds to the summit of 1400 Pillar Mountain, and a view of Kodiak, Shelikof Straits, the distant peninsula, and many more archipelago-like, lush, green islands.

From the size of the harbor and the number of boats, it's obvious that fishing is the main industry of this town of 5,000 people, 700 or so of whom are native Aleuts, mixed with Russians and Scandinavians. The fishing boats and hardy crews brave the stormy Gulf of Alaska and the moody Aleutian Islands.

Kodiak was the greatest loser in the 1964 earthquake, when seventy people died. The tidal waves that followed swept away the whole business district, tossing big fishing boats from their moorings far inland.

Now a rebuilt downtown with fine shopping mall and the boat harbor attract tourists and photographers. The waterfront, lined with marine suppliers and other fish-oriented businesses, plus the assorted fishboat traffic, keeps them snapping. Norman's has photo supplies plus a large choice of ivory carvings, gold nuggets and furs. Don't be misled by Solly's Office; it's a restaurant and bar with country rock music. For atmosphere, stop in and bend an elbow at the dock-side B & B Bar. It stands for Beer and Booze, and the place is a popular fisherman's hangout.

Besides fish and its Russian American background, Kodiak claims two giants, one on land, the other in the sea. The Kodiak brown bear, weighing up to 1,200 pounds, is the largest carnivore on earth and is a prized hunter's trophy. King crab may spread 4 feet or more, pincer to pincer. You can meet up with this sea monster in one of 15 seafood processing plants, or at lunch or dinner along with other seasonal Kodiak specialties: shrimp, halibut, salmon, and tasty local scallops.

If you want to pursue a Brownie, or other game animals for trophies or photos, allow time to arrange for an expert guide. Bear harvesting and hunting areas are closely regulated for preservation. Otherwise, if you want to bear-watch or take photos, charter planes fly to salmon streams where bears gather to fatten up on fish. Other flightseeing tours take tourists over Afognak and Raspberry Islands where elk graze, and around the Barren Islands, home of seals and sea lions.

Every August, Kodiak puts on Frank Brink's "Cry of the Wild Ram" at the Frank Brink Amphitheater at Monashka Bay. Out-of-doors, rain or shine, the historic drama about Baranof goes on, so dress for the occasion accordingly.

Celebrations come often in this lusty fishing town. Notable ones are the three-day early May King Crab Festival with crab races, St. Herman's Day on August 9, the Jaycee Rodeo in mid-August, and the facetious Great Buskin River Raft Race, usually in mid-June. Five beer (or grapefruit-juice) breaks are written into the rules.

Kodiak National Wildlife Refuge

The same Alaska Land Act, adopted in December 1980 to enlarge and preserve Denali National Park, enlarged the Kodiak National Wildlife Refuge. Most people think of Kodiak bears in connection with this almost two-million-acre refuge, but it is also the natural habitat of abundant other wildlife, some of it transplanted there in the 1920s. The red squirrel, Dall sheep, blacktail deer, mountain goat, beaver, snowshoe hare and muskrat are doing well along with the natives: land otters, brown bats, red fox, tundra vole, and weasels. Offshore is the domain of seals, whales, sea otters, and porpoises.

The refuge is also for the birds—in great numbers. Waterfowl like the shallows and marshes along the 800-mile coastline of the refuge. In winter, among the common ones are various ducks and geese and some twenty seabird species. Bald eagles are commonly seen nesting in cottonwood trees or high on the cliffs and pinnacles along the shore.

But the Kodiak bears, starting life at less than a pound and weighing 1,200 full grown, are the main attraction. They are readily seen in July and August feeding along salmon spawning streams. Local airlines make charter flightseeing trips to the area, and tales of incidents involving these impressive beasts flow freely (and are often exaggerated).

It's also possible to use one of twelve free recreation cabins within the Refuge for up to seven days. The catch is that reservations are determined by drawings in January, April, July and October. What's left over is on a first-come, first-served basis. Good idea to learn all you can about the area—especially bear facts—before you go.

PRACTICAL INFORMATION FOR
SOUTHCENTRAL AND INTERIOR ALASKA

 HOW TO GET THERE. By air: Anchorage and Fairbanks, main cities of Southcentral and the Interior, respectively, are served by carriers flying direct from gateway cities in the lower 49 states and abroad. (See *Practical Information for Anchorage* and for *Fairbanks.*) Kodiak is served by Wien Airlines and interstate carriers, also flying to other towns and "bush" operations.

By car: The *Alaska Highway* is kept open the year-round, but most of the traffic is from May to September. It's a 1,529-mile stretch from Dawson Creek, British Columbia, to Fairbanks, if you pass up the opportunity to head east on the Glenn Highway that leads to Southcentral and Anchorage. The various access routes necessary in order to reach the start of the Alaska Highway at Mile 0, Dawson Creek, easily add another thousand miles. Some 900 miles through the Yukon Territory are good, wide, graded gravel. The paving starts at the Alaska border. Maintenance is difficult due to annual freezing and thawing; the pavement may be rough in spots. Take it easy and allow more time for Alaskan miles.

The alternative to driving the whole distance is to con⊥ect with the *Southeastern Alaska Marine Highway System* ferry ports at Prince Rupert, BC, and at Haines and Skagway in Alaska—all with road access to the Alaska Highway.

By bus: *Canadian Coachways,* 222 First Avenue Southwest, Calgary, AB Canada T2P 0A6, to Whitehorse, YT; on to Fairbanks via *Alaskan Coachways,* 2157 2nd Ave., Whitehorse, YT, Canada Y1A 1C6. Also look into the routes of *Alaska-Yukon Motorcoaches,* 349 Wrangell, Anchorage, AK 99501; (907) 275–1305 or 555 4th & Battery Bldg., Seattle, WA 98121; (206) 682–4104; and *White Pass & Yukon Motorcoaches,* P.O. Box 100479, Anchorage AK 99510; (907) 277–5581, toll-free (800) 544–2206.

By rail: Alaskans are excited about having bought their railroad, an important transportation link stretching from Fairbanks to tidewater port Seward on the Kenai Peninsula. They plan to use it to expand industries such as agriculture, mining, and tourism. Besides the run between Anchorage and Fairbanks, there is passenger service south of Anchorage to Portage, on Turnagain Arm. A spur running between Portage and seaport Whittier shuttles passengers and vehicles cruising or ferrying across Prince William Sound to or from Valdez. Charters for large parties to events not served by regular trains—to Seward for the Salmon Derby or 4th of July Marathon, for example—are also possible. *Tour Alaska,* 2555 76th S.W., Mercer Island, WA 98040; (206) 236–1592 or (800) 835–8907 toll free, reserves three 60-passenger vintage luxury dome cars for their Midnight Sun Express tour groups riding the rails between Anchorage and Fairbanks. Others may purchase tickets on a limited, space-available basis. Food and beverages are served in dining cars aboard the trains. Young high school hosts and hostesses, trained in railroad and Alaska lore, answer questions and point out sites of interest along the way during the 12-hour trip. For reservations, winter schedules, and other information write Pouch 7–2111, Anchorage 99510. In Fairbanks contact the depot at 280 North Cushman, 99701.

CLIMATE AND WHAT TO WEAR. In the Southcentral and Gulf of Alaska regions, winter relinquishes its hold to capricious spring late in April, so prepare for changeable weather and dress in layers you can add or peel off as needed. Overshoes, hat, gloves, and an all-purpose coat will come in handy. During summer the temperature average is in the middle 60s. Be prepared with a sweater for cooler evenings, though they are long and light. During this area's spectacularly colorful fall—golden trees, blue skies—light wool shirts, slacks, and pants are ideal. Though temperatures are rarely extreme in winter, they can range the Fahrenheit scale from the 30s to 15° below zero. Bring appropriate dress for whatever outdoor activities attract you as participant or spectator—perhaps skiing, snowmobiling, or skating.

The Interior offers surprises, particularly those hot summer days in Fairbanks when the temperature sometimes tops 90° F. Lightweight clothes feel best, but if you are heading for wilderness areas such as Denali National Park, take a coat or jacket. Spring weather is changeable and cool, as is autumn, when everyone wants to be out enjoying nature's fall color and wildlife display. Bring warm layers of clothing you can adapt as needed, including long underwear, plus stocking cap, earmuffs, wool socks, gloves and overmitts, and warm boots. Winter is cold. On top of the warm layers, add a winter coat or down jacket.

 HOTELS AND MOTELS. Sometimes taking "potluck" leads to unexpected pleasures, whether it's a place to stay or a place to eat. This is especially true of the smaller communities explored outside of Anchorage and Fairbanks. The state's free *Vacation Planner* lists accommodations of all kinds (though without recommendation). It's a help for those who like to travel independently without being tied down to a rigid schedule requiring advance reservations.

The following (alphabetically) are some Fodor editors' choices, bolstered by comments of those who've tried them, and qualified by this advice: Approaching day's end, keep an eye out for promising-looking places, and don't be trepid about inquiring. If they are full, the proprietors will know about other possibilities in the vicinity.

What you'll pay for lodging will depend on the local prices. Generally, they'll be *Moderate,* according to the following categories, based on double occupancy. *Expensive:* $80–100; *Moderate:* $60–80, *Inexpensive:* below $60.

ANCHOR PT.
(Zip Code 99556)

Anchor River Inn. *Moderate.* At Mile 156.9 Sterling Hwy., Anchor Pt.; (907) 235–8531, 16 miles north of Homer. Motel with food and lounge. Home-made baked goods and R.V. hookups. Great fishing on the Anchor River.

ARCTIC CIRCLE HOT SPRINGS
(Zip Code 99730)

Arctic Circle Hot Springs Resort. *Moderate.* Write to the Resort, Box 69, Central; (907) 520–5113. Lodge with newly renovated rooms, cabins, swimming. Over 50 operating gold mines nearby.

CHENA HOT SPRINGS
(Zip Code 99701)

Chena Hot Springs. *Expensive.* 60 miles from Fairbanks on Chena Hot Springs Rd. Write: Drawer 25, 1919 Lathrop St., Fairbanks; (907) 452–7867. Rent rooms or cabins here and enjoy the natural hot water pool. Picnicking, volleyball, hiking in summer; downhill skiing, ice skating in winter.

COPPER CENTER
(Zip Code 99573)

Copper Center Lodge. *Moderate.* Write: Copper Center; (907) 822–3245. Built during the 1897–98 gold rush, this is on the National Register of Historic Places. Dining room and cocktail lounge.

Tonsina Lodge. *Moderate.* Write SRA 152–A, Tonsina AK; (907) 822–3206. Cafe and Mangey Moose Saloon and Cantina.

CORDOVA
(Zip Code 99574)

Prince William Motel. *Moderate.* Box 848, Cordova; (907) 424–3201. Sixteen units in downtown Cordova, with café and cocktail lounge. TV.

Reluctant Fisherman. *Moderate.* Forty rooms, some with views. Coffee shop, restaurant, bar with live entertainment. Hunting and fishing trips. By boat harbor. Box 150, Cordova; (907) 424–3272.

DELTA JUNCTION
(Zip Code 99737)

Evergreen Inn. *Moderate.* Mile 266 Richardson Highway, across from Tourist Information Center. Box 485, Delta Junction; (907) 895–4666. 24-hour restaurant plus nightclub. Photo and flightseeing tours; guided hunting and fishing trips.

Kelly's Motel. *Moderate.* Junction of Richardson and Alaska Highways. Box 827, Delta Junction; (907) 895–4667 or 4973. Quiet, clean, open all year.

DENALI NATIONAL PARK AND PRESERVE
(Zip Code 99755)

Denali National Park Hotel. *Expensive.* At McKinley Station of Alaska Railroad. Denali National Park and Preserve; (907) 683–2215. Open summers with a variety of accommodations—even some renovated railroad cars. Snack shop, saloon, dining room, gift shop. Hiking, nature walks, wildlife tours available.

McKinley Chalets. *Expensive.* Outside the park, but not far from the entrance. Denali National Park and Preserve; (907) 683–2215. 120 attractive suites overlooking Nenana River. A new, growing resort, noted for fine food prepared by an expert chef. Gift shops and lounge; open end of May–Sept.

Mt. McKinley Village. *Expensive.* About 6 miles from park entrance. Box 66, Denali National Park and Preserve; (907) 683–2265. 50-room hotel open mid-May–late Sept. Restaurant, service station, "Village Pub."

Denali Cabins. *Moderate.* 231 Parks Hwy., overlooking Nenana River. Box 427, Denali National Park and Preserve; (907) 683–2234; after April 15: 683–2643. New private cabins, bathouse with hot tub.

McKinley Wilderness Lodge. *Moderate.* 12 miles south of the park, along Carlo Creek. Box 85, Denali National Park and Preserve; (907) 683–2277. Supper club in main building serving daily, 6:00–10:00 P.M., Mid-May–mid-Sept.

GLENN & RICHARDSON HIGHWAY JUNCTIONS

Ahtna Lodge. *Expensive.* Box 88, Glennallen, Ak 99588; (907) 822–3288. Locally owned by "People of the Copper River." 30 rooms, restaurant, bar, gift shop.

Gakona Lodge and Trading Post. *Moderate.* Near Gakona, Mile 2, Tok Cutoff. Box 101, Gakona, AK 99586; (907) 822–3482. Historic, rustic log building houses the *Carriage House Restaurant* and *Trapper's Den Bar.* They sell natural foods, plus much more at the Post.

HOMER
(Zip Code 99603)

Baycrest Motel. *Moderate.* Three miles from town center, Box 2447, Homer; (907) 235–8716. 12 units, some with kitchens and a suite with fireplace. Great mountain-water view.

Best Western Bidarka Inn. *Moderate.* Mile 172, on Kachemak Bay in Homer. Box 1408, Homer; (907) 235–8148. Restaurant, lounge, 46 units, kitchenettes.

Driftwood Inn. *Moderate.* 135 Bunnell, Homer; (907) 235–8019. Close to all; a block from the beach. Halibut fishing charters; car rentals.

Heritage Hotel. *Moderate.* 147 E. Pioneer Ave., Box 2447, Homer; (907) 235–7787. 46-room log hotel in downtown area is landmark, recently expanded and renovated. Some kitchenettes, open year-round. A favorite with Alaskans. Cafe next door.

KENAI
(Zip Code 99611)

Katmai Pines Lodge. *Moderate.* Spur Hwy. and Main St., Kenai; (907) 283–4846. 34 rooms with private baths, telephones and TVs. Yellow Rose Restaurant, open 6 A.M. to midnight; live entertainment nightly.

Kenai Merit Inn. *Moderate.* 260 S. Willow, Kenai; 283–7566. 60-room, two-story motel, centrally located (half mile from airport); courtesy car pickup. TV, 24-hour direct-dial phones. Coffee shop, dining room, bar.

Uptown Motel. *Moderate.* Box 1886, downtown Kenai; 283–3660. 52 rooms, all conveniences and room service. 30,000-year-old Woolly Mammoth Tusk among displays. V.I.P. Lounge and Restaurant.

Harborview Hotel. *Inexpensive.* Box 4133, Kenai; (907) 283–4133. 13 comfortable rooms. Coffee shop and dining room, and banquet facilities for 60, but shared baths, and without telephones or TVs—enjoy the view, instead.

KODIAK
(Zip Code 99615)

Kodiak Sheffield House. *Expensive.* 234 S. Benson; 486–5712. Across from fascinating fishing boat harbor. 90 rooms and suites. Regional giant, Kodiak Bear (stuffed) on display. Coffee shop, dining room, bar.

Buskin River Inn. *Moderate.* State Airport, 487–2700. 51 rooms; new in 1985. Lounge, restaurant (local seafood, freshest available).

Shelikof Lodge. *Moderate.* Overlooking town and harbor at 211 Thorsheim Ave., Kodiak; (907) 486–4141. Recently remodeled two-story building downtown. Restaurant and cocktail lounge. Alaskan artifacts featured in gift shop.

Kodiak Star Motel. *Inexpensive.* 119 Brooklyn Terrace, Box 553, Kodiak; (907) 486–5657. 26 rooms, some with kitchenettes. Laundry facilities.

MANLEY HOT SPRINGS
(Zip Code 99756)

Manley Roadhouse. *Moderate.* Elliott Hwy., Manley Hot Springs; (907) 672–3161. Rooms, bar, and "grub." Historic and prehistoric objects are displayed.

SEWARD
(Zip Code 99664)

Breeze Inn. *Moderate-Expensive.* Downtown, at small boat harbor Box 935, Seward; (907) 224–5237. Lounge and restaurant.

Marina Motel. *Moderate.* Box 1134, Seward; (907) 224–5518.

Murphy's Motel. *Moderate.* 4th and D streets, Box 736, Seward; (907) 224–5650. 11 units overlooking Resurrection Bay. TV, coffee in all rooms. Near small-boat harbor.

New Seward Hotel and Gift Shop. *Moderate.* Box 675, Seward; (907) 224–5211. Handy to bus and ferry terminals. Round-the-clock courtesy coffee. Half a block to food and drink.

Van Gilder Hotel. *Inexpensive.* Box 775, Seward; (907) 224–3079. Seward's oldest hotel, with vintage look, old-fashioned charm and hospitality, and view of lovely Resurrection Bay.

SOLDOTNA
(Zip Code 99669)

International Hotel. *Moderate.* At Mile 95, Sterling Hwy. Box 910, Soldotna; (907) 262–4451. Two-story motor inn on Kenai River. Comfortable rooms, attractive furnishings. TV. Direct-dial phones. Fishing (license required). Bar; *Riverside House* restaurant specializes in steaks and Alaska seafoods.

Soldotna Inn. *Moderate.* At Kenai Jct. Box 565, Soldotna; (907) 262–9169. This motel offers units with private baths, some kitchenettes. Restaurant and lounge. Free TV and coffee.

Bunk House Inn. *Inexpensive.* 44701 Sterling Hwy. Box 3100, Soldotna; (907) 262–4584. Twenty pleasant rooms, TV, radio, restaurant, lounge

TOK
(Zip Code 99780)

Tundra Lodge. *Expensive to Moderate.* At Mile 1315, Box 336, Tok; (907) 883–2291. 45 new deluxe rooms bring the total to 78. Large restaurant, separate cocktail lounge, gift store, liquor store, and laundromat. KOA campground also remodeled and enlarged to 54 sites—full hookup, many drive-thru sites. Tenting area with fire pits. Campground facilities: shower house, car/truck wash, sanitary dump, and ice machines. Tundra Lodge and KOA are the largest, most modern on the Alaska Highway between Whitehorse and Fairbanks.

Golden Bear Motel. *Moderate.* Glenn Hwy., ¼ mi. S of jct. Alaska Hwy., Box 276, Tok; (907) 883–2561. 44 units; 8 rustic log. With private baths, kitchenettes or full kitchens. Coin laundry. Gift shop. Campground, trailer park, and free picnic area. Small wildlife museum. Open year-round. Gold panning; free Alaskan movies nightly in summer.

Tok Lodge. *Moderate.* Box 135, Tok; (907) 883–2851. 28 rooms with bath. Restaurant serves hearty Alaskan meals. Bar, game room, liquor store.

Alaska North Motel & Campground. (Formerly Young's.) *Moderate.* Mile 1313.3 Alaska Hwy. (Box 508); 883–5555. Near Husky Lounge and liquor store. Laundromat next to lounge makes it easy to do your wash while imbibing or eating at nearby restaurant.

VALDEZ
(Zip Code 99686)

Lamplighter Hotel. *Expensive.* 208 Egan Dr., Valdez; (907) 835–4485. 50 rooms, restaurant, bar. Close to shopping.

Sheffield House. *Expensive.* Box 468, Valdez. Toll-free continental U.S. (800) 426–0600; in Alaska, call collect 274–6631; in Canada, Zenith 06003. 100 units with full baths and showers. Dining room and bar. Marina, dock, boat and motor rentals. Fishing tackle & bait shop. Daily custom smoking and canning service. No pets. At Valdez's small-boat harbor.

Totem Inn. *Moderate.* Richardson Hwy. and Meals Ave. Box 648, Valdez; (907) 835–4443 Alaskan touches in lobby include mounted wild game and cheery fireplace. Restaurant and lounge.

Valdez Motel. *Moderate.* Box 65, Valdez; (907) 835–4444. With assorted singles, doubles, and family units among its 27 rooms. Restaurant. Features "Pipeline Club."

Village Inn. *Moderate.* Downtown near waterfront. Box 365, Valdez; (907) 835–4445. 60 new rooms; 21 cottages with kitchen. *Gay Nineties* lounge and restaurant. Children, pets O.K.

WHITTIER
(Zip Code 99693)

Sportsman's Inn. *Expensive to Moderate.* Box 698, Whittier; (907) 472–2352. Boasts it's Alaska's largest seaside resort, for it faces on Prince William Sound. Restaurant, bar.

YOUTH HOSTELS. See also *Facts at Your Fingertips.* In **Delta Junction:** North of town on Tanana Loop Rd., about a mile to a right turn on the Tanana Loop extension, then left on a dirt road to the hostel; (907) 895–4627. Open Memorial Day through Labor Day.

In **Homer:** On Pioneer Ave., Box 3366, Homer, AK 99603; (907) 235–6711. A dormitory for 30 with community room and kitchen; women's dorm upstairs; men's down. Breakfast included in AYH member charge of $7.50; nonmembers $9.50.

CAMPING AND CABINS. There are numerous campgrounds, public and private, in the Southcentral and Interior regions of Alaska. (See "Camping" in *Facts at Your Fingertips* for addresses of federal and state agencies offering camping facilities.)

The U.S. Forest Service maintains campgrounds and cabins in the national forests, including **Chugach National Forest.** Some may charge $3 or $4 per night. Remote area cabins reached by trail, boat, or plane are a bargain at $10 per night per party. Flights to the well-equipped cabins on fishing water may run about $200 per hour (rising fuel costs make prices unpredictable), up to 5 persons in a small plane. Reserve ahead. Write: Chugach National Forest, Cabin Reservations, Box 10–469, Anchorage, AK 99511.

You may find a campground space problem in **Denali National Park and Preserve,** even though there are several campgrounds within it. Write for camping information: Superintendent, Box 9, Denali National Park and Preserve, AK 99755; (907) 683–2294. For cabin information: Gary Kroll, Box 427, Denali National Park and Preserve, AK 99755; (907) 683–2643 or 2234.

Don't overlook the Bureau of Land Management campgrounds (mostly free) and their 3 cabins (with fee), in the **Fairbanks area** and on the **Gulf of Alaska.** Write: BLM District Office, Box 1150, Fairbanks, AK 99701.

Some campgrounds worth noting: in **Homer:** *Homer Spit Campground.* $9 a vehicle, up to 6 people; $12 for electric hookups. Hot showers extra. Open May–Sept.; no reservations. Visitor information; fishing gear rentals. On Homer Spit; phone (907) 235–8206.

Near **Kenai:** is the *Scenic View Camper Park.* It's on the bluff overlooking the ocean—a great view of Cook Inlet, volcanoes, and oil platforms. A path leads to the beach. Full hookups, 20 spaces, showers and laundromat. Drive through Kenai and out 7 miles on the North Road and you'll see them on the bluff. Write Rt. 1, Box 205, Kenai, AK 99611; (907) 283–3369.

See also "State Parks," "National Forests, Parks and Preserves," later in this *Practical Information.*

WILDERNESS LODGES. The lodges included here are a sampling of places tried and declared worthy by some Alaska travelers and by wilderness enthusiasts with assorted interests. The State's Travel Directory (see "Tourist Information Services," *Facts at Your Fingertips*) lists many more, alphabetically, and by region. You can drive to some, but most can be reached only by air and water.

Perhaps your travel agent has brochures and can make a recommendation. See also "Tours," in *Facts at Your Fingertips.* Or write the following for information to help you make up your mind. If your main interest is fishing, some of the best lodges and resorts with sportfishing packages are rounded up by *Alaska Sportfishing Packages,* (206) 382–1051 or (800) 426–0603. At any rate, be sure to make advance reservations for the lodge of your choice, for space may be limited.

Denali National Park and Preserve. *Camp Denali* is about 90 miles into the park, in the midst of alpine and sub-Arctic terrain. Its primitive facilities are more than offset by its surroundings, a friendly staff of enthusiastic, nature-minded young people, and the owners, whose individual attention leads toward an in-depth wilderness experience. June through August, the camp offers week-long Sourdough Vacations and Wilderness Workshops. They're all-inclusive: lodging, nutritious meals, guiding, interpretive programs, recreational equipment, and transportation round-trip from McKinley Station, a most enlightening and photo-worthy drive. Write Camp Denali, P.O. Box 67, Denali National Park, AK 99755. Phone in winter (907) 683–2302; in summer (907) 683–2290. *North Face Lodge,* surrounded by the park, near Wonder Lake, has regular plumbing and offers complete wilderness packages including meals and transfers for one or two nights. These mini-vacations in the wilderness are in connection with *Mt. McKinley Village.* (See "Hotels and Motels," above.) For information for North Face write Box 66, Denali National Park, AK 99755; (907) 683–2265.

Kenai Peninsula. Across Kachemak Bay from Homer, the *Kachemak Bay Wilderness Lodge,* China Poot Bay, Homer, AK 99603, (907) 239–8910, is open year-round and reached only by boat or floatplane. From about $2,000 for 5- to 10-day packages: meals, cabin, and all activities, including sauna. *Land's End Resort,* (Box 273, Homer, AK 99603; (907) 235–8900 or 8119) in a fascinating location at the tip of almost 5-mile-long Homer Spit, has just had a million-and-a-half dollar renovation. It's handy to downtown Homer and to large runs of king and silver salmon and super-sized halibut caught in deep, mountain-and-glacier-bordered Kachemak Bay. The extraordinary saltwater fishing, beach exploring, bird watching, crabbing, clamming, and shrimping make this a fast-growing recreational area. Near the tip of the peninsula is *Willard's Moose Camp* on Caribou Lake, SRA Box 28; Homer, AK 99603, 235–8830. A master guide and outfitter leads hunts for moose, Dall sheep, caribou, goat, elk, and bear, and there is assorted outdoor recreation around the camp's lodge and cabins.

Nabesna. *Sportsmen's Paradise Lodge* is Mile 28 Nabesna Rd. Bar, sandwiches. Photography and sportfishing for grayling. Write the lodge, Gakona, AK; (907) 822–3316.

Soldotna. *Sportsman's Lodge* is on the Kenai River at the confluence of the Russian River, Mile 55, Sterling Hwy., Cooper Landing, AK 99572; (907) 595-1294. Cabins and campgrounds here; river float trips, and many conveniences, including a grocery store.

HOW TO GET AROUND. By air: They still rely heavily on air transportation here, despite the ease of road travel. The state has the world's highest ratio of licensed pilots. There are more than 150 air-taxi and contract-carrier lines operating in the state, including those of the famed bush pilots, who offer dependable transportation to isolated points. Inquire locally.

The following carriers offer service throughout the Southcentral and Interior regions: *Air North,* Box 60054, Fairbanks, AK 99706; *Kodiak Western Alaska Airlines,* Box 2457, Kodiak, AK 99615; *40-Mile Air,* Box 539, Tok, AK 99780; *Valdez Airlines,* Box 6714, Anchorage, AK 99502.

For information on scheduled air service from and around the *Yukon,* contact: *CPAir,* 1004 W. Georgia St., Vancouver, BC, Canada V6E 2Y2, (604) 682-3411; *Pacific Western Airlines,* 1018 W. Georgia, Vancouver, BC, Canada V6E 2Y2, (604) 684-6161; *Trans North Air,* Box 4338, Whitehorse, YT, Canada Y1A 3T6, (403) 668-6616; *Trans Provincial Airlines,* Box 280, Prince Rupert, Canada V8J 3P6, (604) 627-1341.

By water: The *Southcentral System of the State Ferries* does not connect with the Southeast System. You'll have to fly or drive to one of its ferry ports in the Gulf of Alaska. Two ferries connect ports on Cook Inlet and Prince William Sound. *The Bartlett,* named for a revered Alaskan senator, covers Prince William Sound from Valdez to Cordova and Whittier, where passengers and cars are portaged by rail through a mountain tunnel to connect with the Anchorage-Seward and Sterling highways leading down to the Kenai Peninsula, or along Cook Inlet to Anchorage. The *Tustumena,* another glacier namesake, links Gulf of Alaska and Kenai Peninsula towns: Seward, Homer, Seldovia, and island towns Port Lions and Kodiak. For reservations write Alaska State Ferry System, Pouch R, Juneau, AK 99811; (907) 465-3941 or 3940.

The *Glacier Queen II* crosses Prince William Sound; contact Columbia Glacier Cruises, 547 W. 4th, Anchorage, AK 99501; (907) 276-8866 or toll free (800) 544-2206.

Passenger ferry service is available between Homer and Seldovia. Contact *Rainbow Tours,* on the Boardwalk, Homer Spit: Box 1526, Homer, AK 99603; (907) 235-7272.

By car: The modest highway system covers about a fifth of the state in the Southcentral to Interior sections, from the Kenai Peninsula to Fairbanks, and to the Yukon Territory. Besides the Alaska portion of the Alaska Highway, these highways are also paved: the Richardson, Glenn, George Parks, Anchorage-Seward-Homer, and Haines (except for the Canadian portion). Many of the feeder roads near Alaska's larger cities are also paved. Besides cars, recreation vehicles, and motorcoaches, there'll be people traveling by bicycle, motorcycle, and by thumb, usually with backpacks. (See "Hints to Motorists," in *Facts at Your Fingertips.*)

By bus: With advance planning you can get around Southcentral and Interior Alaska and the Yukon by scheduled bus service, although it is not as frequent as in other, smaller states. Contact these for current fares and schedules: *Alaska-Yukon Motorcoaches*, 349 Wrangell St., Anchorage, AK 99501, or 555 4th and Battery Bldg., Seattle, WA 98121; *Norline Coaches* (Yukon) Ltd., 3211A 3rd Ave., Whitehorse, YT, Canada Y1A 1G6, to Tok and Beaver Creek, with Yukon Stage connection to Fairbanks; *Valdez/Anchorage Bus Lines*, Box 867, Valdez, AK 99585, or 743WW. 5th, Anchorage, AK 99501; and *White Pass & Yukon Motorcoaches*, Box 100479, Anchorage AK 99501, between Anchorage and Haines and Whitehorse and Skagway. Together they cover way-points on highways connecting main cities and towns. Alaska Yukon's schedule coincides with ferry arrivals and departures at Skagway and Haines.

By rail: The *Alaska Railroad* runs between Fairbanks and Anchorage via Denali National Park and Preserve. Reservations should be made at least 2 weeks in advance. The railroad also extends south of Anchorage; passenger service is available from Anchorage to Portage, with shuttle service between Portage and Whittier in summer. No reservations for the shuttle (passengers connecting with the ferry in Whittier have first priority). Contact the railroad for schedules: Pouch 7–2111, Anchorage, AK 99510.

 TOURIST INFORMATION. Make a point, when traveling on your own, to stop in at the visitor centers at towns along your route. Almost every community has one. Invariably you'll find the staff (often volunteers) friendly, helpful, and hospitable. They're eager to see that you don't miss anything they treasure in their area; historic sites, museums, churches, or viewpoints. Listed here are centers in some of the larger towns in southcentral Alaska and the Interior.

Delta Junction Chamber of Commerce: Box 987, Delta Junction, AK 99737; (907) 895–4941 (in summer); 4439 (in winter). Open daily 9:00 A.M.–6:00 P.M., June to Labor Day.

Homer Chamber of Commerce, Box 541, Homer, AK 99603; (907) 235–7740. Open 10:00 A.M.–6:00 P.M. Memorial to Labor Day, or contact Kachemak Bay Convention and Visitors Bureau, 3691 Ben Walters Lane; 235–8196. The best information source in town is probably the Pratt Museum, 3779 Bartlett St., 235–8635. Open daily 10:00 A.M.–5:00 P.M. in summer. (Closed Jan.)

The **Kenai** visitors information center is in "Moosemeat John's" cabin off Kenai Spur Rd., Box 497, Kenai, AK 99611; (907) 283–7989. Open 9:00 A.M. –5:00 P.M. Mon.–Fri. year-round; in summer 10:00 A.M.–2:00 P.M. on Sat.

In **Kodiak** local volunteers dispense information at Center & Marine Way, May 15 to Sept. 15. Rest of year contact Chamber of Commerce, Box 1485, Kodiak, AK 99615, (907) 486–5557.

In **Seward** visitors information is dispensed from the Information Cache, an old railroad car at Third and Jefferson. Write: Box 756, Seward, AK 99664;

224–3094 (3046, in winter). Open daily 9:00 A.M.–5:00 P.M. Memorial–Labor days.

The **Tok** Visitor Information Center and Museum is open 7:00 A.M.–10:00 P.M. daily in the summer. Located at mile 1,314.1 Alaska Hwy.; (907) 883–5667.

Valdez Chamber of Commerce is at 245 E. North Harbor Dr. Write: Box 512, Valdez, AK 99686; (907) 835–2330. Open daily in summer 9:00 A.M.–9:00 P.M.; weekdays 9:00 A.M.–5:00 P.M. in winter.

Whitehorse Chamber of Commerce, 302 Steele St., Whitehorse, Yukon, Canada Y1A 2C5; (403) 667–7545.

TOURS. Besides the *Alaska Sightseeing* (349 Wrangell, Anchorage, AK 99501) and *Gray Line Tours* (300 Elliott Ave. W., Seattle, WA 98119), check out *Alpine Llamas,* Box 1557, Homer AK 99603; 296–2217. Pack trips by llama into Kachemak Bay State Park for trout fishing, canoeing, birding, and exploring glaciers. For train tours see "How to Get There: By train," above.

Air tours: In Denali National Park. A thrill while in the park is flightseeing with *Denali Wilderness Air,* headquartered in the railroad station. Ask about their reasonable and exciting air tours for close-up views and photography of rugged Mt. McKinley's glaciers and cirques. Contact them at Box 82, Denali National Park and Preserve, AK 99755; (907 683–2261) (in summer). Also ask about their *Denali Wilderness Lodges* flights.

Around Homer: *Homer Air* offers air charters for flightseeing, sport fishing, and clam digging. Office is located at Homer airport. Write: Homer Air, Box 302, Homer, AK 99603; (907) 235–8591.

Maritime Helicopters offers tours to lower Cook Inlet, Augustine Island, McNeil River, Barren Islands, Harding Icefields. Box 357, Homer, AK 99603; (907) 235–7771.

To Fort Yukon: *Air North,* Box 60054, 456–5555.

Around Kodiak: Tours of the area are offered through *Island Air Service,* Box 125, Kodiak, AK 99615; (907) 486–6196. Their office is at the Kodiak Municipal Airport.

Water tours: To Columbia Glacier: Daily cruises to the glacier from Valdez aboard the *Columbia Queen* can be arranged through Valdez Charter Service, Box 947, Valdez, AK 99686; (907) 835–4461.

From Homer: On Homer Spit *Wilderness Adventures* (235–6094) sells and rents outdoor recreational equipment and offers custom adventure trips, such as skiing, climbing, dogsledding, and horseback riding in the Kachemak Alps; guided and fully outfitted. *Rainbow Tours* (235–7272) offers Kachemak Bay sightseeing of marine life, bird life, and wildlife; halibut and salmon sportfishing charters; passenger ferry service between Homer and Seldovia; and tours of secluded Seldovia.

From Dawson City: Paddle to ghost town Moosehide during a 2-hour tour on the *Yukon Lou.* Contact *Yukon River Tours* (in the birch cabin on Front St.), Box 1, Dawson City, Y.T., Canada Y0B 1G0; (403) 993–5482.

Riverboats gave up in 1952 when the year-round Canada-Alaska highway was completed. Now the brand-new catamaran, M.V. *Klondike,* named for the last of the great sternwheelers, follows in the wake on the Yukon River. Starting in June 1985 this modern (all the amenities with a Gay '90s decor) *Klondike* can take up to 220 passengers on daily 5-hour cruises between Dawson City, Yukon, and Eagle, Alaska.

Leaving from Dawson at 8:00 A.M. (or the reverse cruise, leaving Eagle in the early afternoon) makes a fascinating, well-narrated addition to package tours to and from Alaska via the highway. Besides the colorful history at both ends of the run, highlights along the beautiful, winding Yukon include gold mine sites, abandoned trapper and miner cabins, working homesteads, and a sternwheeler graveyard. Contact Yukon River Cruises, P.O. Box 100034, Anchorage, AK 99510; (907) 276–8023.

Resurrection Bay: Tours of the bay from Seward, costing around $40, are available aboard *Shaman.* Write: "Shaman," Box 881, Seward, AK 99664; (907) 224–3664. Tickets are also available aboard the boat, slip D-18, Seward small-boat harbor, or at the Fish House in Seward.

From Whitehorse: Cruise up the Yukon River on the lakeboat *Schwatka.* Tours depart twice on a day from Schwatka Lake, near the dam. Contact *Atlas Tours,* Box 4340, Whitehorse, YT, Canada, Y1A 3T5; (403) 668–3161.

 STATE PARKS. See "State Parks" in *Facts at Your Fingertips* for general information about the system. In Southcentral and Interior sections of Alaska you may want to visit *Chugach State Park,* just outside of Anchorage. A 494,000-acre park, it offers year-round access to the outdoors. The many summer hiking trails become dogsled, cross-country ski, and snowmobile trails in winter. Camp at a state-maintained campground or on your own in secluded wilderness. Write to the park for more information: 2601 Commercial Dr., Anchorage, AK 99501; (907) 279–3413.

Denali State Park, accessible via the George Parks Hwy., allows excellent views of Mt. McKinley. There's a campground here and trail system. Write for more information: District Superintendent, Denali State Park, Box 182, Palmer, AK 99645; (907) 745–3975.

Kachemak Bay State Park and *Kachemak Bay State Wilderness Park* are undeveloped parks, accessible by boat or plane from Homer. They contain wild, mountainous terrain and spectacular ocean shoreline. Boating and fishing are perfect activities here. Write: District Superintendent, Kachemak Bay State Park, Box 1247, Soldotna, AK 99669; (907) 262–5581.

Captain Cook State Recreation Area is on North Kenai Rd., outside of Kenai, accessible by car or float plane. Here you can fish, view waterfowl, explore the beaches, and camp. Contact: District Superintendent, Kenai District, Alaska State Parks, Box 1247, Soldotna, AK 99669; (907) 262–5581.

NATIONAL FORESTS, PARKS AND PRESERVES.
The Russians found Eskimos living in the Prince William Sound area when they called there—descendants of those who had arrived thousands of years ago, according to evidence from archeological diggings. The Natives called themselves a name (picked up by the Russians) that has evolved to the present Chugach, pronounced Chew'gatch.

Chugach, with 6,000,000 acres, second in size among national forests only to the Tongass, stretches along the coast of the Gulf of Alaska, taking in the islands and most of the land bordering Prince William Sound. Naturalists are aboard the ferries plying the Marine Highway through this watery section of the forest. They interpret the prolific and fascinating sea and bird life and the immense, iceberg calving Columbia Glacier. The Chugach reaches to Seward on the Kenai Peninsula and is just across Turnagain Arm from Anchorage. To this area is added Afognak Island, first set aside as a reserve in 1891 by President Harrison.

Formerly of considerable importance for its copper deposits, the Chugach area has in recent years been geared to military operations centered around Anchorage, with multiple-use development of commercial fishing, timber, and recreational resources in the forest itself. The fault that brought the disastrous Good Friday earthquake of 1964 just about bisects the forest, and an excellent interpretive program has been established to help the public understand the powerful natural forces that have shaped the rugged landscape. A visitor center is operated during the summer within the Portage Glacier Recreation Area, about 50 miles southeast of Anchorage and in the heart of the area most dramatically affected by the quake. Accessible from Alaska Route 1, open 9:00 A.M.–7:00 P.M. Memorial–Labor Day; 345–5700. Nearby towns to the forest are Anchorage, Cordova, Kodiak, Seward, Valdez, and Whittier.

Within the forests are Kenai moose, Dall sheep, brown and black bears, mountain goats, and elk—animals among the largest in North America. The forest is also nesting ground for one of the largest concentrations of trumpeter swans, Canadian geese, and other waterfowl and shore birds. Most of the saltwater fishing in Prince William Sound is concentrated in the streams and waters around Valdez and Cordova. Some king salmon are caught in the fall and winter, while silvers are taken in quantity from July into September. Razor clams, Dungeness and king crab are among shellfish found on the forest shores. The lakes and streams of the forest offer an exciting challenge for freshwater fishermen.

The U.S. Forest Service maintains campgrounds and cabins on the Chugach; minimal fees. (See "Camping and Cabins," above.) Contact U.S. Forest Service, Box 1628, Juneau, AK 99802, or 2221 E. Northern Lights Blvd., Anchorage, AK 99504, or write Chugach National Forest, Cabin Reservations, Box 10–469, Anchorage, AK 99511.

Denali National Park and Preserve, despite its name change, remains the best-known and most visited in Alaska. The park can be reached by plane (a 3,000-foot airstrip is maintained for light aircraft); three times a week, by rail, from Anchorage or Fairbanks; by paved road, Alaska 3, from Anchorage or Fairbanks; and by the gravel, summer only Denali Highway, Alaska 8, a 135-mile road, of which some 20 miles leading from Paxson are paved. The road extends from Paxson, on Milepost 185.5 on the Richardson Highway, Alaska 4, to the village of Cantwell, located 1.8 miles beyond the junction of the Denali Highway with the Anchorage-Fairbanks Highway (George Parks Highway). Charter flights are available from Anchorage or Fairbanks. *Alaska-Yukon Motorcoaches* schedules daily bus service between Anchorage and Fairbanks via Denali National Park.

A visit to the park is a highlight of most package tours, including a wildlife-viewing "safari" deep into the park. Tundra wildlife tours are conducted daily in summer by experienced driver guides. The fare for the 130-mile round trip to Eielson Visitor Center (open daily throughout summer, early A.M. into the evening) includes a picnic lunch. Frequent stops are made to photograph flowers, birds, mountains, and animals, particularly grizzly bears, caribou, sheep, and moose. On clear days, from the center, the north summit of Mt. McKinley, 19,470 feet, is visible, though 31 miles away to the southwest. In the foreground is Muldrow Glacier.

There are several campgrounds within the park. (Those at Riley Creek and Morino are open year-round, although without facilities in winter.) Beyond Mile 14 at the Savage River Bridge, permits to drive private vehicles are issued only if you have a reservation for one of the 72 campsites available beyond. Campers should bring a camp stove with plenty of fuel, as well as all the supplies they think they will need. The nearest store is many miles away. Free shuttle buses run often along the Park Road to serve the public. Check at the Riley Creek Visitor Center near the park entrance. Open in summer from early morning until late evening, they'll have the latest information on shuttle buses, rules and regulations, campsite availability, hiking trails, and other worthwhile park activities: campfire talks, nature walks, wildlife tours, and sled dog demonstrations. Write for information: Superintendent, Box 9, Denali National Park and Preserve, AK 99755; (907) 683–2238. May–Sept; year round, write Anchorage office, Box 85; 274–5366. Also, ten miles north of the park entrance the *McKinley KOA Kampground* has groceries, laundromat, and a restaurant nearby.

Kenai Fjords National Park is over 500,000 acres of wilderness, including mountain valleys and fjords, glaciers, and a huge icefield. The park can be reached from Seward or Homer. Its a great place to explore by boat: you may see seabirds, sea lions, seals, porpoises, whales. The fishing is wonderful. Contact the Superintendent, Box 1727, Seward, AK 99664. You can also call the park office in Seward for information: 224–3874, or stop at the visitor center at Seward's small-boat harbor, across from the Harbormaster's office. Open 8:00 A.M.–5:00 P.M., daily, in summer; no weekends the rest of the year. The visitor center has exhibits and slide programs, as well as information.

Kluane National Park, Canada, is easily reached from the Alaska and Haines hwys. Hikes, tours, campfire talks, slide shows are available. Write Superintendent, Kluane National Park, Haines Junction, Yukon, Canada Y0B 1LO; (403) 634–2251.

WILDLIFE REFUGES. The *Kenai National Wildlife Refuge* is about a mile south of Soldotna. Here you can hike, canoe, camp, drive scenic roads. The visitor center will give you all the information you need, open 8:00 A.M.–4:30 P.M., daily. Write for details: Box 2139, Soldotna, AK 99669; (907) 262–7021.

The *Kodiak National Wildlife Refuge* is accessible only by air. Although there are many kinds of animals here—including red fox, land otter, weasel, whales, porpoises, seals, sea otters, and sea lions—it is the Kodiak bear that most visitors come to see. The bears become readily observable in July and August when they congregate along streams to feed on salmon. 12 recreation cabins are available, free of charge, but reservations are needed and determined by lottery. Cabins may be reserved for up to 7 days. Contact: Manager, Box 825, Kodiak, AK 99615; (907) 487–2600.

SPORTS. Rafting: *Denali Raft Adventures's* 12-mile float down the Nenana River in Denali National Park ($30) through moose, sheep, and other wildlife country suits most everyone. You should be fairly hardy; it's required that you be at least 12 years old for the 4-hour "Healy Express" ($40) through Nenana Canyon and its exciting white water. They have an assortment of rafting adventures—all day, an evening, overnight or longer, or a few hours. Rafting is combined with fishing, bird watching, and photography on other wilderness rivers throughout the area and farther afield. For specific information write: Gary Kroll, Box 427, Denali National Park and Preserve, AK 99755; (907) 683–2234.

Raft trips can also be arranged at Portage Glacier Recreation Area, June 1–Sept. 7. Contact *Portage River Adventures,* Box 261, Girdwood, AK 99587. Reservations: (907) 783–2266. From $25; children half-price.

Skiing: *Mt. Alyeska Ski Resort* is 40 miles southeast of Anchorage on the Seward Hwy. A resort complex with complete facilities, it is Alaska's largest ski area, offering glacier skiing, night skiing, five chairlifts. In summer, the chairlift makes a wonderful sightseeing ride. Box 249, Girdwood, AK 99587; (907) 783–2222.

Cross-country skiing, snowmobiling, and snowshoeing can be enjoyed at *Turnagain Pass,* south of Anchorage on the Seward Hwy. A sign at 988 feet elevation indicates safe and possible-avalanche areas. The restrooms look like snow caves in the winters. The area west of the highway is for snowmobiling; the area east is for cross-country skiing and snowshoeing. Information available from the Seward Ranger District, Chugach National Forest, 334 4th Ave., Seward, AK 99664; (907) 224–3374.

HISTORIC SITES AND HOUSES. Dawson City: *Jack London's Cabin* on Eighth Ave. is built from half the logs used in London's original wilderness cabin. Open 9:00 A.M.–6:00 P.M.; interpretation daily at 1:00 P.M. Admission is free.

The SS *Keno* was the last steamboat to sail the Yukon River. Free tours are given daily of the sternwheeler, now on the riverbank, near Queen St. Open 9:30 A.M.–6:00 P.M.; call 993–5566 for information.

Robert Service's Cabin: The Yukon poet's cabin has been completely restored. On Eighth Ave. Open 9:00 A.M.–6:00 P.M. daily. At 10:00 A.M. and 4:00 P.M., local actor Tom Byrne recites Service's poems. Admission is free.

Eagle: *Fort Egbert* was established by the U.S. Army in 1899 and abandoned 12 years later. Today the town historical society is working to restore this fort, as well as other historic buildings in town, including the old *Courthouse* and the *cabin of Norwegian explorer Roald Amundsen.* Open to the public in the fort are the carriage house, dog houses, stables, officers' quarters. Free tours of the town's historic areas are held on summer mornings, 10:00 A.M. daily; they start from the courthouse.

Fort Yukon: A 19th-century *log church* houses an intricately beaded white moosehide alter cover, crafted by Athabascan women.

Kenai: The *Russian Orthodox Church,* built in 1894, is considered one of the best preserved examples of such a 19th-century church. It is the oldest one in Alaska and contains a number of religious and art objects imported from Russia. Across from Fort Kenay, regular services are held here, and tours may be arranged by appointment: 283–4122.

Kodiak: The *Russian Orthodox Church* here, in the oldest such parish in Alaska, contains paintings, icons, and other objects—many almost 2 centuries old. Visitors are welcome by appointment: 486–3854.

Seward: *St. Peter's Episcopal Church,* at the corner of Second Ave. and Adams St., features a unique painting of the Resurrection. Dutch artist Jan Van Emple painted the picture in 1925, using Alaskans as models and Resurrection Bay as the background.

Whitehorse: The *Old Log Church,* Elliott and Third, was built in 1900 for the Church of England. It and the log rectory next door are in the process of being gradually restored. A museum in the church displays pioneer artifacts.

The SS *Klondike* once traveled the Yukon River, and is now completely restored to its original condition. It's at rest beside the Yukon River near the Robert Campbell Bridge and open in summer 8:00 A.M.–8:00 P.M. Free guided tours are conducted June 1–Sept. 15; make reservations at the nearby information center: 667–7545.

LIBRARIES. Seward: The *Seward Community Library,* across from the State and City Office Building, holds a slide show at 2:00 P.M. called "Seward Is Burning." The show illustrates the damage done to the town in the 1964 Earthquake. (This slide show is held in the City Hall basement in summer.) Also displayed in the library are Russian icons and paintings by Alaskan artists. The library hours are 1:00–8:00 P.M. Mon.–Fri.; 1:00–6:00 P.M. Sat.; 224–3646.

Whitehorse: The *Yukon Archives,* part of the Yukon Government Building on Second Ave., displays art about the Yukon and the gold rush—as well as having numerous books on the topics. Open 10:00 A.M.–9:00 P.M. weekdays; shorter hours on weekends and holidays; 667–5321. (Also in the Government Building is the *Whitehorse Public Library,* call 667–5239.)

MUSEUMS. Dawson City: The *Dawson City Museum* on Fifth Ave. displays a large collection of Yukon artifacts, including a collection of narrow-guage locomotives. Open daily in summer, 10:00 A.M.–6:00 P.M.; 993–5291. Small admission fee.

The *Gold Room,* on the second floor of the Canadian Imperial Bank of Commerce, houses an exhibit of early equipment used for weighing, measuring, and melting gold. Open 10:00 A.M.–3:00 P.M.; no admission fee.

The *Mining Museum,* Front and Queen sts., is outdoors and has a collection of mining artifacts.

Eagle: The *Amundsen Cabin* and the *old courthouse* are now museums and part of the town's historic district, through which the town historical society conducts tours. Tours are held in summer at 10:00 A.M. daily, starting at the courthouse. (See "Historic Sites and Houses" earlier in this *Practical Information.*)

Fort Yukon: The *Dinjii Zhuu Enjit Museum* displays articles dealing with the culture and history of the people of Yukon Flats. 662–2487.

Homer: The *Pratt Museum* on Bartlett St. has exhibits focusing on pioneer, Russian, and Indian history and land and sea animal life. Visitor information is also dispensed here. Open daily, 10:00 A.M.–5:00 P.M. in summer. 235–8635. Small admission charge.

Kenai: The *Fort Kenay Museum,* Mission and Overland aves., is a collection of artifacts dating back to early days of this town. Included are primitive tools, heirlooms from gold mining days, Russian church icons. Open May–October. Hours vary. 283–4156 or 7294. Voluntary donations; also a gift shop.

Kodiak: The *Baranof Museum* was built in the 1790s by Alexander Baranof to store sea otter pelts. Now it's a museum housing a collection that dates from the early days of Kodiak: antique Russian samovars, handcrafted silver jewelry, Aleut basketry. Open daily in summer 10:00 A.M.–3:00 P.M.; Saturdays and Sundays noon to 4:00 P.M. In winter it's open weekdays except Thursdays, 11:00 A.M.–3:00 P.M.; Saturdays and Sundays, noon to 3:00 P.M Small admission charge. 486–5920.

Seward: *The Seward Museum* is in the basement of the State and City Office Building, Fifth and Adams. Here there are artifacts and photographs from Seward's past: including Indian baskets, ivory carvings, and photos of the 1964 earthquake. Open mid-June–Labor Day; hours vary. Small admission fee.

Tok: The *Visitor Information Center and Museum* displays Indian arts and artifacts and wildlife exhibits. It's located near the intersection of Hwys. 1 and 2; open 7:00 A.M.–10:00 P.M.; 883–5113.

Valdez: The *Valdez Museum* is in the Centennial Building at the corner of Egan and Chenega. The emphasis of the exhibits here is on town's past: household items of the pioneers, old mining and fire-fighting equipment. Open 10:00 A.M.–7:00 P.M. daily in summer; shortened winter hours. Free. 835–2764.

Wasilla: This museum is a historical park with early buildings of the area, stewarded by the Wasilla–Knik–Willow Historical Society (376–2005).

Whitehorse: The *MacBride Museum* is on First Ave. Featured here are displays on the history of the Yukon, including animal, gold rush, and riverboat exhibits. Sam McGee's cabin is on the grounds. Open summers 9:00 A.M.–9:00 P.M. Small admission charge. The *Old Log Church,* Elliott and Third, is a museum displaying pioneer artifacts.

 THEATER AND ENTERTAINMENT. Dawson City: *"The Gaslight Follies"* run from late May to mid-September in the restored Palace Grand Theater. Its an old-time variety show, and just the theater itself is worth the price of the ticket. Shows are held nightly (except Tuesdays) at 8:00; advance tickets available at the theater: (403) 993–5575.

Kodiak: *Cry of the Wild Ram* is a historical drama about 30 years in the life of Alexander Baranof. It's held outdoors in the Frank Brink Amphitheater, rain-or-shine. Evening performances first two weeks in August. Contact Kodiak –Baranof Productions, Box 1792, Kodiak 99615 (486–5291) for dates and information.

Whitehorse: The *"Frantic Follies,"* a local-talent, family vaudeville show, has a gold rush flavor. Held nightly June-mid-Sept. in Sheffield Hotel. Tickets should be obtained early, through Atlas Travel (403) 668–3161.

 LOCAL ART. Homer: This is an art-conscious community, and locals will help direct you to where it's all displayed.

Homer Artists Gallery, 111 W. Pioneer Ave., was started by Hazel Heath, a homesteader and Homer's former mayor. Open year-round, Tues.-Sat., 10:00 A.M.–5:00 P.M.; 235–8944.

The *8 x 10 Art Gallery* on Pioneer Ave. displays and sells wild berry prints, watercolors, and drawings of the area. It also dispenses wildflower information. Open daily 10:00 A.M.–5:00 P.M.; closed Sun.

Kenai: *Olde Towne Gallery* displays work of Kenai Peninsula artists, as well as providing artist workshops. It's off Main St. on Cook Ave. and open Mon.-Sat. 10:00 A.M.–4:00 P.M.; 283–7040.

Seward: You can see paintings by Alaskan artists in the *Seward Community Library,* across from the State and City Office Building. It's open 1:00–8:00 P.M. Mon.-Fri.; 1:00–6:00 P.M. Sat.; 224–3646. (See "Libraries" earlier in this *Practical Information.*)

SHOPPING. Copper Center: At Mile 93 on the Richardson Hwy. is the *Grizzly Gift Shop,* selling a variety of goodies—fun to browse through and take with you.

Gakona: The *Little Alaska Cache,* north junction of Glenn and Richardson hwys., open May-Oct., sells Athabascan baskets, moccasins, mittens, diamond willow and burl items, jewelry and beadwork.

George Parks Hwy: At *Hoag's Hollow,* Mile 271 (from Fairbanks), they create native art, serve free coffee, and dispense information.

Homer: *Alaska Wild Berry Products* on Pioneer Ave. manufactures jams, jellies, sauces, syrups, and juices made from wild berries hand picked on the Kenai Peninsula. They ship orders, too: Box 347, Homer, AK 99603; (907) 235-8858.

Kodiak: *Norman's,* on the mall, photo supplies and a large choice of ivory carvings, gold nuggets, and furs.

Tok: *The Burnt Paw* is located at intersection of Hwys. 1 and 2. They sell jade and ivory, Alaskan ceramics, crafts, paintings, smoked salmon, "squaw candy"-even dogsled puppies.

Between Anchorage and Valdez: the oldest Alaskan store on this route is the *Cracker Barrel,* Mile 187. Though expanded to supermarket stock, it keeps its old-time flavor and photo display.

PANNING FOR GOLD. To pan for gold at "Poverty Bar" on Bonanza Creek, Dawson City, visitors can contact "Poverty Bar Placers," on Bonanza Creek Rd., 8 miles from Dawson City. Open 9:00 A.M.–5:30 P.M. daily in summer. Equipment and instructors furnished. Also ask at any local visitor center.

DINING OUT. As with accommodations, don't hesitate to ask locals for advice: where they eat—when they want to splurge and when they want to eat inexpensively. Often, eating at the "only place in town" turns out to be a delightful, delicious, and convivial experience. In the fish-and-game-filled Kenai Peninsula you might discover local delicacies on the menu, perhaps bear roast, mooseburgers, king crab, and salmon.

Though mostly *Moderate* (as categorized below), restaurant prices may vary, with higher prices for meals that include items shipped from a distant source of supply. We've categorized the restaurants roughly: *Deluxe* $30 and up; *Expensive* $20–30; *Moderate* $15–20; *Inexpensive,* under $15. Many establishments accept credit cards, although it's always wise to double-check in advance.

See also "Hotels and Motels," earlier in this *Practical Information* for lodging spots that offer food as well.

HOMER

Chartroom Restaurant. *Expensive.* At *Land's End,* year-round resort at the tip of the Spit; 235-8900.

The Bunk House. *Moderate.* 5 miles out east road, overlooking Kachemak Bay. 235–8644. Very popular. The locals head there for good food and dancing.

Don Jose's. *Moderate.* On Pioneer Ave. Specializes in Italian & Mexican food, 7 days a week.

Mallard Restaurant and Lounge in Homer's newest Lakewood Inn, corner of Lake St. and Ocean Drive, overlooking Beluga Lake. 235–6144.

Porpoise Room. *Moderate.* Located on the Homer Spit and overlooking the small-boat basin and Kachemak Bay, this dining room specializes in fine steaks and Homer seafood. Bar. 235–7848.

Sterling Café. *Moderate.* By Heritage Hotel. 235–8644. Grade-A meats and seafood, homemade pies.

Waterfront Bar and Dining. *Moderate.* In downtown Homer. 235–8747. Dinners only at this cozy dining room.

The Parfait Shoppe. *Inexpensive.* 235–6774. For hamburgers, milk shakes and soft ice cream.

The Soup Bowl. *Inexpensive.* At the Lakeside Mall. The name describes it.

KODIAK

Buskin Bar & Restaurant. *Expensive.* Next to airport 487–2700. Local seafood, homemade pastries, desserts.

Chartroom. *Expensive.* Fine dining with harbor view at the Sheffield, downtown waterfront; 486–5712.

El Chicano. *Moderate.* Second floor, Center St. Plaza; 486–6116. Authentic Mexican cuisine, including the beer and margaritas. Take-outs.

Shelikof Restaurant & Lounge. *Moderate.* In Shelikof Lodge, overlooking city and harbor; 486–4141.

Solly's Office on the Mall. *Moderate.* 486–3313. Bar, restaurant, and country rock music.

SEWARD

Captain's Table. *Moderate.* Next to the Breeze Inn; 244–5237. Overlooking the beautiful Seward small-boat harbor, rebuilt after 1964 earthquake.

Sourdough Bar & Dining Room. *Moderate.* In the Van Gilder Hotel, National Historic Site; 224–3079. Near shops, ferry, and bus.

The Fairweather Cafe. *Moderate to Inexpensive.* Downtown; 224–3907. Quiches, soups, sandwiches, and desserts.

Shamrock Deli. *Inexpensive.* In Murphy's Motel (of course), 4th & D., 224–5650. Eat your order in the shadow of Mt. Marathon, or take it with you.

VALDEZ

Pipeline Club. *Inexpensive.* In Valdez Motel; 835–4444. Salmon is so fresh it may not be on the menu yet—ask the waitress.

Sheffield House. *Expensive.* Restaurant overlooks picturesque boat harbor. 835–4391.

Pizza Palace. *Moderate.* 201 Harbor Dr.; 835–4686 or 2365. View of pipeline terminal site from Harbor Club Bar. Plus ravioli, spaghetti, lasagna. Valdez history in wall decor.

Village Inn Dining Room. *Moderate.* Corner of Richardson Highway and Meals Ave.; 835–4445. They also reserve for the Valdez Salmon Bake at The Lakehouse on Robe Lake, home of trumpeter swans. 5–9 P.M. daily, June 15-September. Travel Service desk, 835–4401, will help arrange an Alaskan adventure—including hydrofoil to Columbia Glacier.

Hanger 9, *Inexpensive.* At the airport; 835–4999. "Cook your own steak" is a bargain. Live music at night and breakfast all day.

 BARS AND NIGHT LIFE. Your establishment may have a bar; if not, ask locals for some of their favorites. Here are a few notable night spots. **Chitina:** The *Chitina Saloon* (can't miss the location in this small town) offers live music on Saturday and Sunday nights. A real down-to-earth atmosphere.

Dawson City: *Diamond Tooth Gertie's Gambling Casino* is on Queen St. at Fourth Ave. The Klondike gambling tables are specially licensed in the Yukon. There's bar service and cancan girls perform the floor show. Open every night but Sunday, late May to mid-Sept. You must be 19 to enter.

In **Homer,** the *Salty Dawg Saloon* has an old-fashioned atmosphere and great views of boats and glaciers; near Homer Spit. Close by is the *Waterfront Bar,* a favorite of fishermen.

Kodiak: The *B&B Bar* at the downtown waterfront is a popular fishermen's hangout. *Solly's Office,* on the mall, is a bar and restaurant and a place to listen to country-rock music.

THE FRINGES OF ALASKA

Nome, the Arctic Circle, and More

Even though a "bush" airline advertises "Fly the Arctic before it's paved" and "See the Arctic Circle before it's a traffic circle," no public roads lead to the fringe areas in far northern and far western Alaska. To rub noses with Eskimos, you'll have to fly. But the end of the road does not signal the end of adventure. Planes head far north and west out of gateway cities. Some fly to the Bering Sea Pribilof Islands, headquarters for guided seal and bird watching tours and superb nature photography. Some fly out the Alaska Peninsula to the Katmai National Monument. Here fishing and nature watching are the main course with baked Alaska for dessert. A highlight of the Monument is the eerie, seared, moonscape-like area called the Valley of Ten Thousand Smokes. Other package tours from Anchorage and Fairbanks make large flying circuits across that intangible Arctic Circle. These modern Arctic expeditions combine facets of gold rush, Eskimo and Russian heritage, and the North Slope oil fields.

Practically speaking, it's best to take a package tour. They come in sizes from a day to several, and they are priced accordingly. Generally, the prepaid and thus noninflatable (for duration of your trip) package tour prices cover the many air miles round trip to the Arctic destination, airport transfers, hotel, and services of an in-residence "expedition leader," perhaps a Native. A good tour guide can be a valuable catalyst as he interprets the unusual environment, scrupulously delivers all promised tour features, issues warm parkas for outdoor activities, if needed, and orients his charges to the essential establishments: hotels, restaurants, shops, churches, and bars, if any. Some communities are dry, or vote liquor in or out depending on whether such revenue is currently needed.

Meals are not included, and the price may seem high. Eating can add $30 to $35 a day; more, if you research the local bars also. The source of supply is far away, and freighting is expensive, whether by air or water—only possible during the summer when the Arctic seas are liquid. But eating can be an interesting experience. In the past, the brave could sample muktuk—whale skin with some blubber still attached—or even order a whale steak. With conservation concerns and hunting quotas, the Eskimos may not be able to spare any. However, the menu may feature other Arctic delicacies such as reindeer steak, salmon, or sheefish in season.

The main tour destinations, reached by jet, are Nome, Kotzebue, Barrow, and Deadhorse at Prudhoe Bay. Smaller Eskimo villages, such as Gambell, Point Hope, Shishmaref, Savoonga, Selawik, Kiana, and Noatak, may be visited via smaller bush planes. It's possible to stay overnight by making arrangements ahead—usually through local airline offices, if no other package tours are offered.

Flying north, the change in terrain is obvious soon after leaving Fairbanks. There are views of the multibillion dollar pipeline and the meandering Yukon River, as the last snowy mountain barrier gives way to the flat vast treeless plain, gently sloping north to the Arctic Ocean.

If it's your first trip, the first sight of an Arctic community is rather grim. The tiny weathered buildings are almost lost in the expanse of tundra, the vegetation that covers the permanently frozen ground. The top few inches melt and vegetate in summer, supporting flowers, berries, and other low-growing plants. It's also the home and feeding grounds for nesting birds and small Arctic animals—lemmings, parka squirrels, foxes—and larger ones—caribou and reindeer. The polar bears will be off on icepacks lurking in the distance off shore; rarely near settlements.

Waves constantly wash the shore, and it appears that a big one might easily inundate the roadway and houses stretched along the beach. At Point Hope, on a small peninsula jutting into the Chukchi Sea not far from the U.S.S.R.-U.S. International Boundary, erosion compelled the Eskimos to move their centuries-old whaling town inland. The site is a favorite dig for archaeologists. They have found evidence of Eskimo culture and habitation going back some 4,000 years. The uprooting hasn't been easy. It is hoped visitors will continue to be welcome to attend the happy whaling festivals held after each successful season, and that some of the intriguing facets of old Point Hope will be saved.

For example, the graveyard, with its fence made of giant whalebones, is the town's landmark, and very photogenic. A sod, whalebone, and driftwood home should also be preserved as an outdoor-indoor museum-piece. These time-mellowed dwellings are an amazing adaptation to the harsh environment. Even when lighted and heated only by seal oil lamps, they are surprisingly cozy and comfortable inside.

Kotzebue, Barrow, and Nome

Both Kotzebue and Barrow are above the Arctic Circle. Kotzebue, about 30 miles north of it, was established as a reindeer station and permanent trading post about 1897. The area was influenced by "outsiders" long before that, however, including Baron von Kotzebue exploring for Russia. He sailed into the sound off the Arctic Ocean in the first part of the 19th century. Some souvenirs his party left behind include blue Russian trading beads on display in the Ootukahkuktuvik ("place for having old things") museum and some Eskimos with Russian names.

Barrow's unique location has always attracted visitors, too: explorers, adventurers, and Arctic researchers. During World War II, its strategic position made it a key point in the Defense Early Warning System (DEW Line). The adaptable, durable Eskimos, naturally best fitted for Arctic survival, played important roles in all the activity. Barrow is now gearing up for more development activity at Pet 4, the nearby Naval Petroleum Reserve.

The Arctic has been changing, no doubt about it, and the Natives welcome the addition of creature comforts: utilities, medical facilities, shopping malls, schools, and communication systems. Yet many are reluctant to forego the ways of the past.

In the Eskimo towns you'll see new ways versus the old, and combinations of both. Skin boats have outboard motors. Women carve up seal meat and prepare sealskin storage pokes and wouldn't think of using any knife but the ancient, efficient ulu *(ooloo)*, with its sharp, curved blade opposite a handle just right to grasp and manipulate.

Along with the seal meat, walrus, whale, fish, and caribou meat still stored in their natural deep freezers dug out of permafrost, they may also stash TV dinners. Fur parkas and mukluk footwear are still the practical Native garb, but store-bought jackets and boots, and tennis shoes and T-shirts, especially on the smaller set, are making inroads.

On the surface, the smiling Eskimos appear happy in their changing way of life. However, deep social studies indicate it's been a traumatic transition, often leaving deep scars. Yet, they seem exceptionally friendly with visitors, and enjoy entertaining tourists with shows built around their cultural past. Tourism seems to be an industry that they can live with—even develop—with enthusiasm. Native corporations have been investing capital from land claims settlements in new, modern hotels with all the comforts they think visitors want. And most of the residents are willing to share aspects of their fascinating way of life, past and present.

Visitors are sometimes surprised to learn that Alaskan Eskimos never have lived in igloos, as did their Canadian cousins. In the Arctic villages, where building material is scarce and freight rates high, houses are mostly built from driftwood and salvage. Now some prefabricated modest frame houses have also appeared.

You'll visit with Eskimos in Nome, too, though Nome was a white man's town in the beginning. The King Island Eskimos who lived on a rocky island in the Bering Sea had been coming to the area for centuries to pick berries, and to fish in summer. After gold rush Nome was established at the turn of the century, the King Islanders continued to make the 13-hour trip from the island. They paddled large oomiaks (skin boats) filled with families and supplies, prepared to camp under their oomiaks on the beach. In 1959, when the Bureau of Indian Affairs school was closed, they moved to Nome permanently and settled in frame houses.

Many of these Eskimos still go back to hunt and to check on their homes in the old ghost town clinging to the cliffs of King Island. Flightseeing trips often swing by for a look. The Natives have continued their excellent ivory carving, and a dance group—tots to senior citizens—entertains with age-old story-telling dances and songs.

Gold rush memorabilia are all over Nome. Tour groups get a short course in gold rush history in the audio-visual "Story of the Gold Rush," a blend of old pictures and narration. Then they strike out to see what's left. This includes gold fields still with giant dredges sitting in their private lakes and surrounded by piles of rocky tailings. Some are working now, because of profits made possible by the higher price of gold. Gold fever proves contagious when visitors practice panning at a small private operation on the tour agenda. What you pan you have to give back, but they'll give you a tiny free sample in a vial for a souvenir. If you get the hang of it, then try gold panning along Nome's famous beach, where anyone can pan and keep it, just like in the old days.

Nome's night life is notorious, naturally, because of its gaudy, lusty reputation in the past, and there are a number of bars willing to help prove it. However, the most sensational night show takes place above the Arctic Circle, starring the midnight sun.

For 36 days in summer, the sun doesn't drop below the horizon in Kotzebue. In Barrow it stays on stage for 82. Photographers snuggle down in their warm, colorful, borrowed parkas and shoot away. Sometimes all night. By fixing your camera in one spot (on a tripod is best) and shooting at 15-minute intervals, you can catch multiple exposures on the same film, as the sun arcs from east to west, without touching down in midsummer.

No two Arctic tours will be exactly alike, but you'll see the most of whichever place you choose to stop overnight. In all the towns, you'll be exposed to things Eskimo, from entertainment (dancing and games) to watching them go about their summer work of garnering food for winter. With almost 24 hours of light there is activity round-the-clock as they mend nets, fish, bring in seal and beluga, a small white whale, which they butcher on the beach.

In each town there are good shopping possibilities. You'll find typical and beautiful hand-crafted items in the stores, or perhaps make your purchase directly from the artist. After the dances, they spread out their wares.

Some towns boast of specialties. Kotzebue, for example, has *a* tree, referred to as the "Kotzebue National Forest." Several years ago, some tree-hungry fellows at the nearby Air Force Station brought in the lone spruce, planted it, nourished it, and coaxed it to grow.

Not to be outdone, Barrow brags about having the purest air in the world, give or take some whiffs agreeable to Eskimo noses but a bit ripe for cheechakos (newcomers). The adjacent Naval Arctic Research Laboratory backs up the claim. It's noted for Ice Island exploits, oil exploration, and experiments in Arctic living. They say that dust and pollutants caused by vehicles, fires, etc., are soon whisked away by brisk Arctic breezes.

Prudhoe Bay

In each place there are unusual museums to browse through, with displays you aren't likely to see elsewhere. Deadhorse, the "town" for the Prudhoe Bay area, might well be preserved as a huge museum complex, for now and future generations. The costly, much-publicized Arctic oil and gas project is complex and varied. One-day tours there explore activity on the tundra from oil pipes to sandpipers. Among the birds, wildflowers, summer-migrating caribou, and abundant ground squirrels, the guide will show you Prudhoe's forest, too, a stand of mature willow trees that grows only to seedling height on the edge of the Arctic Ocean.

The field tour surveys the scene: wells, stations, and oil company living complexes, small cities in themselves. The guide is prepared to explain things you may have read about, including the multimillion dollar research programs for preserving the ecology, and special tundra vehicles called Rolligons. Their great weight is distributed so that it scarcely makes a dent as it passes over the delicate terrain.

When to go? Most people visit in summer, but you can sample the Arctic in winter, too, with appropriate activities such as dog sledding, snowmobiling and fishing through the ice. The Visitors Bureau can help you arrange such activities. May to June Arctic visitors, may encounter the "break-up" of shore ice as the scene shifts from winter to a fleeting spring, then into summer.

We've barely touched on the magnificence and stark beauty of the Arctic, and the lifestyle of its fascinating, durable residents. Still with one mukluk in the past, they appear to be looking forward to a prosperous future. Go visit as soon as you can.

The Katmai

The Katmai National Park and Preserve is a wild, remote landscape on the Alaska Peninsula, bordering Shelikof Strait across from Kodiak Island.

Moose and almost 30 other species of animals, including foxes, lynx, and wolves, share the scene with bears fishing for salmon from stream banks or standing in the water. Ducks are common; so are whistling swans, loons, grebes, gulls, and shore birds. Bald eagles can be seen perched on rocky pinnacles by the sea. Altogether, more than 40 species of songbirds alone can be seen during the short spring and summer season. Marine life abounds in the coastal area, with the Steller sea lion and hair seal often observed on rock outcroppings.

Compared with roads and facilities at Denali National Park, it is quite primitive, but therein lies its charm.

Valley of Ten Thousand Smokes

Visitors have been coming to Alaska's Katmai area for over 4,000 years, except for a four-year lull. For centuries, the original Natives used to summer here, attracted by plentiful fish and game that they used for stocking up their winter larders.

On the morning of June 1, 1912, a green valley, more than 40 miles square, lazed below a mountain called Novarupta. Then the earth quaked, and for five days the violent tremors continued. On June 6, the quakes subsided, and the green valley breathed peacefully again. But a few hours later rivers of white-hot ash were pouring over the valley. A foot of ash fell on Kodiak, 100 miles away. Winds carried the ash to eastern Canada and Texas.

While Novarupta was belching forth pumice and scorching ash, another explosion took place six miles east. The peak of Mt. Katmai collapsed; where there had been a mountaintop there was suddenly a chasm almost three miles long and two miles wide. Simply put, the molten andesite that held up Mt. Katmai had rushed through newly created fissures to Novarupta and been spewn out. Sixty hours after the first thunderous blast from Novarupta, the great eruptions were over. More than seven cubic miles of volcanic material had been ejected; the green valley lay 700 feet under ash. Though no one was killed, the Natives fled from Katmai, Savanoski, and other villages.

By 1916, things had cooled. A National Geographic expedition, led by Dr. Robert F. Griggs, reached the valley. It seemed full of steaming fumaroles. What they reported inspired Congress to set it and the surrounding wilderness aside as a national monument in 1918. At first sight, Dr. Griggs came up with an apt name, Valley of Ten Thousand Smokes.

The Natives never came back, but they have been replaced by sight-seers, fishermen, hikers, and outdoor enthusiasts, who migrate here in summer, attracted by the fish and wildlife, and by the volcano-sculpted Valley of Ten Thousand Smokes (which have now cooled down to only a few, after over 70 years). No roads lead to the monument, at the base of the volcano-studded Alaska Peninsula, 290 miles southwest of Anchorage. Getting there is an all-Alaskan wilderness fly-in experience, in order to visit this remote Alaskan wilderness.

From Anchorage, planes wing along Cook Inlet, rimmed by lofty snowy peaks of the Alaska Range. They land at King Salmon, near fish-famous Bristol Bay, where passengers transfer to a smaller plane, at home both on land and water, for the next hop. In twenty minutes, the amphibian plane splashes down in Naknek Lake, in front of the Park Headquarters, next to Brooks River Lodge. A motorboat lassos the plane, tows it to shore, and then everyone walks a plank from plane hatch to the beach.

From Brooks Lodge, a daily tour bus with a naturalist aboard drives 23 miles through the monument to the Valley Overlook, where those who wish can hike the easy one-and-a-half-mile trail for a close-up look at the pumice-covered valley floor. The depth of the sand flow is evident where the rushing Ukak River has cut a deep channel, leaving a sheer cliff of pinkish layered residue, called volcanic "tuff." Cross sections are 200 to 300 feet high.

A flightseeing tour with Katmai Air Services, for example, will allow you to experience from the air early trade and hunting trails and deserted Native villages. In season, roaming moose and brown bears are spotted. Jade-green lakes now fill some old volcano craters, and the sulphur smell of some "smokes," still sending up signals in the valley, wafts into the plane.

Brooks River and Naknek Lake are hot spots for fly fishing. In fact, the trophy rainbow fishing is so fantastic, only artificial lures and single hooks are permitted. Fish watching is another popular sport. A short walk up river to Brooks Falls, salmon are easily seen and photographed as they leap the eight-foot barrier in their compulsive, epic struggle to reach their native grounds during the spawning season.

Besides Brooks Lodge, there are other fly-in camps and lodges in "Angler's Paradise." Outdoor-minded families can headquarter there and satisfy assorted interests. From Grosvenor Lake and Kulik Lodge on Nonvianuk Lake, the avid fishermen can fly off with a pilot/guide to fish for Arctic char and grayling, northern pike, and rainbow trout that reach trophy size, feeding on the abundant natural food in myriad lakes and streams. Nonfishers can take float trips, boat trips, hike, rockhound, plus observe and photograph birds and wildlife, hard-working beaver to bears, who are also avid fishermen. They say if the fisher appears extra big, shaggy, and has four legs, use caution and common sense, and allow plenty of elbow room. Usually there's no problem. Accommodations are mostly shared cabins, but with hot and cold water, private bathroom with shower, heat, and lights. Anywhere it's otherwise, they'll tell you what to expect.

The Most Remote Areas

Beyond the Katmai and the Alaska Peninsula lie the farthest reaches of Alaska. Separating the North Pacific Ocean from the Bering Sea, the Aleutian Islands, termed "The Chain," stretch from the Alaska Peninsula in a southwesterly arc toward Japan. The distance from the point nearest the Alaska mainland, Unimak Island, to the most distant island, Attu, is over one thousand miles. This semivolcanic, treeless archipelago consists of about 20 large islands and several hundred smaller ones.

Before the Russians came, the islands were dotted with Aleut villages. Today there are communities only at Nikolski, on Umnak Island; Unalaska, on Unalaska Island; Atka on Atka Island; Pilot Point on the Alaska Peninsula, and Cold Bay at its tip. The hardy Aleuts work at commercial fishing or in canneries and as expert guides for hunters and fishermen. With the exception of U.S. Naval bases, the settlements are quite small, and accommodations are scarce. Visitors are not encouraged to visit the complex facilities of the U.S. Navy at Adak and Shemya. No passenger ships reach the Aleutians; the chain is served by Reeve Aleutian Airways.

Bethel, on the Kuskokwim River, north of Bristol Bay, is 80 miles inland from the Bering Sea. From an Eskimo village it has grown to the largest town in western Alaska, population about 3,400. Commercial fishing and freezing are the mainstay of the economy. It is the transportation center and administrative headquarters for the lower Yukon and the Kuskokwim delta areas, encompassing about 70 native settlements. Bethel is as important to Alaska as it is little known to outsiders. Though visitor accommodations are limited, Bethel boasts a library, museum, radio and television station, theater, hotel, bank, newspaper, maternity home, child-care center, regional office of the Alaska State Troopers, the largest Alaska Native Service field hospital in the state, an $8.8-million regional high school, and a $3.5-million regional dormitory for boarding students. (Like many Native settlements, Bethel has voted to be dry; no liquor for sale within city limits.)

This river delta area abounds with moose, wolf, beaver, and muskrat. To the northwest, the Yukon Delta Wildlife Refuge takes in one of the largest waterfowl breeding grounds in the world. Thus, despite modern encroachment, these Yupik Eskimos in the delta also opt to continue their centuries-old subsistence lifestyle.

Just north of Kuskokwim Bay and off the Southwest Bering Sea coast is another important wildlife refuge. Nunivak Island, home of the Nunivak National Wildlife Refuge, is noted regionally for its large herd of reindeer, a transplanted herd of musk oxen, and the Eskimo settlement of Mekoryuk. This is one of the least-touristed parts of Alaska. Visitors, lured by fine ivory carvings, masks, and items knit from qiviut (musk oxen) wool, should check with airlines flying there about accommodations, which are limited and far from deluxe.

In the Bering Sea some 200 miles northwest of Cold Bay are the Pribilof Islands, misty, fog-bound breeding grounds of fur seals. Five islets make up the Pribilof group, tiny, green, treeless oasis, with rippling belts of lush grass contrasting with red volcanic soil. In May the mating seals come home from far Pacific waters, and the islands see scenes of frenzied activity. When a thousand bulls scold at the top of their lungs or roar jealously, the sounds roll out several miles to sea.

Tours fly to St. Paul, and St. George, the two largest Pribilof Islands. For the most part, these outposts, almost in tomorrow in time and next door to Siberia in space, are visited (by air and sometimes by sea) by those who have business there, or by persistent, inveterate travelers addicted to way-out destinations.

Getting to the Pribilofs today points up the amazing development of air transportation in the last 30 years. It's a 2,000-mile round trip from Anchorage over massive snowy peaks of the Alaska Peninsula, tapering down to the rocky sea-level islands of the Aleutian Range. This was the supply route for U.S. forces during World War II, when Japan tried to use the islands as stepping-stones to invasion via Alaska.

A veteran bush pilot, Bob Reeve, pioneered the flights, and his Reeve Aleutian Airways is still the "only way to fly" out the Chain. His planes, mostly prop jets, are bigger and better now. Otherwise, it's the same informal delivery operation.

Space is blocked off as needed for freight, and there are usually 30-some seats left over for passengers. Aleuts, like other natives living in far-out places, became members of jet sets before auto clubs. Some passengers will be government workers, many in wildlife jobs. The others heading for St. Paul or St. George Island may be on a 3-, 4-, or 6-day wildlife tour.

The pilot and crew obviously enjoy being "tour guides." They point out old lava flows, some still-smoking volcanic peaks, rusting debris and Quonset huts left at Cold Bay base after the war, and sea life. During the 200-mile Bering Sea leg, there may be a pod of playful whales.

On arrival at St. Paul Airport, tours are met by the resident guide, eager to reveal the wildlife treasures supported in this sanctuary 250 miles from the nearest land. During their stay, nature-lovers will have opportunities to watch seals and birds and take pictures in the accessible rookeries, and to get acquainted with some of the town's friendly residents. About 500 descendants of Aleut-Russians live here now, practically all of them members of the Old Russian Orthodox Church, an attraction for visitors, along with vestiges of Aleut culture remaining in the town.

Two hundred years ago, the Russians transplanted Aleut Natives here to harvest fur seals—almost to extinction. However, they are in business today, with the herds now restored to full strength, about 1¼ million, due to careful management and monitoring of the annual harvest by the U.S. Government and protection by international treaty from the rapacity of large-scale hunters.

In addition to the largest seal herd in the world and other sea mammals, the Pribilofs offer a richness of subarctic and alpine flora and over 180 varieties of birds. Thousands of sea birds nest on the cliffs. Away from the cliffs and the village, it is not unusual to see Arctic blue fox and reindeer herds.

This—the Southwest, Far West, Far North Fringes, or Southcentral, Interior, or Southeast—all this, then, is Alaska, a state catapulting out of the past. In two or three decades some say it will be far tamer, less awesome, more comfortable and some of it preserved only in story-books. Meanwhile, the increasing annual number of visitors surpasses the state's over 500,000 population of hospitable residents. They appear pleased to share their treasures with kindred souls wherever they meet them, in the cities and towns or in the "bush."

PRACTICAL INFORMATION FOR THE FRINGES
OF ALASKA

HOW TO GET THERE AND HOW TO GET AROUND. By air: *Alaska Airlines,* 4750 International Airport Road, Anchorage, AK 99502; or Box 68900, Sea-Tac International Airport, Seattle, WA 98168, flies within the state to Prudhoe Bay, Nome, and Kotzebue. *Alaska Aeronautical Industries,* Box 6067, Anchorage, AK 99502, flies to Homer, Kenai, Kodiak, and (in summer) Denali National Park. *MarkAir,* 6441 So. Air Park Place, Anchorage, AK 99502; (907) 266–6233, flies within Alaska to Arctic, far west, and Southwest destinations, with frequent flights between Anchorage and Fairbanks. *Reeve Aleutian Airways,* 4700 West International Airport Road, Anchorage, AK 99502, flies to points on the Alaska Peninsula, the Aleutian Islands, and to the Pribilof Islands. Information is always available at *Alaska Airlines, Alaska Aeronautical, MarkAir,* and *Reeve* ticket counters at the Anchorage International Airport terminal.

Ryan Air Service (formerly *Munz Northern*) flies to many Native villages out of Nome and Kotzebue. For information, or to go along on a flightseeing "milk run," write Box 790, Nome, AK 99762. Or stop by their Nome and Kotzebue Airport offices.

Many air taxi and charter services have offices at airport terminals. Space permitting, they'll make on-the-spot arrangements for flightseeing tours or take you where you want to go.

CLIMATE AND WHAT TO WEAR. Fringe area residents boast that, tempered by the oceans, it doesn't get as cold there as in the Interior region—even at far north Barrow. When the ice moves out in Arctic regions in early June, things start to warm up, even into the 50° Fahrenheit ranges during summer. However, you should be prepared with full Arctic gear for a winter visit, as discussed in *Facts at Your Fingertips.* If you are on a modern "Arctic expedition" they'll outfit you with an Eskimo-style, lined parka to wear outdoors, if needed, during your visit. Otherwise, better have handy a warm windbreaker that can also handle some rain.

In the Pribilof Islands, where it is likely to be damp and misty (perfect seal weather!), tour groups can borrow ponchos during their stay. The main thing is to be comfortable during the hours spent out-of-doors observing nature's wonders in these unusual regions in the wilderness rim. Even with bus transportation on the tours, you'll be inspired to walk a lot, around the villages, and "in the field," so comfortable sturdy shoes are essential. A pair of binoculars will definitely enhance wildlife viewing, and you'll be sorry if you don't bring plenty of film for your camera.

 HOTELS AND MOTELS. Do be sure to reserve before you go. In the wilderness fringes, accommodations are few, and space may be limited unless you are with a tour group. (Then you will probably stay in the finest—which may well be the only—hotel in town.) It's also a wise idea to double-check on your reservations a week or so before you plan to arrive. Though no bed-and-breakfasts, as such, exist in these areas, it is sometimes possible to arrange to stay with a family through bush airlines serving outlying villages. Rates, based on double occupancy, are as follows: *Deluxe,* $100 and up; *Expensive,* $80–100; *Moderate,* $60–80; *Inexpensive,* under $60.

BARROW
(Zip Code 99723)

Arctic Hotel. *Deluxe.* Barrow; (907) 852–7788. Over $100 at this 43-room establishment buys comparative luxury on the edge of the Arctic Ocean. The town is dry at this writing, so there is no lounge, but restaurants are close by.

Top of the World. *Deluxe.* Box 189, Barrow; (907) 852–3900. Summer tour groups stay in this 40-room, relatively luxurious establishment. Overlooking the ocean, and with adjoining restaurant (*Pepe's*); open year-round.

Barrow Airport Inn. *Expensive.* Box 933; 852–2525. Town's newest hotel, one block from airport, includes free breakfast at *Pepe's Restaurant.*

BETHEL
(Zip Code 99559)

The Kuskokwim Inn. *Expensive.* Box 218; (907) 543–2207. Open year-round. Coffee shop and dining room. (No bar, town is currently dry.)

KOTZEBUE
(Zip Code 99752)

Nul-luk-vik Hotel. *Deluxe.* Box 336; (907) 442–3331. A prefabricated, flown-and barged-in Native-corporation-built hotel. 85 rooms with phones, bar, gift shop. Very well managed and decorated. Features finest buffets in town in restaurant overlooking Kotzebue Sound of Arctic Ocean. Fine midnight sun viewing rooms on all 3 floors (no elevators). Houses tours. Open year-round.

NOME
(Zip Code 99762)

Nugget Inn. *Deluxe.* Box 430; (907) 443–2323. On Front St. Arctic tours stay here. Otherwise on space-available basis. Some rooms overlook restless Bering Sea. Attractive gold rush decor and spacious lobby with bar, *Gold Dust Saloon.*

Polaris Hotel. *Moderate.* Box 741; (907) 443–2000. Bar and liquor store. 12 double rooms with private baths in new section; other 23 rooms use baths down the hall. Space may be scarce because of renewed interest in gold prospecting.

 YOUTH HOSTELS. Nome: Operated by the Community United Methodist Church, W. Second and D St. Box 907, Nome, AK 99762; (907) 433–2865. Open year-round. No meals are served but kitchen facilities available.

 CAMPING AND CABINS. See "Camping" in *Facts at Your Fingertips* for addresses of the federal and state agencies offering camping facilities. The Bureau of Land Management offers campgrounds (most are free) and a few cabins (a fee for these) in Nome and Taylor on the Seward Peninsula. Write BLM, Fairbanks District Office, Box 1150, Fairbanks, AK 99701. See also "National Parks and Preserves," below.

 WILDERNESS LODGES. Lodges located in these remote wilderness rim areas excel in assorted fishing experiences as well as other activities: float trips, boat trips, hiking, rockhounding, observing and photographing birds and other wildlife—very likely bear, who are also avid fishers—and flightseeing tours. **Gates of the Arctic National Park and Preserve.** *Wiseman Lodge,* Box 10224, Fairbanks, AK 99701, is a historic gold rush camp area, about 200 miles north of Fairbanks, adjacent to the park and the Haul Rd. to the North Slope. Reserve early for June–Sept. Stay at the historic lodge, or to take wildlife photos here, bird and natural history tours, trail rides, backpacking or camping trips.

Katmai. Some of the lodges in "Angler's Paradise" are described above in the Katmai section of the text. *Katmailand, Inc.,* 455 H St., Anchorage, AK 99501; (907) 227–4314, offers *Brooks Lodge, Grosvenor Camp,* and *Kulik Lodge,* accessible by air, summers only. Fish here for rainbow trout, Arctic char, grayling, lake trout, salmon. *Exploration Holidays* "Land of Katmai Tours" overnights at Brooks Lodge. See "Tours" in *Facts at Your Fingertips.*

Around Nome. *Camp Bendeleben* is open year-round, by reservation. It's located at Council, an early-1900 goldmining camp, about 75 miles northeast of Nome. Tall, expert hunter/fisherman John Elmore guides small-game hunting and ice-fishing trips in winter. The rest of the time he leads the way to the best Arctic char, grayling, pike, and salmon (four species), combined with sightseeing and photography expeditions. Write him at Box 1045-S, Nome, AK 99762; (907) 443–2880.

Silvertip-on-the-Unalakleet River is near the Eskimo town of Unalakleet on Norton Sound of the Bering Sea, southeast of Nome. The river, long cherished by the Eskimos as a source of the food obtained during prime summer salmon runs, attracts fishermen from the world over, bent on battling the fighting Pacific salmon. Among the comforts of this beautiful, all modern log lodge that fishers look forward to after their exhilarating day, is a fully stocked "open bar." Box 6389, Anchorage, AK 99502; (907) 243–1416.

Southwest. *Aleknagik Mission Lodge,* Box 165, Aleknagik, AK 99555; (907) 842–2251, is beautifully recycled from a Seventh-Day Adventist mission school. It promises trophy salmon and trout fishing in the heart of the Bristol Bay area. The *Golden Horn Lodge* (Box 6748, Anchorage, AK 99502; [907] 243–1455) in the Wood River-Tikchik lakes area has daily flyouts to remote waters for 12 species of sportfish, and they also feature overnight excursions. *Iliamna Lake Lodge* (921 W. 6th Ave., Suite 200, Anchorage, AK 99501; [907] 274–1541), open year-round, has all kinds of sportfishing, photo/wilderness expeditions, and fly-fishing seminars with experts. *Iliaska Lodge,* also on Lake Iliamna, is a full-service flyout operation catering to fly-fishermen only. Contact the Manager, Box 28, Iliamna, AK 99606; (907) 571–1221.

Don't let the name—*No-See-Um Lodge*—keep you away. They take only up to 7 guests for their 7-night package stays, and every day is tailored to each guest's fishing interest. It's on the Kvichak River 35 miles south of Lake Iliamna; inquire Box 934, Palmer, AK 99645; (907) 745–5347 or 345–1160. *Valhalla Lodge,* exclusive (up to 12 people) and deluxe, is operated by a licensed master guide and commercial pilot with years of experience. On Six Mile Lake between Lake Iliamna and Lake Clark, Valhalla is in the midst of the best of Alaska sportfishing territory. A nearby attraction is a 200-foot waterfall in the Tazimina River. Contact: Box 6583-N, Anchorage, AK 99502; (907) 276–3569.

Isolated *Woodriver Lodge,* 40 miles north of Dillingham, is another example of luxury in the bush. Each day guests fly out from the lodge to fish in the Woodriver-Tikchik Lake region, which offers many tempting, hardly tapped choices among the lakes, streams, mountains, fjords, and forests of a 2-million-acre wilderness. Write to 4437 Stanford, Fairbanks 99701; (907) 479–0308.

Detailed descriptions of many of the lodges mentioned above, including the Silvertip, Valhalla, and No-See-Um; what's included in their sportfishing packages; and prices, are available from *Alaska Sportfishing Packages,* Suite 1320, 4th & Blanchard Bldg., Seattle, WA 98121; (206) 382–1051 or toll free (800) 426–0603.

TOURIST INFORMATION. Kotzebue. There's a *National Park Service Information Center* at the west end of the Living Museum of the Arctic. Open in summer, Mon.–Fri., 7:00 A.M.–5:00 P.M. in summer; 8:00 A.M.–4:30 P.M., winter. Write Supt. of Northwest Alaska, National Park Service, Box 287, Kotzebue, AK 99752; (907) 442–3890.

Nome. Stop by the *Nome Visitor Bureau* on Front St. at Perkins Plaza (or write Box 251, Nome, AK 99762; [907] 443–5535) to learn there is more here than gold rush nostalgia and bars. The Bureau is open whenever tour groups are coming through, which is daily in summer. If it does happen to be closed, talk to the staff at the *Nugget Inn* on Front St., (907) 443–2323. The *Carrie McClain Museum* on Front St. also dispenses tourist information: open summers Tues.–Fri., 9:00 A.M.–5:00 P.M., Sat. afternoons; winters, Tues.–Sat. afternoons. 443–2566.

TOURS. Overall, the best source for information and brochures on optional tours leaving from Anchorage and Fairbanks to explore the Arctic, the Katmai, and other wilderness areas is *Alaska Exploration Holidays & Cruises* (See "Tours," *Facts at Your Fingertips*). Their Anchorage office is at 547 W. 4th Ave., 99501; (907) 277–5581. Another good bet is someone who has been there, such as your travel agent.

Here are some of the regional possibilities to contact for information: In the **Bristol Bay** area, Chip Marinella's *Wild Country River Guides,* 12020 Timberlane Drive, Anchorage, AK 99515, [907] 349–9173, are highly regarded for their experience and knowledge of the whole area.

Reeve Aleutian Airways has scenic flights (weather permitting) of the **Cold Bay** area and the **Izembeck National Wildlife Refuge.**

Katmai Air offers floatplane flightseeing, sportfishing, and transportation charters in **Katmai National Park,** King Salmon, AK 99613; June–September; contact Sonny Petersen, Kulik Lodge, Box 275–S, (907) 246–3465.

A flight tour that will give you a good bird's-eye view of **King Island** can be arranged through *Munz Northern Airlines* at the Nome Airport, Box 790, Nome, AK 99762; (907) 443–5482.

NATIONAL PARKS AND PRESERVES. *Gates of the Arctic National Park and Preserve* is north of the Arctic Circle, about 199 miles north of Fairbanks. The park is mostly covered with shrubs and tundra, being north of the northern limit of trees. It is considered one of the finest wilderness regions remaining in the world. No National Park Service facilities; access is by air only. Write: Superintendent, Gates of the Arctic National Park, 201 First Ave., Box 74680, Fairbanks AK 99707; 456–0281.

Katmai National Park and Preserve is a haven for outdoor enthusiasts, offering an unspoiled setting in which to enjoy great fishing, boating on island-studded lakes, and virtually unlimited hiking. Wildlife abound; the chance of seeing moose and brown bears, among other animals, is excellent. Katmai was also the scene of one of the most violent volcanic eruptions in modern times. The *Valley of Ten Thousand Smokes* was inundated with volcanic ash and pumice—and received its name because of the smoking fumaroles that existed in the once-verdant valley. There are wilderness lodges within the Katmai (see above in this *Practical Information*), cabins, campgrounds, and a convenience store. You can rent fishing equipment and boats (with guides) at Brooks River and Lake Grosvenor. Charter aircraft can be taken from King Salmon, about 40 miles from park headquarters. For information contact the Superintendent, Katmai National Park and Preserve, Box 7, King Salmon, AK 99613; 246–3305. The Alaska Regional Office, Parks & Forest Information Center, 2525 Gambell St., Room 107, Anchorage AK 99503 (271–4243) offers information on all National Park Service lands in Alaska. (See also "National Parklands" and "Camping" in *Facts at Your Fingertips.*)

WILDLIFE REFUGES. *Izembek National Wildlife Refuge* is a valuable waterfowl breeding area at the tip of the Alaska Peninsula. The continent's entire black brant population can be found in the refuge's tidal lagoons for two to three months each year. Brown bears and caribou prowl the upland regions. Limited accommodations are available at Cold Bay. Contact the Manager, Pouch 2, Cold Bay, AK 99571, for additional information.

The *Yukon Delta National Wildlife Refuge* is the largest such refuge in Alaska. Large numbers of birds can be found here, including whistling swans and white-fronted, emperor, and cackling Canada geese. The *Nunivak National Wildlife Refuge* is considered part of the Yukon Delta and is the home of a flourishing herd of musk ox. Contact the Manager, Yukon Delta National Wildlife Refuge, Box 346, Bethel, AK 99559.

MUSEUMS. In **Bethel,** the *Yugtarvik Regional Museum* holds Eskimo artifacts and is the marketplace for contemporary crafts of southwestern Alaska and the Yukon-Kuskokwim delta area. Open Tues.–Sat., 10:00 A.M.–6:00 P.M. No admission charge. 543–2098.

Kotzebue: The modern *Living Museum of the Arctic,* funded by the Northern Alaska Native Association (NANA), has dioramas of the Arctic environment: animals, birds, and sea life. Natives also give live demonstrations here of crafts, such as skin sewing and ivory carving, and they perform cultural dances in Eskimo native dress. Here you can see an Eskimo blanket toss. Call 442–3304. In summer there are usually two 2-hour shows a day given in the museum to coincide with the tour schedule. For those not on tour, inquire at the Nul-luk-vik Hotel (442–3331) or at the NANA office in the building across from the airport. Guides will also have information. There'll be a charge if you are not with a group. *Ootukahkuktuvik* (Place Having Old Things) is the name of a museum containing masks, whaling guns, and many more of the fascinating antique items relating to Kotzebue's early trading history, including Russian trading beads made of blue glass. On Second Ave., the museum is open summers 8:00 A.M.–4:30 P.M. Mon.–Fri. By appointment at other times. Appointments can be arranged through City Hall, 442–3401. Donations only.

Nome: The *Carrie McClain Museum,* Front St., allows visitors to learn about the sea mammals and birds such as the sandhill cranes that migrate—often right over the town—in May to summer on the Seward Peninsula. Also displayed are exhibits on Eskimo art, and the gold rush history of Nome, as well as photo collections. Tourist information provided. It's a popular place. Open summers, Tues.–Fri., 9:00 A.M.–5:00 P.M., Sat. afternoons; winters, Tues.–Sat. afternoons and by appointment. 443–2566.

SHOPPING. You'll encounter some intriguing possibilities for purchasing Native arts and crafts that you'll know are authentic. The creator may be putting finishing touches on, say, an ivory carving, or the last stitches into a pair of mukluks (fur boots). In Nome, Kotzebue, and Barrow, the Eskimos bring items to their Native dances, for sale afterward: yo-yos of fur and skin, baskets of baleen (the black plankton-strainers from a whale's mouth), masks—perhaps one a dancer was wearing—and dolls, dressed Eskimo-style in fur parkas.

In **Kotzebue,** the *Nul-luk-vik Hotel Gift Shop* on Front St. and the *Arctic Rivers Trading Co.,* Second St., keep a good supply of masks, paintings on animal skins, jade and ivory jewelry and carvings, raw jade, and furs. In **Nome,** the *Arctic Trading Post,* Bering and Front, has an extensive stock of authentic Eskimo ivory carvings, and other art works and books by Alaskans. Also stop in the *Polar Jewelry and Gift Shop* on Front St, and the *Billikin Bakery.*

PANNING FOR GOLD. Gold pans are a hot item in **Nome** stores; if you don't bring your own, buy one there. Panning on the beach is free, or you may want to sign on with a tour group that is going to a panning demonstration. "Blueberry" John Andrews is a long-time tour guide whose hobby is gold panning. Ask for him, and for other panning information, at the Visitors Bureau (443–5535), on Front St.

DINING OUT. Since supplies are barged or flown in, prices may seem relatively high here. Prices for restaurants in Alaska's fringes are categorized as follows, based on a complete dinner: *Deluxe:* $30 and up; *Expensive:* $20–30; *Moderate:* $15–20; *Inexpensive:* under $15. See also "Hotels and Motels" earlier in this *Practical Information* for lodging establishments that have restaurants.

BARROW

Pepes. *Expensive.* Adjoining the Top of the World Hotel. The best Mexican food in town—and an amazing decor.

Sam & Lee's Chinese Restaurant. *Expensive.* Fine food.

Mattie's. *Moderate.* Just north of main Barrow in a section called Browerville. Good food in an 1883 whaling shelter.

Ken's Restaurant. *Moderate to Inexpensive.* Above the airport terminal building. Burgers and good bakery items.

KOTZEBUE

The Arctic Dragon. *Expensive to Moderate.* 301 Front St. 442–3776. Specializes in fine Chinese dishes.

Dairy Queen Brazier. *Expensive to Moderate.* Second and Lagoon sts. 442–3269. Eat here to say that you've been at the farthest north DQ in the U.S. It serves steak and seafood as well as the usual DQ fare.

Kotzebue Deli. *Moderate.* 4th and Mission. Pizza here, but this place is really noted for its gourmet burgers, priced from $8 to $11, depending on which amazing things you order to top them.

Hamburger Hut. *Moderate to Inexpensive.* Front St., along the beach. A good selection of burgers here, starting at under $3.

NOME

The Fort Davis Roadhouse. *Expensive.* 3 miles east of town on the Nome-Council Rd. 443–2660. Reindeer steaks a specialty. Newly expanded, it's a place to meet convivial locals. Nome's ex-mayor may be tending the bar. Order his concoctions, a "Tanglefoot" or a "Bering Ball." Entertainment.

Milano's Pizzeria. *Moderate.* For Italian food.

The Polar Cub. *Moderate.* Behind Front St., next to sea wall. Serves breakfast, lunch, and early dinner, then the staff moves to the Roadhouse for serving late diners. Try some goodies from their Billikin Bakery.

Twin Dragon Restaurant. *Inexpensive.* On Bering St., 2 blocks from the sea. Delicious Korean and Chinese food: Cantonese, Mandarin, Szechwan; chow mein; egg foo yong; beer, saké, and house wine.

BARS AND NIGHT LIFE. In Nome, especially, there's no lack of bar-hopping possibilities, among them the *Bering Sea Saloon* and the *Board of Trade,* oldest bar on the Bering Sea. They're both on Front St. and both exude the rugged north. Do be aware that some of these communites may have recently voted to be dry, including at this writing Barrow and Bethel.

INDEX

The letter H indicates hotels & motels. The letter R indicates restaurants.

GENERAL INFORMATION

GEOGRAPHICAL INDEX

215

INDEX